THE POETRY
OF
MICHAEL LONGLEY

ULSTER EDITIONS AND MONOGRAPHS
General Editors
Robert Welch
Joseph McMinn

ULSTER EDITIONS AND MONOGRAPHS SERIES
ISSN 0954-3392

1. *Joyce Cary Remembered.* Compiled and edited by Barbara Fisher
2. *Swift's Irish Pamphlets - An Introductory Selection.* Edited by Joseph McMinn
3. *Charles Lever: New Evaluations.* Edited by Tony Bareham
4. *The Achievement of Brian Friel.* Edited by Alan J. Peacock
5. *Strangers to that Land: British Perceptions of Ireland from the Reformation to the Famine.* Edited by Andrew Hadfield and John McVeagh
6. *Louis MacNeice and His Influence.* Edited by Kathleen Devine and Alan J. Peacock
7. *Modern Irish Writers and the Wars.* Edited by Kathleen Devine
8. *Charles Lever, the Lost Victorian.* S. P. Haddelsey
9. *The Cock and Anchor.* Joseph Sheridan Le Fanu, edited by Jan Jędrzejewski
10. *The Poetry of Michael Longley,* Edited by Alan J. Peacock and Kathleen Devine

THE POETRY OF MICHAEL LONGLEY

Edited by
Alan J. Peacock
and Kathleen Devine

Ulster Editions and Monographs: 10

Copyright © 2000 by Alan J. Peacock, Terence Brown, Douglas Dunn,
Peter McDonald, Robert Welch, Elmer Kennedy-Andrews,
Neil Corcoran, Michael Allen and Michael Longley

First published in Great Britain in 2000
by Colin Smythe Limited, Gerrards Cross, Buckinghamshire

British Library Cataloguing in Publication Data

A catalogue record for this book
is available from the British Library

ISBN 0-86140-412-2

Distributed in North America by Oxford University Press
198 Madison Avenue, New York, NY 10016

The right of Alan J. Peacock, Terence Brown, Douglas Dunn,
Peter McDonald, Robert Welch, Elmer Kennedy-Andrews,
Neil Corcoran, Michael Allen and Michael Longley
to be identified as the Authors of this work has been asserted in
accordance with the Copyright, Designs and Patents Act, 1988

All rights reserved. Apart from any fair dealing for the purposes of research
or private study, or criticism or review, as permitted under the Copyright,
Designs and Patents Act, 1988, this publication may be reproduced, stored
or transmitted, in any forms or by any means, only with the prior
permission in writing of the publishers, or in the case of reprographic
reproduction in accordance with the terms of licences issued by the
Copyright Licensing Agency. Enquiries concerning reproduction outside
these terms should be sent to the publishers at the above address.

Produced in Great Britain
Typeset by Art Photoset Ltd., Beaconsfield, Buckinghamshire
Printed and bound by T.J. International Ltd., Padstow, Cornwall

CONTENTS

ABBREVIATIONS	vi
INTRODUCTION. Alan J. Peacock	ix
ACKNOWLEDGEMENTS	xxii
MICHAEL LONGLEY AND THE IRISH POETIC TRADITION. Terence Brown	1
LONGLEY'S METRIC. Douglas Dunn	13
LAPSED CLASSICS: HOMER, OVID, AND MICHAEL LONGLEY'S POETRY. Peter McDonald	35
MICHAEL LONGLEY AND THE WEST. Robert Welch	51
CONFLICT, VIOLENCE AND 'THE FUNDAMENTAL INTERRELATEDNESS OF ALL THINGS' IN THE POETRY OF MICHAEL LONGLEY. Elmer Kennedy-Andrews	73
MY BOTANICAL STUDIES: THE POETRY OF NATURAL HISTORY IN MICHAEL LONGLEY. Neil Corcoran	101
LONGLEY'S LONG LINE: LOOKING BACK FROM *THE GHOST ORCHID*. Michael Allen	121
'HOW DO YOU SEW THE NIGHT?': *THE WEATHER IN JAPAN*. Alan J. Peacock	143
ETRURIA. Michael Longley	169
NOTES	171
NOTES ON CONTRIBUTORS	181
INDEX	183

ABBREVIATIONS

The following abbreviations are used to refer to volumes of poetry by Michael Longley:
- P   *Poems 1963–1983* (London, Secker & Warburg Ltd., 1991, first published in 1985, Edinburgh, The Salamander Press; Dublin, The Gallery Press).
- GF *Gorse Fires* (London, Secker & Warburg Ltd., 1991).
- GO *The Ghost Orchid* (London, Jonathan Cape, 1995).

ILLUSTRATIONS

Manuscripts of poems by Michael Longley   65–72

Between pages 138 and 139

Portrait of Michael Longley, 'Light from Two Windows' by Jeffrey Morgan.

ML's father, Captain Richard Longley MC, London, 1918.

A photograph taken at the wedding of ML's parents, Clapham Common, February 1927.

ML's mother, Constance, c. 1937.

ML with twin Peter (on the left), at their fourth birthday party, 1943.

Lena Hardy, ML's sister Wendy and Joan Gilbert, at Tyrella Beach, Co. Down, 1937.

ML, with sister Wendy and twin Peter, 1947.

ML as a sixth former at the Royal Belfast Academical Institution, 1957.

ML as an undergraduate at Trinity College, Dublin.

ML with Derek Mahon, John Hewitt and Seamus Heaney at Cushendall, Co. Antrim, 1969.

A literary evening at the Lyric Theatre, Belfast, with Paul Muldoon, John Hewitt, Patrick Galvin, Frank Ormsby, Ciaran Carson, Seamus Deane, John Boyd and ML, c. 1975.

ML with Francis Stuart and Neil Shawcross at The Queen's University English Society, c. 1985.

ML with co-tutor Paul Muldoon at the Arvon Foundation, Lumb Bank, Yorkshire, 1985.

ML with John Montague, Donald Hall and Frank Ormsby, in the Crown Bar, Belfast, November 1998.

ML with his daughter Rebecca, 1969.

ML photographed at the Arts Council of Northern Ireland in 1985.

ML with his wife Edna, and children Dan and Sarah, Summer, 1986.

INTRODUCTION

In the course of the last decade Michael Longley has definitively established himself as a prime figure not just in Irish poetry, but within the wider domain of poetry in English. The key event for this consolidation of reputation was the appearance in 1991 of *Gorse Fires*, a volume which marked a momentous return to inspiration after a character-testing lean period following *Poems 1963–1983*. The austere lyric intensities of *Gorse Fires* condensed Longley's ability to image the macrocosm in the microcosm, to elide distinctions between the human and the natural world and to conflate personal and larger histories. There followed the more restless, protean energies of *The Ghost Orchid* (1995). Here once again every poem is stamped with the impress of a relaxedly authoritative poetic personality, drawing on a wide spectrum of cultural and literary influences in a technique which ranges between concentrated, imagistic delicacy and scabrous, sardonic humour. There is a sureness of touch, an assimilative confidence in the use of (particularly ancient) sources of reference and allusion, and a measured poise in the rhythms and inflections of language which token a major talent, secure in its direction. Another outstanding volume, *The Weather in Japan*, has now been published, to extend Longley's range and achievement even further (see the final essay in this volume); and a booklet of poems, *Broken Dishes*, appeared in 1998.[1]

The 1996 Symposium at the University of Ulster on which the present volume is based was projected in 1994 in the wake of the success of *Gorse Fires*. In the interim, *The Ghost Orchid* was published, so that in the event the proceedings provided a very timely vantage-point for a review, assessment and celebration of Longley's career, given edge and topicality by the stimulus of important new work. The previous Symposium was devoted to the work of Louis MacNeice and, in his piece on MacNeice and Longley deriving from that event, Michael Allen went so far, in the face of Longley's remarkable recent return to form, as to say that, arguably, 'not until *Gorse Fires* (1991) and *The Ghost Orchid* (1995)' did Longley achieve 'a single self-integrative and uniquely recognisable stylistic mode . . .'[2] *Gorse Fires* did indeed, in a way dramatised by the fallow years of the mid-to-late 'eighties, suddenly seem to project Longley's achievement and reputation onto a new plane (in this sense echoing MacNeice's radical revival of powers at about the same time of life in *The Burning Perch*). At the same time, though, Longley's resurgence is also very much a development on the themes, preoccupations and techniques of his earlier books (cf., e.g., Douglas Dunn's synoptic view of his metric in the present volume) and a continuing assertion of his unswerving, life-long commitment to the exclusive role of lyric poet, evident particularly in his principled ('sooner silence than forgery')[3] negotiation of what MacNeice identified as the difficult 'middle stretch'. Another cogent comparison might be with Patrick Kavanagh's 're-birth' after the set-back of his near-fatal illness in 1955 and the production of such poems as 'The Hospital' and 'Lines Written on a Seat on the Grand Canal, Dublin'.

In all these cases, there is a sudden access of creativity in circumstances where diminution might have been expected. Already substantial careers are augmented in a way that gives them a new overall configuration. In particular, there is the production of a number of outstanding poems which immediately assert their place within a broad tradition of modern Irish poetry. Beside the two works by Kavanagh just mentioned one might place, say, MacNeice's 'Charon' and 'Budgie' from *The Burning Perch*, 'Between Hovers', and 'Detour' from Longley's *Gorse Fires* and 'Autumn Lady's Tresses' and 'Ceasefire' from *The Ghost Orchid*. Like MacNeice, as a classicist, Longley would, in the production of these volumes, be aware of Horace's rueful misgivings about continuing in the lyric mode beyond one's fifth decade. But like Kavanagh in his 'canal-bank' poems he was able to relax, in *Gorse Fires*, into a quietly exultant, affirmative mode, effortlessly discovering the extraordinary in the ordinary in poems which combine an easy, intimately human colloquial tenor with a now instinctive sense of form. A development towards a looser metric and a more spacious line continues on through *Gorse Fires*.

In an essay on *The Ghost Orchid*, Brian John has stressed the importance of these recent technical developments in Longley's work:

The publication of his latest volumes . . . reveals the new, freer line, in deceptively accomplished poetry which indicates that Michael Longley has come into his own.[4]

He feels that 'the nature and scope of the poet's most recent work deserve more general acknowledgement' and, more retrospectively, observes that his 'worth' has been 'less widely and enthusiastically recognised' (than that of his contemporaries, Heaney and Mahon). The comparative impact of the recent work is probably more substantial than is suggested, but the general picture is fair. Adequate recognition has been delayed – particularly of the earlier work; and Peter McDonald puts his finger on at least one salient consideration when he writes: 'Longley's poetry, though it has never gone short of respect, has yet to work its way into the discourse of those cultural critics for whom Irish writing occupies a central position'.[5] Longley's is a non-declaratory kind of writing which does not lend itself uncomplicatedly to critical approaches where 'placing' within cultural and socio-political determinants is a central rather than an ancillary or constituent critical concern.

For the record, the facts of Longley's Protestant, middle-class Belfast upbringing (as the son of a commercial traveller and then professional charity fundraiser, who served in both World Wars, Major Richard C. Longley, M.C.) and related cultural experience are vividly recounted in his autobiographical prose writing and interviews. Like the young MacNeice, he experienced predictable socio-religious demarcations where, for instance, contact with Catholics was an exotic experience – though, in class terms, the local geography of his home and schooling in the Lisburn Road area of Belfast afforded more direct exposure to working-class Protestant social realities than was the experience of the English public school-educated son of the Church of Ireland rector and future archbishop. Michael and his twin brother Peter

> attended the local Public Elementary School where, out of a large class of nearly forty pupils, we were almost the only middle-class children. Most of the others lived on 'the wrong side' of the Lisburn Road . . . John and Herbie shared with me their mythology which was mostly concerned with Roman Catholics. Did I know why Taigs crossed themselves? What dark practices lurked behind confession and Mass? . . . The Orange Order and the 'B' Specials marched through our conversations.[6]

However, if social and sectarian division were part of Longley's early (and, according to familiar Northern Irish social paradigms, extended) experience[7] these matters of background are 'givens' of personal history rather than enduring determinants of outlook. They are acknowledged with a mixture of sentiment and unillusioned analysis (notably in the prose writings), but they do not constitute a defining mature identity. In the poetry, they are a source of insight rather than programmed allegiance in a career where the purview has consistently inclined towards the inclusive rather than the exclusive and where wide-ranging cultural and literary analogising has been an instinctive provider of broad historical perspectives. In this, no doubt, his specialization in Classics, first in his secondary schooling at the Royal Belfast Academical Institution and then at Trinity College, Dublin, has been a factor – even if during his Trinity career he 'more or less dropped classics and took up writing poetry and drinking Guinness in O'Neill's bar'.[8] The key consideration here is not the degree of academic commitment to a given discipline, but the negotiation of the challenge provided by an extended literary and cultural vista – the 'enormous gap in my reading between Lucretius and W.H. Auden'. Stretched in this way, the creative imagination may discover patterns of human experience in literature remote in time and location which can have a cogent relevance for the here and now:

When I read a poem like 'Dead Man's Dump' by Isaac Rosenberg I feel as though it's the young Aeschylus or the young Sophocles walking on the muddy duckboards.

The past is a continuum, and literary history provides both touchstones of excellence in this way and also 'stepping stones' of access; and:

The stepping stones for me would be Hughes and Larkin, to a lesser extent Hill, then back to the 'thirties – Auden and MacNeice – then back to the trenches – Owen, Rosenberg, Edward Thomas. And then the great resumption – Hardy, Tennyson, Keats, Clare, Herbert, Donne, back to Propertius, Catullus . . .[9]

'Nature poet', 'love poet', 'neo-classical imitator and translator', 'poet of the Troubles', Longley (like MacNeice) resists any single, defining characterization; and, as with MacNeice again, his intent, minutely observant response to phenomena in the (especially natural) world about him qualifies him, if anything, as a 'philosophical' poet – but one whose scepticism, intelligence and basic humility prevent insight and intuition from hardening into dogma and system. In *The Ghost Orchid*, for instance, his bravura rendition of a section of Ovid's *Metamorphoses* in 'According to Pythagoras' wittily voices a mistrust of systematised 'knowledge', as picturesquely fanciful ancient scientific lore on natural phenomena, punctuated with a demotically confident refrain-element ('any farmer knows that'; 'that's obvious'), builds to a

Introduction

resounding philosophical climax: 'The fundamental interconnectedness of all things / Is incredible enough, but did you know that / Hyenas change sex?' The comic bathos however is aimed not at the bizarre wrongness of the interpreted data (these, as the poem shows, are enjoyable enough and suffer only from the provisionality of all scientific knowledge), but at the totalizing view.

In fact, 'the fundamental interconnectedness of all things' might be said to be the informing vision of Longley's poetry, but implicitly, heuristically and self-effacingly pursued, as in the hauntingly beautiful 'Autumn Lady's Tresses', again from *The Ghost Orchid*:

> How does the solitary swan on Dooaghtry Lake
> Who knows all about the otter as a glimmer
> Among reeds, as water unravelling, as watery
> Corridors into the water, a sudden face,
> Receive through the huge silence of the sand-dunes
> Signals from the otters' rock at Allaran Point
> About another otter, the same otter, folding
> Sunlight into the combers like brown kelp. . . ?
>
> (*GO* 2)

The whole poem is significantly a question voiced in one slowly unravelling, meditative sentence. The human element, the 'you and I' of the poem, is introduced only latterly within an established context of humbly tuned-into connexions in the natural world – and it is the non-human creatures who, within this expansively democratic vision, are credited with access to an invisible system of 'signals'. The approach is the polar opposite of anthropomorphism: it is based on a humility in the face of natural phenomena given edge and specificity by a naturalist's acuity of observation and a philosophical sceptic's openness, as well as wariness, as to implications. (In his first volume, in the final stanza of 'A Personal Statement' (*P* 29), Longley directed 'Body' to 'Sail . . . cargoless towards surprise' and 'Mind' to 'raise your sights – / Believe my eyes'.)

'Interconnectedness' in Longley subsumes geography, flora, fauna, home, love – 'And death of course' (*P* 28); and 'Between Hovers', subtitled 'in memory of Joe O'Toole', discovers a profound ethic in this non-anthropocentric sense of continuity between the human and the natural world:

> And not even when we ran over the badger
> Did he tell me he had cancer, Joe O'Toole

> Who was psychic about carburettor and clutch
> And knew a folk cure for the starter-engine.
> Backing into the dark we floodlit each hair
> Like a filament of light our lights had put out
> Somewhere between Kinnadoohy and Thallabaun.
> I dragged it by two gritty paws into the ditch.
> Joe spotted a ruby where the canines touched.
> His way of seeing me safely across the duach
> Was to leave his porch light burning, its sparkle
> Shifting from widgeon to teal on Corragaun Lake.
>
> (*GF* 5)

The intimate neighbourliness, the casual, close sense of connectedness with fauna and locality, the appreciation of the quotidian – all these memorialize and celebrate a life at ease with its elements. The shift in focus which follows however is haunting in its unsentimental equation of human and animal destiny:

> This morning on the burial mound at Templedoomore
> Encircled by a spring tide and taking in
> Cloonaghmanagh and Claggan and Carrigskeewaun,
> The townlands he'd wandered tending cows and sheep,
> I watched a dying otter gaze right through me
> At the islands in Clew Bay, as though it were only
> Between hovers and not too far from the holt.

No constituent of the natural cycle is privileged, and the human recognition of this shared existential exposure is strangely consoling.

Implicit in the intimate sense of sympathy here with terrain and its natural cycles and processes is Longley's distinctive attitude to place and belonging or 'home'. The familiar political-cum-ideological tropes on this theme in modern Irish literature cede to what develops in his work as an ethical construction. It is not a simple matter of binary options, of choice between North or South, Ireland or England, territory of upbringing or elsewhere. Longley has two identifiable 'homes', Belfast where he was raised and Carrigskeewaun in Co. Mayo – the latter a long-term holiday location which has developed imaginatively and emotionally (as 'Between Hovers' attests) as a second home. He continues to live in Belfast however not simply because he was brought up and schooled there and spent many years working there with the Arts Council of Northern Ireland (1970–91), but because he finds it and the North of Ireland generally a 'stimulating' social and cultural environment:[10] it is a matter of choice, of experience, not simply of origins. Similarly, though the intensities of 'Between Hovers' are called out by Longley's respect for his neighbour's integration with his social and physical environment, his 'home', Longley's is crucially a *neighbourly* response – he shares in what he celebrates. The Kavanagh-esque roster of place-names implicitly tokens his belonging as well as that of his friend. His two homes (and in this open, non-exclusivist attitude there could logically be more) are not therefore alternatives, but foci within a network of experiences, judgements, choices and relations. In a 1985 radio interview, when he was about to go to England for filming, and scheduled to visit areas associated with his parents' background before they moved from Clapham Common to Belfast in 1927, while insisting that he was an 'Irishman' Longley observed that he felt 'just ever so slightly schizoid'. He continued: 'I know when I go to Clapham I shall just have this slight echo of a doubt that perhaps this is home . . . but know home is Belfast where I have lived practically all of my life'.[11] In an interview ten years later he was speaking in much the same terms: 'Home is Belfast. Belfast is home. I love the place. The city, the hills around it, County Down, County Antrim. My home from home is in Mayo. But home is Belfast'. As ever though, the outlook is open: 'My sense of Ireland continues to develop as I discover more of it. It's as simple as that . . . I hate the notion that there are degrees of Irishness. One of the ways of defeating it is to experience as much of the island as you can'.[12]

At the first public reading from *Gorse Fires* at the University of Ulster at Coleraine,[13] Longley offered the view that the lyric poet has, basically, only two themes: love and death; and his work over three decades might be said, in the last analysis, to bear out this dictum – with the proviso of course that the exploration and expression of this basic antinomy may include the totality of individual experience as well as the accumulated precedents of history and the literary tradition (cf., in this connection, his Latin models, Tibullus and Propertius). Moreover, since his career has spanned the period of the current Troubles, the lyric programme has been under constant pressure from contemporary political realities; and the love/death antithesis is certainly relevant to his compassionate witness in this connection. Between the poles represented by, say, 'The Linen Workers' (*P* 149), with its mixture of nightmare surrealism and stark documentary detail, and the gentle tact of 'The Ice-cream Man' (*GF* 49), where a list of 'wild flowers of the Burren' is remembered as assuaging, for a child (his daughter, Sarah), the reality of a neighbourhood murder, Longley has shown a forthright but humanely attuned response to civil disorder and sectarian outrage. Characteristically too he has shown an ability to mediate his response to violence in Northern Ireland by reference to other conflicts in other times, as in 'Wounds', where memory of his father's First World War experience and his comrades' confused motives at the Somme ('...a boy about to die, / Screaming "Give 'em one for the Shankill!"') is dovetailed in with episodes from the current Troubles ('I bury beside him / Three teenage soldiers, bellies full of / Bullets and Irish beer . . .') in a way that allows a treatment of contemporary violence that is both starkly realistic and compassionate:

> Also a bus-conductor's uniform –
> He collapsed beside his carpet-slippers
> Without a murmur, shot through the head
> By a shivering boy who wandered in
> Before they could turn the television down
> Or tidy away the supper dishes.
> To the children, to a bewildered wife,
> I think 'Sorry Missus' was what he said.
>
> (P 86)

The chilling domestic intimacy of 'neighbourly' murder is unblinkingly registered but, as the First World War perspective helps to assert, 'the poetry is in the pity'. A sense of the 'interconnectedness' of human experience is central to the poem in its humane conflation of the experience of generations; and, on a much wider scale, the same sense of commonality is the key to the dynamics of Longley's classicizing. The *exempla* of human conduct provided by a literature remote in time and place may provide vital templates for coming to terms with current experience; and in Longley's work this has proven particularly valuable in the discovery of techniques for canvassing *positive* perspectives on contemporary Northern Irish conflict. Here, given the notorious intractability of the problem and the entrenched attitudes involved, the oblique, quasi-parabolic potential of such intercultural analogising has provided a means of hopeful comment, based on implication. where more direct hortatory techniques might seem like brash sermonizing.

The poem 'Peace', for instance, in *The Echo Gate* is a free translation or 'imitation' of a work by the first century B.C. Roman love-elegist, Tibullus; its function however as a response to the

Introduction

Northern Irish Peace People's request for a poem is a matter of oblique linguistic signalling:

> Who was responsible for the very first arms deal –
> The man of iron who thought of marketing the sword?
> Or did he intend us to use it against wild animals
> Rather than ourselves? Even if he's not guilty
> Murder got into the bloodstream as gene or virus
> So that now we give birth to wars, short cuts to death.
> Blame the affluent society: no killings when
> The cup on the dinner table was made of beechwood,
> And no barricades or ghettos when the shepherd
> Snoozed among sheep that weren't even thoroughbreds.
>
> (P 169)

The infiltration of modern terminology ('arms deal', 'affluent society') into the version of Tibullus 1, 10 jolts ancient topoi into contemporary immediacy ('Murder got into the bloodstream as gene or virus') and provides a context in which reference to the Troubles ('barricades', 'ghettos') is unmistakable but not exclusive. The anti-war, anti-violence sentiments of the poem are thus generalised and the witty, uninsistent analogising subtly authenticates the positive, hopeful tone of the poem as it develops. Producing a 'peace poem' was a tall order in the depths of the 1970s Troubles, but humour and obliquity enabled Longley to fulfil his commission in a way which did not involve didacticism or pious hopes. The more recent 'Ceasefire', in *The Ghost Orchid*, is even more remote in its frame of reference – a passage from the *Iliad* with only the title to touch off any implication for the situation in Northern Ireland. 'I get down on my knees and do what must be done / And kiss Achilles' hand, the killer of my son' says the aged Priam, petitionary for Hector's corpse, as he is graciously received by Achilles:

> Put in mind of his own father and moved to tears
> Achilles took him by the hand and pushed the old king
> Gently away, but Priam curled up at his feet and
> Wept with him until their sadness filled the building.
>
> (GO 39)

The eirenic scene is moving and exemplary, but shadowed by the ongoing tragedy of the war at Troy. The fragile possibility of humane empathy between antagonists is thus canvassed in luminous but unillusioned terms.

What qualifies contemporary hopes is of course, as the ancient analogy suggests, the course of actual events on the 'nightmare ground' of Ulster, as Longley terms it (P 78), echoing the Second World War phrase of Keith Douglas; and he has responded, sometimes in stark nightmarish terms ('Letters'; 'The Linen Workers') to those realities, but also, notably, with a human sense of appalled compassion ('Wounds'; 'The Greengrocer'), avoiding sectional partisanship and, as in 'Wounds', opening out analogies to other areas of conflict and division – specifically the two World Wars, where his father's service and status as 'belated casualty' provide a poignant personal link. This kind of nexus is central to Longley's art and imagination: humane, integrative, obliquely autobiographical, culturally assimilative – and by the same token not *assimilable* to any *parti-pris* political or sectarian interest-grouping. Similar qualities are also evident in his role as a founder-member (1988) of the Cultural Traditions Group, with 'its aims . . . to encourage in Northern Ireland the acceptance and understanding of cultural diversity; to replace political belligerence with cultural pride';[14] and he brought the same determinedly open and culturally ecumenical outlook to his professional career with the Arts Council of Northern Ireland, which he joined in 1970 (after a post-Trinity spell school-teaching in Dublin, London and Belfast) and from which he took early retirement as Combined Arts Director in 1991.

The assertion of liberal values, the search for the 'middle way' between extremes, the adoption of a 'humane perspective' (in the humanitarian as well as the philological sense), the avoidance of ideology – all these inscribe Longley as a successor of MacNeice whose *Selected Poems* (1988)[15] he has edited and on whom he has written as a critic. His commitment to the discovery of common ground within the polarized context of Northern Ireland also affiliates him to the humanitarianism of John Hewitt, and aspects of his regional programme. Perhaps more instinctively though than Hewitt Longley is able to embrace and internalize an extended cultural purview in social and territorial, as well as literary, terms.

In 'Detour' in *Gorse Fires*, with rich irony and genial good humour he imagines his own funeral procession – not in Belfast, but through the streets of a small market town. The town is not identified in the poem. It corresponds in its detail with Louisburgh, Co. Mayo, just along the road from Carrigskeewaun, but is intended more generally as 'a hymn to those wonderful Irish small market towns':[16]

Introduction

> I want my funeral to include this detour
> Down the single street of a small market town,
> On either side of the procession such names
> As Philbin, O'Malley, MacNamara, Keane.
> A reverent pause to let a herd of milkers pass
> Will bring me face to face with grubby parsnips,
> Cauliflowers that glitter after a sunshower,
> Then hay rakes, broom handles, gas cylinders.
>
> (*GF* 7)

Unpresumptuously, this is only a 'detour'. The location of the main event is left open. Yet the intimate immersion in the everyday particularities of localised place tokens a level of 'belonging' that is all the more powerful for being unasserted. Longley wittily and movingly acknowledges his objective 'outsider' status (his cortège seems to have minimal impact on the quotidian tempo of small-town life, the cows being given their customary rural priority); and like Kavanagh rejecting the notion of a 'hero-courageous / Tomb' in favour of a memorial 'canal-bank seat for the passer-by' in his adoptive corner of Dublin 4, Longley cedes 'reverence' to the 'milkers' and embraces the realm of the everyday. Here:

> From behind the one locked door for miles around
> I shall prolong a detailed conversation
> With the man in the concrete telephone kiosk
> About where my funeral might be going next.

In a typically self-deprecating way, he is 'at home' in his 'home from home' (*P* 94) territory – the belonging signified precisely in the relaxed irony with which he contemplates his meandering, yarning obsequies.

That 'interconnectedness' at the level of habitat and society can be put through this ironic register is the measure of Longley's consistent ability to achieve a personalised and often idiosyncratic 'take' on issues of wide human resonance, eluding canalisation into glib, received modes and attitudes. In the love-poetry, for instance, the conventional love-death conflation is seen not as a simple antithesis, but as a gradual, synthesized *process*. 'Love Poem' (*P* 115) – 'If my nose could smell only / You . . .' – pursues a relentless trope of love as biological destiny, imaged in details of somatic process and decay where 'death' is given the last word. Equally uncompromisingly, 'In Mayo' posits speaker and beloved as evanescent figures in a landscape where 'separating vertebrae / And scapulae litter a sandy wind' where 'Dawns and dusks here should consist of / Me scooping a hollow for her hip-bone . . .' – but:

> Then a slow awakening to the swans
> That fly home in twos, married for life,
> Larks nestling beside the cattle's feet
> And snipe the weight of the human soul.
>
> (P 119)

The rising lyric note is securely 'earthed' in a sense of attunement to a network of biological and zoological interrelations within a given habitat.

David Wheatley has written, reviewing *The Ghost Orchid*, how 'increased range' goes along with a continuing aspiration to 'rootedness'; and he remarks on the sense of continuity in Longley between the microcosm and the macrocosm:

> Great and small, far and near are constantly placed in alignment, as when the water-gourd of 'Chinese Objects' leads him to the conclusion that 'the world / Is not so big, the gourd so small' after all; as if in confirmation of this, another oriental poem, 'Chinese Occasions', turns out to be set in Belfast.[17]

Longley's ability to combine 'rootedness' with inclusiveness of range and reference, to 'watch Lesbos rising' from 'the high ground of Carrigskeewaun' (GF 1), to envision the more general through a close attention to the intimately particular, is central to his sense of place and 'home'.

It is also a developing and unifying principle of his lyric enterprise – focused and centred, but open in reference and implication. 'Terezín' can evoke the Holocaust in one haunting haiku-like couplet –

> No room has ever been as silent as the room
> Where hundreds of violins are hung in unison.
>
> (GF 39) –

and in Longley's elegiac booklet of poems, *Broken Dishes* (1998), private loss can mesh once again (cf. 'In Memoriam' and 'Wounds') with the century's larger experience:

> He would have been a hundred today, my father,
> So I write to him in the trenches and describe
> How he lifts with tongs from the brazier an ember
> And in its glow reads my words and sets them aside.
>
> ('January 12, 1996')

Introduction

Ezra Pound famously defined the epic as 'a poem including history';[18] and Longley has been able to fulfil something of that prescription within the more concentrated, subjective scope of the lyric or shorter poem. Certainly, in his run of Homeric poems he has developed a lyric mode which, in a synecdochic way, 'includes' epic. Part and whole, great and small, microcosm and macrocosm are interdependent concepts in his work and minima have their importance next to maxima – as in 'Phosphorescence', where stepping stones across a stream reveal 'at every stride the Milky Way', and a reflected Venus can bloom 'like brookweed next to the Pleiades' (*GF* 2).

Whether in this reduced, imagistic way or in more extended stanzaic patterns or discursive structures within a freer metric, Longley's work has remained essentially that of a lyric poet in that the overall dynamic of the poetry is centripetal – i.e., elaborating, only as necessary, outwards from a lyric core, rather than extending centrifugally *towards* large-scale form. Expansion is followed characteristically by contraction, and *An Exploded View* (1973), for instance, contains a number of poetic sequences, including the substantial 'Letters'; but six-line poems, 'To the Poets' and 'An Image from Propertius', begin and end the volume – the former, like the more discursive 'Letters', a reflection on the role of the poet in troubled times, but registering the sense of marginalization in stark, spare terms ('The dying fall, the death spasm, / Last words and catechism...' (*P* 61)).

Within such defined but tensile parameters Longley has unwaveringly pursued his career as a lyric poet ('I'm a lyric poet; I feel no need to get away from it at all'),[19] accommodating a wide range of public and private themes within an inclusiveness always given edge and vitality by its relation to an individual, and at times even idiosyncratic, angle of approach or sense of interconnection. Accordingly, the present volume, based on papers delivered at the 1996 session of the Ulster Symposium, seeks to take stock of his range, development and achievement as a poet so far. It is hoped that a substantial sense is given of the complex social, intellectual and literary contexts and traditions which inform and influence the work; the main focus though is upon critical analysis of the central lyric achievement.

ACKNOWLEDGEMENTS

The editors wish to express their thanks to the University of Ulster for financial support towards the present volume. Thanks are also extended to the Dean and Faculty of Humanities of the University, to the Arts Council of Northern Ireland and the Cultural Traditions Group of the Community Relations Council of Northern Ireland for support towards the 1996 session of the Ulster Symposium from which the present volume derives; also, to the staff of the University library.

Particular thanks are due to the General Editor of the Series, Professor Robert Welch, for his unflagging interest and practical support.

We are especially indebted to Michael Longley for generously making available the manuscript and photographic materials which are reproduced in the volume, for permission to print the text of his poem 'Etruria', and for pre-publication access to the typescript of *The Weather in Japan*. Our appreciation is also extended to Jeffrey Morgan for kind permission to reproduce his portrait of Michael Longley, now the property of Belfast City Council.

Acknowledgements to reproduce extracts from the published works of Michael Longley are as follows:

from *The Ghost Orchid*, published by Jonathan Cape, reprinted by permission of the Random House Group; in the USA reprinted by permission of Wake Forest University Press;

from *Gorse Fires*, published by Martin Secker & Warburg, reprinted by permission of the Random House Group; in the USA reprinted by permission of Wake Forest University Press;

from *Poems 1963–1983*, published by Martin Secker & Warburg, reprinted by permission of the Random House Group; in the USA reprinted by permission of Wake Forest University Press.

MICHAEL LONGLEY AND THE IRISH POETIC TRADITION

TERENCE BROWN

Michael Longley's forty-year career as a poet has represented a complex engagement (in which his awareness of English poetic modes has played a vital part) with the Irish poetic tradition. His work has in fact illuminated, extended and in crucial respects helped to redefine that tradition in quiet, subtle, unforced but intriguing ways.

To begin with, in his *oeuvre* lines of filiation with other Irish poets can be detected that have made his writing life a distinctive yet deeply rooted contribution to late twentieth-century Irish poetry. This essay will initially seek to trace those threads as they wind through the poetry, Longley's prose writings and the interviews he has given over the course of the years. It will then reflect on the way Longley has made English modes amenable to Irish experience in ways that extend the possibilities of the Irish poetic tradition.

A feature of Longley's earliest enthusiasms as a poet was an exuberant eclecticism. As he emerged as promising poet at Trinity College, Dublin in the late 1950s and early 1960s, after a period of literary inhibition at his Belfast grammar school (R.B.A.I. valued Rugby and getting-on in the Belfast way of the period), he read voraciously. He took the English tradition and contemporary verse as a whole as his proper field of engagement. In this he was aided and abetted by a well-informed companion who took him 'with joy' on an exciting voyage of discovery, a wide-ranging, engagingly unscheduled, poetic grand tour. Derek Mahon had arrived at T.C.D. a couple of years after Longley, but surpassed his friend in critical and aesthetic self-confidence. These were heady days:

We inhaled with our untipped Sweet Afton cigarettes MacNeice, Crane, Dylan Thomas, Yeats, Larkin, Lawrence, Graves, Ted Hughes, Stevens, Cummings, Richard Wilbur, Robert Lowell, as well as Rimbaud,

Baudelaire, Brecht, Rilke – higgledepiggledy, in any order. We scanned the journals and newspapers for poems written yesterday. When Larkin's 'The Whitsun Weddings' first appeared in *Encounter*, Mahon steered me past the documentary details, which as an aspiring lyricist I found irritating, to the poem's resonant, transcendental moments. He introduced me to George Herbert who thrilled me as though he were a brilliant contemporary published that very week by the Dolmen Press.[1]

The list of poets cited here is telling, for Longley's brilliant contemporaries (from the seventeenth century to the twentieth) include only two Irish poets, neither of whom was published in Dublin by Liam Miller's Dolmen Press. And the list is strikingly internationalist in scope. One gets an impression of an instinctive imaginative open-mindedness of the kind that has marked Longley's sensibility throughout his career. Yet here are significant exclusions. There is no mention of T.S. Eliot, nor of the Ezra Pound whom Longley's poetic predecessor at Trinity, Donald Davie (he lectured in English in the university in the 1950s) so admired. Nor of Austin Clarke, the learnedly obscure Irish poet whom Davie as critic had begun to sponsor during his time in Dublin. A certain disregard for high Modernism and wilful experimentalism may perhaps be inferred. Nor is Patrick Kavanagh one of the 'brilliant contemporaries' although his *Collected Poems* would appear in 1964. At his death, however, both Longley and Mahon contributed to a memorial edition of *The Dublin Magazine* in the spring of 1968.

Longley had in fact encountered Yeats (one of the Irish poets mentioned) at school when he had requested as a third-form prize for English the Collected Yeats, published in 1950. Yeats was also included in the examination syllabus for the Northern Ireland Senior Certificate, in the set anthology, *A Pageant of English Verse*. From Yeats it is possible that he derived his perennial sense that traditional poetic form is a poet's best resource; in Yeatsian terms that 'ancient salt is best packing'. And Longley's according poetry a kind of sacral numen in a secular world may also have its source in his early reading of Yeats. However it was Louis MacNeice (whose wonderfully sensuous philosophic lyric 'Snow' was included among the modern offerings in *A Pageant of English Verse*) who was the major Irish influence on the neophyte poet, who would also number as key texts among the work of his contemporaries Geoffrey Hill's *Mercian Hymns*, Philip Larkin's *The Whitsun Weddings* and Ted Hughes' *Lupercal*.[2]

The publication in 1966 of E.R. Dodds's edition of *The Collected*

Poems of Louis MacNeice was the occasion which allows us to see the young Longley engage critically with the recently dead, Belfast-born, elder poet (MacNeice died in the autumn of 1963), for he contributed a review article of the volume (entitled 'A Misrepresented Poet') to *The Dublin Magazine*, in the spring number, 1967. This was a remarkably assured, insightful piece of critical writing from the hand of a twenty-seven-year-old. It displays a keen eye for the strengths and weaknesses of individual poems (this was the period of practical criticism, in which Longley had been instructed by Philip Hobsbaum in the Group which met informally in the 1960s at Queen's University, Belfast) and for the high points of a career which had included, it must be admitted, rather extensive swathes of dull versifying.[3]

Longley noted immediately, among the juvenilia of the early pages of the volume, the formal and rhythmic assurance of 'Trains in the Distance'. He cites what he identifies as 'lines of an authority unusual for a poet in his early twenties':[4]

> Trains came threading quietly through my dozing childhood,
> Gentle murmurs nosing through a summer quietude,
> Drawing in and out, in and out, their smoky ribbons,
> Parting now and then, and launching full-rigged galleons
> And scrolls of smoke that hung in a shifting epitaph.
> Then distantly the noise declined like a descending graph . . .

Longley comments: 'The lines and their rhythms are bold and efficient, the rhyming is effortless, and the poet's senses are as alert to the physical minutiae of his environment as his intellect is to their significance. Indeed, this little poem exhibits what were to remain MacNeice's major strengths as a poet'.[5] He might perhaps have observed too of this poem, but did not, that MacNeice, like himself, is a master of the sentence, allowing it to weave down lines of verse to compose a poem that possesses a curious, block-like form on the page and in the mind (Longley elsewhere refers to Auden's notion of poems as 'oblongs and squares' and associates his own 'fascination with what can be achieved through syntax, the arrangement of a sentence' with his interest in Latin syntax).[6]

Longley's essay on MacNeice is also notable for the way it accurately establishes the overall shape of MacNeice's career. He notes the early lyrical successes, the drab middle years, with the Second World War, rightly I believe, read as a particularly fruitful period of MacNeice's life.[7] He grants 'the ease and scope of *Autumn Journal*' ('one of the luckiest poems . . . in which everything somehow falls into place').⁸ He responds to the revived lyric tones of the later books, of *Solstices* (1961) and the posthumously published *The Burning Perch* (1963), when MacNeice 'was working towards a new kind of music – hard, stark and adaptable'.⁹ He acknowledges MacNeice's achievements as a love poet for as such he avoided his besetting weakness as a poet: 'that refusal to let his ideas settle to a depth, which in his lesser poems results in surfaces made brilliant in order to cover up imaginative inconsistencies, and in verbal ingenuities which distract from what is being said'.¹⁰

Since Harold Bloom's challenging book *The Anxiety of Influence* we have become accustomed to the concept of poetic influence as an agonistic thing, compact of oedipal stress and straining ambition. Longley's relationship with MacNeice, by contrast, has been less a Bloomian attempt to supersede a precursor, than a generous, admiring, absorbent capacity, a negative capability if you like, to allow MacNeice's sensibility an extended though altered existence in his own poetic. A further reflection on MacNeice's poetry which Longley published in 1971 suggests how his own work developed under the enabling influence of MacNeice as example.

Longley in 1967 had recognised how MacNeice is often superficial, too wordly to be really wise, though he had exempted the love poetry from such strictures. By 1971 he had come to feel that when set against MacNeice's Ulster background 'the dizzy word play and the riot of imagery' that for many English critics mars his work, can be read in quite different terms:

> A proper consideration of his background, however, should help us to understand that all the gaudy paraphernalia of his poetry is finally a reply to darkness, to 'the fear of becoming stone'. His games are funeral games: the bright patterns he conjures from the external world and the pleasures of being alive are not fairy light and bauble but searchlight and icon.¹¹

In a more measured, reflective way, Longley's own love poetry can be said to share something of this dialectic. For his love poems are often elaborate conceits whose complex, elegantly detailed metaphors often carry rumours of war, of individual and mass slaughter (the Great War and Irish 'troubles' constitute Longley's primary historic horizons):

> September grew to shadows on Mweelrea
> Once the lambs had descended from the ridge

> With their fleeces dyed, tinges of sunset,
> Rowan berries, and the bracken rusting.
>
> Behind my eyelids I could just make out
> In a wash of blood and light and water
> Your body colouring the mountainside
> Like uncut poppies in the stubbly fields.
>
> ('On Mweelrea', P 178)

For all the heavy-breathing, forced psycho-drama of Bloom's Freudian vision of influence he is surely right however when he celebrates that moment of poetic power, of burgeoning authority, when a poet writes in a manner which makes the precursor seem the imitator (as when the Stevens of 'Notes Towards A Supreme Fiction' makes Keats seem to anticipate the poetics of the American poet – he makes Keats sound Stevensish). At a crucial moment in Longley's 1967 account of MacNeice he alerts us to how he performs a similar feat. He isolates a moment in MacNeice's verse which in fact seems to anticipate some of his own poetic characteristics. He categorises MacNeice's 'Mayfly' as 'a masterpiece' and cites four lines:

> Who make the mayflies dance, the lapwings lift their crests,
> The show will soon shut down, its gay-rags gone,
> But when this summer is over let us die together,
> I want always to be near your breasts.

Longley would later insist that 'these two beautiful lines disclose the nucleus of his imagination'.[12] In fact such frank, slightly plush eroticism with an intimation of decadent satiation is a very unusual note, a Longleyan note indeed, in MacNeice's work. For MacNeice's love poems are notable less for their consciousness of bodily presence than for an intense awareness of time arrested in the passion of the moment, with actual physicality rendered indirectly. 'Trilogy for X' (written, as we know from Stallworthy, for Nancy Sharp) is a telling instance:

> But now when winds are curling
>   The trees do you come closer,
> Close as an eyelid fasten
>   My body in darkness, darling;
> Switch the light off and let me
>   Gather you up and gather
> The power of trains advancing
>   Further, advancing further.

The phrase 'close as an eyelid fasten' is just the kind of surprising, yet exact, physical conceit we might expect to find in Longley's love poetry. But where Longley would elaborate upon it in an exploration of the sheer oddity of bodily experience MacNeice shifts into a more obviously literary trope, to distance the physicality of sexual intercourse, while allowing us to sense its rhythms and intensity. By contrast we may adduce Longley's 'The Linen Industry', whose final lines make us hear the later poet in MacNeice's 'Mayfly':

> And be shy of your breasts in the presence of death,
> Say that you look more beautiful in linen
> Wearing white petticoats, the bow on your bodice
> A butterfly attending the embroidered flowers.
>
> (P 179)

The metaphysical elaboration of this poem, rich in troping (an intimation of Herbert's rather than of Donne's poetics invests the whole with a religiose/erotic, emblematic quality), educates us to the way in which such a poem is both related to yet different from MacNeice's love poems, which are typically poems of sexual tension and bodily absence. Where MacNeice poises the moment of passion against an imagery of temporal movement, when 'the show will soon shut down, its gay-rags gone', when 'the moving stair' will start up again ('Meeting Point'), Longley allows himself to settle into a protracted meditation in 'The Linen Industry' in which Eros and Thanatos are presiding deities at a celebration of the processes of bodily existence. For this is a poem of growth and decay, creativity and decline, hair, cloth, bone, the palpable presence of actual body and bed.

It is, nevertheless, the weighty physicality of 'The Linen Industry', its materialist awareness of things in themselves (flax, flowers, peaty water, grasses, stooks, skirts, in the first stanza alone) that alerts us to a further aspect of Longley's verse that establishes MacNeice as a precursor who has his Longleyan moments.

Longley remarks in his introduction to his *Louis MacNeice: Selected Poems* (1988): 'Like most true poets he relished making catalogues, whether of place-names ("West Meon, Tisted, Farnham, Woking, Weybridge") or film-stars ("Cagney, Lombard, Bing and Garbo") or things ("Cubical scent-bottles artificial legs arctic foxes and electric mops"). Seldom can the lyric have carried so much freight and remained airborne'.[13] Longley himself is a poet of catalogues, who has indeed made the list a principle of composition in some poems, with an exacting deliberation bred of a settled, materialist vision of the world. By contrast MacNeice's list-making seems an exuberant or appalled response to the 'drunkenness of things being various' ('Snow') or to their weary torpor (note 'Flower Show' with its 'cream cheese, paper, glass, all manner of textile and plastic').

Longley's fascination for lists increased over the years until he began to trust the list as a poem in itself. 'The Ice-cream Man' and 'Trade Winds' in *Gorse Fires* (1991) and 'The Fishing Party' in *The Ghost Orchid* (1995) are the crucial instances. Such manifestations of a recurrent obsession also direct us to the way many of Longley's recent poems seem to take a list of objects as a kind of ur-text from which the poem has emerged. In 'The Dry Cleaners' (in *The Ghost Orchid*), for example, a list of named objects is brought into contiguity and relationship by grammar (three complex sentences) and the narrative occasion the poem summons into existence:

> That time I tagged along with my dad to the dry cleaners
> We bumped into Eurycleia whose afternoon-off it was
> And bought her tea and watched her smooth the table-
> Cloth and make her plate and doily concentric circles, then
> Pick up cake-crumbs with a moistened finger, since to us
> There was more to her than jugs and basins, hot water
> And cold, bed-linen she tested against her cheek after
> The rainy trek from clothes-line to airing cupboard.
>
> (*GO* 32)

One notes here the predominately nominative quality of Longley's verse with nouns held lovingly in such writing in a solution of exact grammar. This also contrasts significantly with MacNeice's poetry when in his late verse he too sometimes took lists as poetic ur-text. In MacNeice however such lists are verbs rather than nouns, as they record transient events rather than the secure givenness of material reality Longley values so much. For MacNeice sees the world characteristically in terms of motion and activity:

> Coffee leaps in a crystal knob
> Chugs and glints while birds gossip . . .
>
> ('Country Week-end')

Longley's universe is a naming of things as they palpably are, as in the opening lines of 'Northern Lights' in *Gorse Fires*:

> When you woke me up and showed me through the window
> Curtains of silk, luminous smoke, ghost fires,
> A convergence of rays above the Black Mountain . . .
>
> <div align="right">(<i>GF</i> 32)</div>

It is also a world of the naming of places (the Belfast place-name of 'Northern Lights' is a typical instance). MacNeice could name places too in his poetry, as in 'The Strand' where he memorialised a father who

> So loved the western sea and no tree's green
> Fulfilled him like these contours of Slievemore
> Menaun and Croaghaun and the bogs between

in lines that have a direct echo in Longley's

>   and all the stars are out
> Lighting up hill-tops, glens, headlands, vantage
> Points like Tonakeera and Allaran where the tide
> Turns into Killary, where the salmon run from the sea . . .
>
> <div align="right">('The Camp-Fires', <i>GO</i> 37)</div>

Yet such use of Irish place names, common in Longley's work, is comparatively rare in MacNeice's poetry. He can, it is true, make his own music with the names of his adopted England:

> A smell of French bread in Charlotte Street, a rustle
>   Of leaves in Regent's Park . . .
>
> ('Autumn Journal' Section V)

or

> We drove round Shropshire in a bijou car –
>   Bewdley, Cleobury, Mortimer, Ludlow . . .

But it is Longley who can begin a poem in *The Ghost Orchid*, 'How does the solitary swan on Dooaghtry Lake', weighing a place name in his hand, like a magical talisman, in a distinctly Yeatsian fashion. For Yeats could famously begin a poem:

> He stood among a crowd in Drumahair . . .
>
> ('The Man Who Dreamed of Faeryland')

So it is Longley more than MacNeice who recalls Yeats to mind when he creates his English language music with an echo of Gaelic nomination, in such resonant lines as:

> From the townland of Carrigskeewaun,
> From a page lit by the Milky Way.
>
> <div align="right">('Remembering Carrigskeewaun', <i>GF</i> 12)</div>

In his 1967 review essay of MacNeice's *Collected Poems* Longley did not address at any length the matter of MacNeice's Irishness, beyond observing that 'his poetry is the direct reflection of an ironic Northern Irish personality'[14] and that he had a love-hate relationship with his native land. His 1971 observations on MacNeice, as we saw, took up that topic in a few telling sentences. He saw then how what can seem superficial to an English readership can, with knowledge of the poet's Irish background, allow MacNeice to be reckoned as 'a touchstone of what an Ulster poet might be'.[15] The implication is that context is a part of meaning, the tradition in which a poet works and the culture from which he derives in part determining how his work should be read and judged.

This instinctive early awareness of the ways in which interpretative communities bear on aesthetic experience is in fact a clue to a central aspect of Longley's career and to his recent work in particular. For Longley has been aware from quite early on that Ireland, its experience and imaginative traditions, affect more general ways of apprehending the world, when they are adopted by Irish poets and writers. In a 1972 symposium on 'The State of Poetry', published in England in *the Review* he tackled the question of literary peripherality in interesting ways. Of a recent 'efflorescence of poetry in the provinces' he made the bold claim: 'most of the best contemporary Irish poetry is being written North of the Border' and asserted: 'the Irish psyche is being redefined in Ulster, and the poems are born – inevitably, one might say – out of a lively tension between the Irish and the English traditions'.[16] He wrote of 'a fruitful schizophrenia in someone trying to write poetry in Ireland' appreciative of the contemporary poetic vitality in the provinces of Britain. 'I . . . am', he averred, 'proud to stand on the geographical and, possibly, the cultural edge of a vital tradition which can accommodate a few Irish accents'.[17]

Crucial to this thinking is the idea that lively tension between English and Irish traditions can help to redefine the Irish psyche – can bring something new to birth. It is akin to his view that MacNeice's poetry, apparently superficial in England, in Ulster can be vested with specific significance by an interpretative community. In Northern Ireland certain English traditions (in his contribution he endorses the then fashionable 'well-made poem') can take on new forms and alter Irish consciousness in significant ways.

In the light of this it might be possible to ponder the shape and significance of Longley's career as an engagement not only with the Irish poetic tradition in the work of Yeats and MacNeice (both of course Irish poets whose work also extends the tradition of English language poetry as a whole), but as a semi-conscious programme in which a series of essentially English poetic modes and kinds have undergone a sea-change in an Irish setting. One might list these as follows: the First World and Second World War poem, the topographical poem, the well-made poem of Movement vintage, the natural history poem, the classical poem (that is a poem employing classical allusion or with content derived from classical literature). A hasty reading of each of these kinds of work in the Longley canon might too readily assign them to the English tradition: the First World and Second World War poems with their poetic respects paid to Isaac Rosenberg, Edward Thomas and Keith Douglas, the natural history poems with their roots in essentially English traditions of amateur botanising, the well-made poems, the product of the Movement's post-war reduction of imaginative horizons and empirical circumspection, the classical poems with their modern source in public- or grammar-school education, all might seem to fit comfortably within an English frame of reference. In Longley's work however these poetic kinds are carried over into Irish contexts (in effect they are 'translated'), thereby allowing them to find a new form of life in the context of an Irish poetic tradition.

Longley's imaginative 'importation' of the classical poem is, perhaps, the most striking of his various acts of metamorphosis in which English poetic kinds are remade in an Irish context. One must be careful here. For of course Ireland has no need whatsoever to import classical knowledge as a poetic resource from the neighbouring island.[18] Yet there is a distinct sense in Longley's early deployment in his verse of classical matter that the poems derive from the world of polite learning and gentlemanly education that made the study of the classics in the Protestant Ireland in which the poet had his social formation seem a distinctly English kind of cultural activity. In 'Odyssey', 'Circe', 'Nausicaa' and 'Narcissus' in Longley's first volume, *No Continuing City* (1969), classical occasions and allusions served as imaginative stimuli for elegant, carefully constructed negotiations by a cerebral sensibility of the mythic possibilities of life in general. The tension in these poems between an urbane discourse and the consciousness of mythic dimension in experience does suggest, it is true, that Longley's classicism from the start was thematically driven, that it was no merely conventional literary trope. But the poems' generalised classical provenance remained their most obvious characteristic. It has been his recent work in *Gorse Fires* and *The Ghost Orchid*, however, that suggests how classical occasion and Irish reality can be associated in ways that speak to a twentieth-century Irish preoccupation.

Since the turn of the century, in the work of Yeats and principally in the writings of James Joyce, Irish writers have been redefining a national relationship with the Greek and Latin origins of European civilisation. These have historically been compromised in Ireland in as much as classicism seemed so much a property of the conqueror, and of imperial Victorian England, with its colonial administrators governing by means of the sword and a Latin tag. And the Church, with its Roman imperium mediated through the Latin tongue, added to the sense of a heavily entailed inheritance. Longley's work, as it 'translates' the classical poem for an Irish interpretative community, is therefore part of a process whereby the Greek and Roman legacy has been appropriated to modern Irish experience in fresh ways by twentieth century poets and dramatists (Seamus Heaney, Tom Murphy, Brendan Kennelly and, before them, Austin Clarke spring to mind in this context). Longley's contribution has been to situate Homeric and Ovidian narratives in Irish contexts of locale and event in a strikingly intimate manner. In his versions of the old tales, familiar stories and events are renovated as they become grimly local, domesticated and yet nobly, poignantly strange once again in a fully realised material world (in 1985 Longley spoke of how in Homer, 'still a favourite poet – the sense of physical life . . . comes out of that story beneath its mythological/historical overlay').[19] The ancient Greek world of the epic narratives and a fully Irish topography and nomination are brought together, therefore, with remarkable assurance in a poem such as the already quoted 'The Camp-fires' in a way that enlarges our sense of what an Irish poem can be (note the magisterial control of parenthesis, as if in a brief Irish poem of place, a Homeric simile can unfold in all its spacious grandeur):

> All night crackling camp-fires boosted their morale
> As they dozed in no man's land and the killing fields.
> (There are balmy nights – not a breath, constellations
> Resplendent in the sky around a dazzling moon –
> When a clearance high in the atmosphere unveils
> The boundlessness of space, and all the stars are out
> Lighting up hill-tops, glens, headlands, vantage
> Points like Tonakeera and Allaran where the tide

Turns into Killary, where salmon run from the sea,
Where the shepherd smiles on his luminous townland.
That many camp-fires sparkled in front of Ilium
Between the river and the ships, a thousand fires,
Round each one fifty men relaxing in the fire-light.)
Shuffling next to the chariots, munching shiny oats
And barley, their horses waited for the sunrise.

LONGLEY'S METRIC

DOUGLAS DUNN

W.B. Yeats's imperative, or advice, as stated in 'Under Ben Bulben' –

> Irish poets, learn your trade,
> Sing whatever is well made . . .[1]

is very often supposed to have exercised a profound meaning for Irish poets who have come after him. To so suppose, of course, is to sanitize Yeats's intentions, overrate his subsequent value to a world, and an Ireland, no longer the same as those he left, or neglect the political and social gestures of the lines which follow:

> Scorn the sort now growing up
> All out of shape from toe to top,
> Their unremembering hearts and heads
> Base-born products of base beds.

After that, Yeats's preferred social vision is hard to take – peasantry, hard-riding country gentlemen, monks, porter drinkers, and lords and ladies gay. Even the first two lines of part V of 'Under Ben Bulben' can be questioned. Is 'whatever' the poem itself or the subject it addresses or possesses? But in a very general sense it seems fair to assume that the artistic side of Yeats's objurgations in that remarkable and unnervingly anachronistic poem have sunk deep into Irish poetic consciousness, whether as a programme to be followed, rejected, or ignored.

However, a great deal of contemporary poetry, Irish and otherwise, exemplifies a very marked concern for artistry, for everything Yeats meant by 'learn' and by 'trade', as well as that aspect of it – the 'well made' – sometimes too ruralistically described as 'craft', or too mechanistically referred to as 'technique'. As well as Michael Longley, such contemporary writers as Seamus Heaney, Derek Mahon, Paul Muldoon, Tony Harrison, John Fuller, Peter Reading, Craig Raine, James Fenton,

Mick Imlah, and Sean O'Brien, to mention only a few, have shown a conspicuous engagement with the artistry of poetry at a level which should lead us to realize that it is an essential part of their poetic identities. It is not a grafted on, willed, enforced virtuosity in *how* they say what they say; it is a crucial part of *what* they are saying. Over the past few decades there has been a temptation to suspect that a poet whose characteristic writing shows a degree of scrupulousness, or a devotion to the metrical articulation of poetry, is engaged in a forlorn contest between his or her alleged orthodoxy and the values of modernism, or a self-repressive struggle with the ostensible virtues of spontaneity, or a sly alignment with tame conservative values. What I propose to say is that the actual performance of writing as demonstrated by the poets of this generation is part of a moral project. It has been discovered and expressed instinctively and in different, individual ways, but despite different political affiliations, and different poetic affiliations too, I believe that it displays much recent poetry to be distinctive in its coherence, and that when you take into account also what these poets say, the values by which they are convinced and by which they live, and those of society, then the implications of a phrase like 'moral project' strike me as a lot less ridiculous than when I first thought of putting it in that way.

By 'metric' I mean T.S. Eliot's understanding and use of the term in his early essay on Ezra Pound,[2] that is, a poet's acoustic, or resonance, the organization of a voice, and 'organization' in the sense of deliberate and procedural as well as – more importantly – intuitive and accidental. If we can characterize that aspect of a poet's work then we come close to describing its distinctiveness. It's this dimension of a poet's work which I want to align with moral value in a very general sense, that is, without associating it with excessive intentionalism or alleging that the work serves a didactic purpose. However, I don't go as far as Yvor Winters in *Primitivism and Decadence* where he asserts an 'absolutist' link between poetic form and morality. Where I accept him and find his remarks illuminating is when he writes that

> the poet, in striving toward an ideal of poetic form at which he has arrived through the study of other poets, is actually striving to perfect a moral attitude toward that range of experience of which he is aware. Such moral attitudes are contagious from poet to poet, and, within the life of a single poet, from poem to poem.[3]

In opposition to his 'absolutist' theory Winters finds all other theories of poetry to be, in the main, what he calls 'hedonistic'.

It's Winters's somewhat prissy, precise, and near-pejorative perspective on hedonism that I remember had exactly the opposite effect on me to the one he intended and warmed me to it about twenty years ago when I first read *In Defense of Reason* and at precisely that moment when I'd started to mutter to myself that I was in for a grimly serious read. Pleasure is one of the most powerful of all human objectives. That it takes a central place in my view of the poetry of Michael Longley's generation – which is my generation too – as an underacknowledged 'moral project' is not at all contradictory. Indeed, in Longley's poetry in particular the pleasures of life are clearly implicated in the 'moral attitude' which his poetry seeks to perfect in relation to the 'range of experience of which he is aware'. Hedonism is a potent and important critical concept in the poetry of Longley and his contemporaries. It has very great temporal and temperamental significance, and whatever else it means it does not stand for carelessness.

In his interview with Robert Johnstone[4] Longley declared that the best thing ever said about English prosody was Robert Frost's remark – 'There's strict iambic and loose iambic'. It's a curiously fixated approach to metre and rhythm and rests its case on the old chestnut that English has a tendency to generate iambics. In fact, English does this, when it does, only as a consequence of its animated multiples of indispensable monosyllabic words such as *the, and, but, not, no, yes, is, are, have, had, were, what, where, when, why* etc., etc. English pronunciation normally puts the stress on the first syllable so that bi-syllabic terms in its vast vocabulary are trochaic, and tri-syllables naturally dactylic. To think only in terms of iambic rhythm is to depress the status of such poets as Tennyson, Browning and Hardy, whose metrical repertoires are extensive. Several contemporary poets, notably James Fenton and Mick Imlah, have exploited triple metres with great success. Early in his career, Longley wrote a number of highly skilled and effective formal poems – 'Epithalamion', 'The Ornithological Section', 'A Personal Statement' and 'The Hebrides' being among them.[5] Of 'A Personal Statement' he's said (in the interview with Robert Johnstone) that the technical influence was George Herbert and that he was interested 'in patterns which used lines of varying lengths in a strict way'. At the same time he described the change in his style over the years as one that moves towards 'increasing simplicity' while also revealing a lust to return to 'that kind of technical firework display'. 'I don't think I'll ever be able to,' he continued, 'but solving the problems I set myself in those poems was inspiring in itself'. Remarks like these, and Longley's acceptance of Frost's gruff, allegedly decisive and misleading opinion, indicate an approach to poetic formality of a kind which I distrust – Frost, for example, would have been aware of, and reacting to, the great weight of Tennyson, Browning, Longfellow, and Emerson, as well as the dithyrambic Whitman. Admittedly, though, it's extremely difficult for a poet to be convincing or even coherent on the subjects of form and versification, especially off the cuff. You have to be able to convey several emphases simultaneously. To concentrate only on the technical aspects of poetry leads to aridity, and while you say what you have to on that matter at the same time you have to do more than acknowledge the imaginative, the temperamental, the instinctive, the *involuntary* side of poetry which leads to the authentically mimetic, kinetic, and mythopoeic. Remarks on poetic form given in conversation usually amount to imperfect summaries. At best, they provide an unreliable hint of what happens when a particular poet is writing.

'A Personal Statement', dedicated to Seamus Heaney, begins:

> Since you, Mind, think to diagnose
>   Experience
> As summer, satin, nightingale or rose,
>   Of the senses making sense –
>   Follow my nose,
>
> Attend all other points of contact,
>   Deserve your berth:
> My brain-child, help me find my own way back
>   To fire, air, water, earth.
>   I am, in fact,
>
> More than a bag of skin and bone.
>   My person is
> A chamber where the elements postpone
>   In lively synthesis,
>   In peace on loan,
>
> Old wars of flood and earthquake, storm
>   And holocaust,
> Their attributes most temperately reformed
>   Of heatwave and of frost.

(P 27)

The delightful sense of measure in 'A Personal Statement', using a five-line stanza imitated from George Herbert, distributes lines of four, two, five, three and two stresses, and almost always with full rhymes. Equally impressive is Longley's success in controlling long and short sentences through the **a-b-a-b-a** rhyme scheme and lines of different lengths throughout the poem. What he achieves is a communicable and lucid lyricism taking the ostensible form of a 'statement', which I understand as a near-metaphysical attempt to align Mind and Body, the intellectual with the elemental and sensory, the pure with the impure, and the imaginative with the physically perceived – a series of antitheses perfectly in keeping with my claim of a 'moral project' and the dilemmas which it encounters or which, at least, it doesn't evade. It's noticeable, too, that his skill in rhyming extends to the satisfying (and traditional) insistence on strong, significant terms at the ends of the lines. That is, 'A Personal Statement', like 'Epithalamion' and 'The Hebrides', is a very traditional poem indeed and seems to have been written self-consciously with that end in view. Harder to achieve, though, in a poem of this kind, is the avoidance of the echo of someone else, and the whisper I hear is that of W.H. Auden, who also admired Herbert and who employed stanzas not unlike this one. Indeed, it was Auden who recovered stanzaic verse for modern poetry in the 1930s at a time when it seemed likely to die out with Hardy, or become an American reserve, or be possessed only by light-versifiers and post-Victorian pasticheurs.

In the accomplished poems of his first collection, *No Continuing City* (1969), there are already signs of his later styles. The looser iambic of 'Odyssey' (*P* 30), for example, while firm enough to justify and deliver rhymes, shows a considerable relaxation of the voice. The last stanza:

> You have kept me going, despite delays –
> On these devious shores where we coincide
> I have never once outstayed my welcome
> Though you all seem last resorts, my brides –
> Your faces favourite landmarks always,
> Your bodies comprising the long way home.

'Journey out of Essex' (*P* 56) is even closer to the unrhymed but stanzaic poetry of his later work.

We like to speak of a poet's 'voice' – and I suppose that is what I mean by 'metric', the poet's acoustic, a resonance that over time becomes describable as in a sense a 'system' although devised as much by instinct and involuntary preferences as by deliberation and choice. It is, or ought to be, as natural as the actual intonation of how the poet speaks. One of the trite, banal and damaging commonplaces of some recent criticism is that to follow metrical or stanzaic habits of writing is to erect an obstacle between the poet and the opportunity of achieving the sacred cow of 'voice', a meaningful individuality of poetic utterance. Conversely, so too is the belief that freer or free verse is a disabling obstacle to artistry in the same curmudgeonly class of wicked, ideologically-driven simplifications. In his first collection, and later in his work, what we hear and see is a poet for whom it is necessary always to struggle with the possibility of formal inertia, that abject complacency into which it is possible to slide when the mind closes itself to the chances of modification or larger change. Also, there is an air of inevitability about how a poet's work grows, if it does, and Longley's most certainly has and continues to do so. Notice that I didn't say 'develop'. There's a remark of Peter Levi's that I like – 'Bad poets develop, good poets grow'.[6] Longley's later manner, like his concerns, grows out of his first collection. In 'A Personal Statement' he sets out his stall and I believe he has been faithful to the comprehensive and benevolent intellectual, sentient, and artistic desires expressed there, no matter if he *seems* to have grown into a more spacious, freer range of styles. In fact, he hasn't; instead, he has achieved a truly remarkable formal control, the true spirit of which is ease. But it seems right to regret that in an earlier poem like 'Graffiti' his versification, its accommodation to a speaking voice, gave him more opportunity to exercise humour and panache:

> It would be painful, tedious and late
> To alter awkward monsters such as these
> To charming princes – metamorphoses
> That all good fairy tales accelerate –
>
> One kiss and, in the twinkling of an eye,
> The Calibans accepted, warts and all,
> At long last resurrected from the sty,
> So blond, so beautiful, and six feet tall.

(P 21)

Despite their formality, their shapely making, the poems of *No Continuing City* are beautifully poised in a language just on the colloquial side of vernacular. His idiom, his diction, moves in and out of colloquial and more formal poetic registers in 'A Personal Statement' – for example, phrases like 'Follow my nose', or 'Deserve your berth' – and even in the *terza rima* of 'A Questionnaire for Walter Mitty' (P 20), although Louis MacNeice colloquialised that form stunningly in *Autumn Sequel*.[7] A poet doesn't really *choose* his or her idiom. It feels truer to recognize that it is brought about by personality, by 'moral attitude', as well as through a near-religious exercise of devotion to those poets of the past for whose work the contemporary poet feels a profound affinity. In Longley's earlier work his diction, its mix of both colloquial and formal pitches, generates an impression of a sociable, good-natured dignity. Just as his perceptions look for a purity or lyric hygiene in what is witnessed, his diction seeks a similar vernacular cleanliness while knowing that it is unobtainable and that the only way of achieving it in *contemporary* writing would be to commit a dishonest act of forgery. An idiom exclusive to poetry would be undemocratic. To look too strenuously for such a 'purity of diction' would be to sacrifice too much of an innately liberal intellect – more than a decent 'moral attitude' could stand. It would be to lose one of the most important, and one of the most neglected, perhaps also one of the most embarrassing gifts of lyric poetry, which is its unsentimental benevolence. This, too, it seems to me, is a crucial part of what I referred to earlier as a 'moral project'.

In his first book, then, Longley achieved a contemporary idiom, characteristically in poems of conspicuous concinnity and formal finish. It is an easily-worn elegance, though. Orotund and grandiloquent tendencies, which can be encouraged by metrical strategies, were always kept at bay, or sometimes exploited sportively, as if having been noticed with raised eyebrows, and amended. If poetry is, or can be, a ceremonial or ritualized use of language and rhythm, then there are plenty of examples of that kind of decorum. However, form, diction, and metre in these earlier poems are typically unaffected: the language is not that of the streets – it is a good distance from the demotic – but neither does it draw too much attention to the fraudulent prestige of an educated idiom. There's a touch of the dandy to the poet of *No Continuing City* but he holds it at arm's length at the same time as he courts a manicured flourish. He shows, with considerable avidity, that he knows all about decorum, but he punctures any anticipation of an *orthodox* versification used as a means of conveying predictable meanings.

To put it mildly, I'm skeptical as to whether metricality can contribute decisively to a poet's creation of equilibrium. All it can do is to enhance the possibilities of melody and add a rhythmical resource which is only tentatively present in prose and harder to discover in free verse. In free verse, too, however, these effects can be achieved through surprises of diction and the presence of original imagery and figuration. Indeed, when imaginative power and a new force of perception are present in any kind of writing it is almost always uncannily the case that their embodiment will be rhythmical as well. Through a life's work, however, metricality and everything we associate with versification – rhyme, stanza, an essentially formal and poetic way of confronting the world – can add what I want to call *duration*. I've taken these terms – *equilibrium* and *duration* – from the Preface to Toni Morrison's *Playing in the Dark: Whiteness and the Literary Imagination*[8] where she discusses Marie Cardinal's *The Words to Say It*, which is an extraordinary account of Cardinal's madness. Cardinal suffered her first anxiety attack listening to Louis Armstrong at a concert. The episode is especially harrowing, and surprising: anxiety is not what those of us who love jazz experience when listening to Armstrong's trumpet solos. Awe, emotion, exhilaration, and excitement, but not anxiety – 'What on earth was Louie playing that night?' Morrison asks, understandably. Convinced she was going to die, Cardinal raced from the concert; and it is described by Toni Morrison as 'this curious flight from the genius of improvisation, sublime order, poise, and the illusion of permanence'. Cardinal evokes the impact of the music on her as 'one precise, *unique* note, tracing a sound whose path was almost *painful*, so absolutely necessary had its *equilibrium* and *duration* become; it *tore at the nerves* of those [other than Armstrong, apparently] who followed it' (italics and parentheses Toni Morrison's).

I hope it's not too disrespectful of an individual's dilemma to associate it – that 'curious flight' – with a general aesthetic predicament. But Cardinal's self-eviction from 'the genius of improvisation, sublime order, poise, and the illusion of permanence' is paralleled (or so I believe) by prevailing attitudes to poetic form. It is as if *equilibrium* (sanity, confidence, or a belief in their possibility and value, and the attempt to win, and deserve them) and *duration* (not just the length of a note, but the chance of a lifetime of sustained artistry and its exploration) are despised as hopeless improbabilities or best left in a state of academic relegation in the comfortable category of the historical. Also, it's generally misunderstood that writing which depends on metricality, and ways of writing derived from it, are examples of improvisation, too. Louis Armstrong's trumpet solos wouldn't be the astounding art that they are unless he had first learned how to play the trumpet – although no sooner will I say that than I'll admit that it's a potentially philistine approach to poetry, and the most vulgar simplification possible of what metricality can mean. Implicit in the 'moral project' of Michael Longley and the poets of his generation is an understanding of the aesthetics of poetry that is too broad, too inclusive, for the simplicities that lurk in a command to 'learn your trade', or a dimwitted insistence on scansion. Nor, by inclusiveness, do I mean a mere tolerance of other ways of writing. What this poetry adds up to is an embrace, a willingness to be inclusive. It is a poetry which seeks always to be generous. It is a poetry of those who 'make love and read the newspapers', to adapt a phrase of Albert Camus's.[9] In its concerns with self, domesticity, personal commitments, family, love, the natural, the urban, the local, it is a poetry, too, in which anything and everything might be topical, even whimsy, and while rooted in the particular and quotidian and natural, it seeks constantly to understand the mysterious, the irrational, and the spiritual.

Although Longley appears to have regretted his earlier formal, rhyming verse as now absentee (or he did so, perhaps momentarily, in 1985, during an unproductive phase when he might not have understood the direction in which his talent was leading him) it's possible to see a freer manner as the destination to which his gift was directed. It would be mistaken though, to consider his work as somehow divided between the ostensibly more elaborate poems of his first book and the freer or 'looser' iambic of his work after around 1968. Indeed, a contrast between formal, freer, and free, is a red herring. After all, it is the same poet, the same 'voice', the same or a similar parley with an experience of life and an ongoing experience of poetry. Besides, occupying a large place in *An Exploded View* (1973) is 'Letters' (*P* 76–85), addressed to three Irish poets, James Simmons, Derek Mahon, and Seamus Heaney, and written in octosyllabic couplets, either in six-line stanzas or, in the poems addressed to Mahon and Heaney, in eight. While 'epistolary', and, therefore, to an extent, personal, the formal ploy of 'Letters' associates it with public poetry – the same rhythm as Robert Lowell's 'Waking Early Sunday Morning', but also a Yeatsian measure ('Under Ben Bulben', for example, 'An Irish Airman Foresees His Death', or 'In Memory of Eva Gore-Booth and Con Markiewicz'), with many examples by Auden ('New Year Letter', parts of 'In Memory of W. B. Yeats'), MacNeice ('Letter from India') and a solid seventeenth-century pedigree in Ben Jonson, Marvell, and Milton. Public statements have often been disguised as private epistolary poems – Burns's and Pope's are two obvious instances. Tetrameter often becomes trochaic in English – we need think only of the songs in

Shakespeare's plays: 'Journeys end in lovers' meeting / Every wise man's son doth know'. It's a wise poet who lets this happen. Iambic and trochaic work well together while trochaic measure is perhaps the most intensely ritualistic rhythm in English:

> Earth, receive an honoured guest:
> William Yeats is laid to rest.
> Let the Irish vessel lie
> Emptied of its poetry.[10]

In Longley's 'Letters', then, there occurs an audibly echoic underlay without the poet going out of his way to achieve it:

> Now that the distant islands rise
> Out of the corners of my eyes
> And the imagination fills
> Bog-meadow and surrounding hills,
> I find myself addressing you
> As though I'd always wanted to:
>
> In order to take you all in
> I've had to get beneath your skin,
> To colonise you like a land,
> To study each distinctive hand
> And, by squatter's rights, inhabit
> The letters of its alphabet,
>
> Although when I call him Daniel
> (Mother and baby doing well),
> Lost relations take their places,
> Namesakes and receding faces:
> Late travellers on the Underground
> People my head like a ghost town.

(P 77)

The dynamic of 'Letters' is a playing off of distempered loathing for Irish violence against the security of family and friendships and a deep love of the place in which an affection for character and nature seems the source of both consolation and an irate puzzlement. The poem, too, is written in the context of a son's birth – it is a vulnerable, frustrated, paternal poem. Its anguished loquacity is underlined by the apparent order of its form, by the opposition of what it has to tell us with the poetic procedure used to convey it:

> Now every lost bedraggled field
> Like a mythopoeic bog unfolds
> Its gelignite and dumdums . . .
>
> Blood on the kerbstones, and my mind
> Dividing like a pavement,
> Cracked by the weeds, by the green grass
> That covers our necropolis,
> The pity, terror . . .
>
> I who have heard the waters break
> Claim this my country, though today
> *Timor mortis conturbat me.*
>
> (P 77–8)

And, as a present to Seamus Heaney, he offers

> The mystical point at which I tire
> Of Calor gas and a turf fire . . .

imagining, too,

> That small subconscious cottage where
> The Irish poet slams his door
> On slow-worm, toad and adder . . .
>
> (P 84)

In terms that might allude to 'A Personal Statement' in his previous collection – that contagion, as Yvor Winters remarked, going from poem to poem – he writes,

> Body with soul thus kept afloat,
> Mind open like a half-door
> To the speckled hill, the plovers' shore.

If 'Letters' is, as I've suggested, a public poem disguised as a private one, and touching on hazardous, difficult subjects, then its tactic is not altogether surprising. Increasingly, Longley's poetry was becoming of the kind that is 'overheard' rather than confronted by the reader as a specific addressee. This is not to say that Longley's later or mature writing is inaccessible or that it is always 'overheard' but that its accessibility is sometimes approached from, as it were, the side. 'Mind open like a half-door / To the speckled hill, the plovers' shore' is a concrete image sufficient in itself (that is, if we leave out the metaphysical force of 'mind', a cipher which can never be entirely clarified). But it is also representative of a whole world of peace, landscape and creatures to which the mind has access even if 'half-door' indicates that the freedom to go there is not what it was or that the entire significance and loveliness of the landscape are no longer visible, the previous view of the country being reduced or damaged. In any case, for a public poem arrived at by private poetic means, by letters 'addressed' to other poets implicated in the same emergency, it has an unexpected frequency of lyrical moments as if the poet hoped instinctively that they would cancel the candour and annoyance of what else he was obliged to say and to some of which the friends who received these letters might conceivably object.

Violence and political affront where a poet lives, in the place with which he or she identifies, can be expected to find their reflection in what such a poet writes about and, even more intimately perhaps, in what I've been calling the poet's metric. Although futile and even possibly demeaning in practice, several possible scenarios could be suggested. The poet could withdraw into an equivalent of that 'small subconscious cottage' and devote mind and pen to subjects and manners that have nothing to do with the political and which reject any taint from it. Or the poet could mount a more direct or denunciatory intervention on the political. Another tactic could be to join one side or another, but the expense of poetry involved in such a choice, to say nothing of shame and spirit, is likely to be immense. Regret, grief, mourning, indignation, are all likely to arise whatever course a poet chooses to take in the Northern Irish (or any other) context. How a poet expresses these feelings, however, is likely to depend on two primary factors – skill and honesty in the way in which such feelings are experienced and presented. Pound's maxim – 'I believe in technique as a test of a man's sincerity' – was ever a potent one, and it's my conviction that it restates the wisdom that was once passed on by word of mouth from older poet to younger. There really are NO rules to the making of poems. If it works, it works; what rules there are rely on an individual ear and the extent to which it has been educated in a wide and profound reading of poetry and on that 'range of experience' of which a poet comes to be aware, as well as that original articulation which, in its performance, creates artistry – and also, the point where I diverge from Yvor Winters, on the experience of which the poet was *unaware*, but which is discovered in the act of writing, the experience, that is, to which the poet is led by poetry itself. Faced with very real and dire emergencies in the poet's community, however, and dangers to which the poet and his or her family are exposed, then the pressure must be very real and must insist on being attended to. I admit to guessing – I know something of political frustration, but nothing of political violence: Scottish nationalism, to its enormous credit, hasn't killed anyone, and if anyone has died of it – as a friend of mine likes to say, perhaps unfairly – it's probably through sheer ennui. Of a poet's obligations, Longley said in his interview with Robert Johnstone,

> I think his first obligation is to his art, to the dictates of his imagination. Beyond that, he has the ordinary citizen's obligations. But it would be fatal for anyone sitting down to paint a picture or write a poem to think that he's contributing to society with a capital 'S'. I've always liked a Latin phrase, 'musarum sacerdos', priest of the Muses.

In his poem 'Wounds' Longley approaches terrorist murders through a filial account of his father's service with the Ulster Division in the Great War. It is a gesture of extreme filial piety in which the father's grave is added to by the bodies of three British soldiers and the uniform of a bus-conductor assassinated in his house in front of his family. The evocation of sectarianism in the soldiers of the Ulster Division is unsettling, if predictable, but an equal part of the poem's disturbance is the realization that it is presented in two measured seventeen-line stanzas or paragraphs, and that the 'loose iambic' of its blank verse has been clearly weighed against a metrical frame as well as a speaking voice. The first paragraph is grimly historical; the second is a disconcerting amalgam of morbidly surreal whimsy and topical realism. What I'd like to attend to are the sheer melancholy measure of the lines and the dangerously domestic potion brewed from the conscientious and descriptive:

> Now, with military honours of a kind,
> With his badges, his medals like rainbows,
> His spinning compass, I bury beside him
> Three teenage soldiers, bellies full of
> Bullets and Irish beer, their flies undone.
> A packet of Woodbines I throw in,
> A lucifer, the Sacred Heart of Jesus
> Paralysed as heavy guns put out
> The night-light in a nursery for ever;
> Also a bus-conductor's uniform –
> He collapsed beside his carpet-slippers
> Without a murmur, shot through the head
> By a shivering boy who wandered in

> Before they could turn the television down
> Or tidy away the supper dishes.
> To the children, to a bewildered wife,
> I think 'Sorry Missus' was what he said.

(P 86)

The signature to these lines – and it is an audible signature as well as a visual one – is conveyed by naming, and by objects. Things in a poem are a fundamental aspect of imagery. Badges, medals, compass, bullets, beer, flies, Woodbines, lucifer, Sacred heart of Jesus, night-light, nursery, bus-conductor's uniform, carpet-slippers, and then the domestic details of turning down the television when the doorbell rings or someone comes into the room, and the uncleared supper dishes, are all part of a grim trove for which the poem is the chest. It's the presence of these details that makes the last line so rueful and disheartening, which shows civil war as 'civil' but also lethal and grievous.

Increasingly, the naming of things, places, birds, animals, plants, and people, in Longley's poems becomes more than hoarding or an accumulation of souvenirs against the ravages of public circumstance. In its discreet way, it asks to be associated with the sentiment inherent in such poems as 'Man Lying on a Wall' or 'Ars Poetica'. In the first of these Lowry's oddly portrayed, highly anonymous figure is evoked as a fugitive from self and livelihood:

> He is wearing a pinstripe suit, black shoes
> And a bowler hat: on the pavement
> Below him, like a relic or something
> He is trying to forget, *his briefcase*
> *With everybody's initials on it.*

(P 137)

'Ars Poetica' ends:

> I am on general release now, having
> Put myself in the shoes *of all husbands,*
> Dissipated my substance in the parlours
> *Of an entire generation* and annexed
> To my territory gardens, allotments
> And the desire – *even at this late stage –*
> *To go along with the world and his wife.*

(P 139)

[italics mine, in both extracts]

Longley's Metric

At least part of the persona in his poems, and a large part of his acoustic, or resonance, is that of a Universal Civilian. Even the sustained pull of war – the Great, the Second, and the local Irish – is implicated in Longley's unarmed (as it were) response to terrorism in his native place.

In describing Longley's or any other poet's freer and free verse it is necessary to avoid 'the artificial method', to use T.S. Eliot's phrase for prosody and scansion learned from Latin and Greek and using their terminology. The 'classification of metres' plays only a very minor part in the appreciation of verse in which recurrent or regular metres are absent. Of greater significance, though, is a poet's earlier experience of the kind of versification which it is now a mistake to call 'traditional' – free verse is long established and accepted; it has traditions of its own. Merely to flick through the pages of Longley's books is to see that its 'squares and oblongs' (a phrase of Auden's quoted by Longley) have been there from the beginning and never gone away. His practice of free or freer verse is one that makes his poems look as if they are measured as metrical poetry – and, indeed, they are. Where there are stanzas, they are almost always of the same size and shape, and lines *look* the same length in his stanzaic poems and in those which are not. Equally obvious, too, is that Longley's lines usually end on breaks of grammatical sense, and very often on nouns and verbs – that is, *as if they rhyme*. These lines are from 'Ghetto'.

> Because you will suffer soon and die, your choices
> Are neither right nor wrong: a spoon will feed you,
> A flannel keep you clean, a toothbrush bring you back
> To your bathroom's view of chimney-pots and gardens.
> With so little time for inventory or leavetaking,
> You are packing now for the rest of your life
> Photographs, medicines, a change of underwear, a book,
> A candlestick, a loaf, sardines, needle and thread.
> These are your heirlooms, perishables, wordly goods.
> What you bring is the same as what you leave behind,
> Your last belongings a list of your belongings.
>
> (*GF* 40)

Of these eleven lines, seven have twelve syllables, two have eleven, and two others fourteen. The first line has twelve syllables – 'Because you will suffer soon and die, your choices . . .' – ; but if there are iambic elements in it – 'you will', 'your choice(s)' – it doesn't speak iambically and resists being scanned as such. The second line, though, is iambic (hendecasyllabic), and the third a perfectly accurate English alexandrine – iambic hexameter. It could be possible to hear hendecasyllables and hexameters as the two points of audible departure in Part I of 'Ghetto' and in a considerable number of Longley's later poems. A truer description, however, might be to understand Longley's freer verse as measured by voice and temperament. His list-making – 'Photographs, medicines, a change of underwear, a book, / A candlestick, a loaf, sardines, needle and thread' – are as lovingly entered here in a 'poem as register' as the domestic trove itemized in 'Wounds'; or the long list of wildflowers (twenty-one of them) in 'The Ice-cream Man' (*GF* 49), which is another poem about terrorist murder, a poem of quiet, natural, floral gesture; or kinds of potato in Part V of 'Ghetto'. Idiom, everyday vocabulary, muffled rhythm, and shapeliness, can be seen and heard in Longley's characteristic later work as at the service of a quiet but intense beauty salvaged from horror. His metric, his temperament, as well as the 'moral project' implicit in his poetry creates a thematic atmosphere and reveals his larger meaning or purpose to be the possibility at least of a humane, secular redemption. Part III of 'Ghetto':

> The little girl without a mother behaves like a mother
> With her rag doll to whom she explains fear and anguish,
> The meagreness of the bread ration, how to make it last,
> How to get back to the doll's house and lift up the roof
> And, before the flame-throwers and dynamiters destroy it,
> How to rescue from their separate rooms love and sorrow,
> Masterpieces the size of a postage stamp, small fortunes.

Just as Longley is a poet unafraid of keeping his voice down, he is equally courageous, or individual, or simply being true to himself, in taking the risk of siding with the diminutive and vulnerable. Although effective and often stunning when read aloud by the poet, the last thing anyone would want to claim for Longley's poetry is that it is 'performerly' or written to nudge an audience. The audibility of his poems is customarily of a kind that creates a silence for their setting. In saying that, I'm conscious of wanting to avoid the point being taken as an 'impression'. It is, I submit, a fact of his verse. Perfect and achieved harmony between a poet's general idiom and what the poet says is the artistic objective of any poet for whom poetry is more than a means to making statements or performing in public. 'Terezín', a two-line poem, as well as being read for the disconcerting beauty of its image, also indicates the essential wager of Longley's writing – everything survives, anything can be preserved, dignity can be restored, there are no limits, only surprises, in the extent of human perception, and the power of memory and imagination is as potent as the power of love:

> No room has ever been as silent as the room
> Where hundreds of violins are hung in unison.

(*GF* 39)

Again, the alexandrine is the metrical foundation of these lines: 'No room has ever been ‖ as silent as the room' is practically Racinian in its control of an antithetical mid-line pause, and it is only the relaxed and necessary extra syllable – 'Where', at the beginning of the second line: 'Where hundreds of violins ‖ are hung in unison' – that forestalls the couplet's regularity. Incidentally, an extra syllable at the beginning of otherwise formal lines is frequent in Tony Harrison's poetry, or an iambic foot inverted (i.e. a trochee) – another of these contemporary poets in whose work manner and meaning are significantly interdigitated. It can be read as a token of the power of *speech* over the blandishments of *written* perfections. It is common in Heaney's poetry, too, and in Mahon's, and others. Within an approach founded on a notion of an intuitive 'moral project' it can be seen as, if not the avoidance of easily enough obtainable perfection or 'regularity' in verse, then the acceptance of the impure, or imperfect, as a necessity in the reflection of contemporary facts. Where a poetry is destined to be determined by its subjects and by the temperamental pressures to which the poet is subjected by external, topical, and sometimes political insistencies, then it seems to me that the poetry that is written will be 'inexact' or 'rough' (in John Donne's sense of 'rough verse' in his *Satyres*) rather than aesthetically smooth or 'elegant'. In almost all contemporary poetry with a claim to lyricism there virtually must be an element of the 'satirical', or at least a moment of comment. The great challenge faced by contemporary poetry is to escape from that instinctive response to the actual or autobiographical and find a way of entering the entirely imaginative.

From *The Echo Gate* (1979), through *Gorse Fires* (1991) to *The Ghost Orchid* (1995) Longley has consolidated the longer line that is an obvious feature of his later poems. Whether this is due to the influence of the American poet C.K. Williams, or Ciaran Carson, or Longley's reading or memories of Latin and Greek verse – he has described himself as a 'lapsed classicist' – is neither here nor there.

Indeed, longer lines have become common in recent poetry. The publisher of Peter Didsbury's excellent *The Classical Farm*,[11] for example, actually did the poet a favour and produced a broader volume to avoid the typographical indignity of broken lines. If free or freer verse – *vers libre* and *vers libéré* – are to fulfil the benefit promised by their departures from regular metrical structures then lines can be as long or short as a poet likes. However, it seems likely that Longley's appreciation of classical verse contributed in a large way to the growth of his own longer line – and by 'longer' all I mean is beyond the pentameter. Latin elegiac couplets consist of a hexameter and a pentameter, but it is the hexameter that has had its way with him. It becomes noticeable in his poetry with 'Peace' (*P* 169–71), which is described as 'after Tibullus', an imitation, or poem in response to, the tenth elegy of Book I of the Tibullus Collection. Longley's updated non-translatorese in 'Peace' underlines Eliot's remark in 'The Music of Poetry':

Whether poetry is accentual or syllabic, rhymed or rhymeless, formal or free, it cannot afford to lose its contact with the changing language of common intercourse.[12]

Such a 'contact' is present in virtually all of Longley's poetry, but it is no inhibition to his rendering of his version of Tibullus in seven ten-line stanzas, that is, in reorganizing the original in line with his own formal preferences or what he considered to be appropriate or opportune. One of the two fidelities required of 'Peace' is first of all loyalty to the spirit of the original poem, and then to 'the changing language of common intercourse.' I find Longley's engagement with classical poetry illuminating in that it shows – as if it were insisted by him – that the language of daily use must always win over the temptations of a more 'poetic' idiom which is always on offer when translating from old sources, or in any writing, especially formal verse. Something of the same kind can be seen in the three sonnets 'Sulpicia', 'Florence Nightingale', and 'Grace Darling', (*P* 172–4) where Longley ignores the familiar pentameter and extends his line beyond the usual reach in what otherwise are rhymed or slant-rhymed sonnets in lines departing from iambic pentameters.

In his wonderful sequence 'Mayo Monologues' (*P* 161–4) he tells four stories. Each named part of the sequence consists of twenty-six lines – that alone is enough to tell us that Longley is a poet who gravitates towards symmetry, were it not already clear in his favouring of equable stanzas and the entire tenor of his writing. However, his relaxed and easy handling of blank verse in 'Mayo

Monologues' shows, too, that he is a poet who gravitates towards freedom of use and expression *as much as* formality and that these two tendencies are far from incompatible. At the risk of becoming a bore in defence of the wishy-washy liberalism of yesteryear, which is still dear to my heart, and hazarding an offence to the poet whose work I am discussing, it would seem appropriate (at least to me) to claim that the aggravated, or modified, formality of Longley's verse is an exhilarating display *in form* as well as in content of the best convictions and attitudes inherited from such predecessors as Auden and MacNeice as well as the poets who first came to public attention in the 1950s. Robert Conquest's phrase in his introduction to *New Lines* (1956) comes to mind, where he identifies 'reverence for the real person or event' as a shared moral and intellectual concern of The Movement poets – but inconsistently borne out by Larkin, spasmodically by Amis, and fulfilled largely only by D.J. Enright. While the plainer meaning of Conquest's observation is witnessed in Longley's writing, and its 'moral project', it is possible to extend the sense of 'event' to language and to the poem itself. There is such a cumulative reverence for the poem and the language in which it is written in Longley's work – implicit, to be sure, but unmistakable – that I feel obliged to suggest that it is his signature, his real and tremendous distinction in contemporary poetry. For a poet of his time – although he shares this with Tony Harrison – he has written little in the way of criticism. Like Harrison, his beliefs about poetry are all embodied in his poems. As well as reverential (Clare, Rosenberg, Keith Douglas, Tibullus, Horace, Ovid, Homer) and companionable (his Irish contemporaries), some of his poems about poetry and poets can be crusty and critical. This gives me an opportunity to point to the humour still persistent in some of the work in his recent collection *The Ghost Orchid* (1995). 'After Horace', for example, while proclaiming a classical antecedent, sets about the issue of 'postmodernism'. What I would like to indicate through the poem is Longley's discretion, his characteristic confidence in showing a subject and his attitude to it without proclaiming in advance what he is about. It is as if he puts as much faith in his reader as he places in himself as a reader and writer of poetry – and I would claim that such an approach is not élitist but democratic. Tact is especially significant in 'After Horace' in that the purpose is clearly satirical, and in satire recklessness or ire might be anticipated; however, it would have been uncharacteristic of Longley's poetry had he allowed it to extend to the denunciatory:

We postmodernists can live with that human head
Stuck on a horse's neck, or the plastering of multi-
Coloured feathers over the limbs of assorted animals
(So that what began on top as a gorgeous woman
Tapers off cleverly into the tail of a black fish).

Since our fertile imaginations cannot make head
Or tail of anything, wild things interbreed with tame,
Snakes with birds, lambs with tigers. If a retired sailor
Commissions a picture of the shipwreck he survived,
We give him a cypress-tree because we can draw that.

To relieve the boredom we introduce to the woods
A dolphin, a wild boar to the waves. Ultimate post-
Modernists even in the ceramics department we
May have a vase in mind when we start, or a wine-jug,
But, look, as the wheel goes round, it ends up as a po.

(GO 5)

Gentle satire of that sort shows the poet as amused more than offended. On the evidence of Longley's work, he could hardly be accused of crusty officiousness, although, in 'After Horace', he might be guilty of taking a term like 'post-modernism' too seriously. It is not, in my opinion, a particularly useful term. If anything, it exposes late twentieth-century anxiety before a need for definitions and name-making, one which neglects the positive and ongoing implications of the notion of 'contemporary', and which leads to, and then falls into, the dangerous 'end of history' argument.

Mockery is more potent in 'The Mad Poet' (GO 6), as is resentment, while the sheer rasp of indignation, the pained and wrinkled face of the poem, contains also a puzzlement before the extremist vocation of poetry and its potential fraudulence. Dialect words are counterpointed mischievously within a poem of classical provenance. The result is a weird mixture of the Roman and the local directed at what the poem portrays as unreasonable poetic behaviour. It shows Longley as a poet for whom rational and benign order seems an intellectual priority. However, such a statement invites serious qualifications, for Longley is also a poet of fantasy, dream, and perceptions drawn from an individual vision that is close to idiosyncratic. The tantrum of 'The Mad Poet' is one that should not mislead us into thinking of Longley as some sort of 'neutral tone' Movementeer, tepid common-senser, nature lover and botanist, or over-domesticated version of the wilder beast often represented as 'the poet'. Instead, it points to something like the same anxiety inherent in an idea like that of 'post-modernism'. Longley's 'metric' is based on a classical if also uniquely personal interpretation of the tradition of poetry in the English language, and on his own intimate acquaintanceship with the poetry of Rome and Greece. On the face of it – that is, put that way – it can look solidly Anglo-Irish, or even British, or 'traditional'. But that would fail to take into account the temperamental cadences of his lines as well as what he says. I believe that this is the shared dilemma of most of the poets of Longley's generation. Discontent with a description such as 'post-modernist', perhaps never entirely happy with 'modernism' either, and yet writing in ways which are indisputably (or that is my conviction) of their time, in the shuffle and reshuffle of the cards of criticism and theory they have found themselves, not sidelined, nor marginalized, but identified as more traditional and less contemporary than they are. A 'moral project' – and one of very great moment – has failed to receive a properly coherent account. I believe this to be true of Longley, Heaney, Mahon, and Harrison, and other poets of their time. When it arrives, as I hope it will, it will attend to the social, political and aesthetic benevolence of the work that has been published – but benevolence, since 1979 if not before, has acquired something of the force of a curse word, and in Northern Ireland (or Ireland as a whole) may well be considered especially suspect. Such an account – when it comes – will also have to consider the peculiarly successful harmony – indeed, at times, the utterly harmonious agreement of metric and meaning in the work of such poets as Michael Longley and others of his generation.

LAPSED CLASSICS: HOMER, OVID, AND MICHAEL LONGLEY'S POETRY

PETER McDONALD

I

The title above adapts a remark made by Michael Longley in an interview of 1985: 'At Trinity I did as little work as possible and called myself a lapsed classicist'.[1] Part of the joke here (as I take it) is that, like religion, a classical education can never be erased; and there is something over and above the routine registers of pleasant self-deprecation in what Longley says later in the same interview:

> I've always liked a Latin phrase, 'musarum sacerdos', priest of the Muses. This may go straight into 'Pseuds' Corner', but poetry, the effort to write it, reading it and living it, is, if you like, my religion. It gives me something akin to religious experience. Perhaps one of the things an artist should do is suggest the sacerdotal values of life – in a completely secular way, of course.[2]

Whether or not this ought to have gone to *Private Eye*, it is a claim for the significance and efficacy of poetry which seems to set the stakes high. Poetry as a substitute for religion is an idea with a long pedigree, and its more recent roots stretch back into the Victorian period; even so, Longley is no more able than, say, Matthew Arnold to present poetical 'sweetness and light' as a fully *satisfactory* substitute. What underwrites the attempt, however, as it has always underwritten such attempts, is the notion of the poet as 'musarum sacerdos', and behind this is the weight of classical authority. As the interview shows, Longley is accustomed to wearing such things lightly; at the same time, he is inclined to present himself as the 'lapsed classicist' who can yet, by virtue of his poetic calling, continue in the priesthood.

Although this essay will look particularly at Longley's poetic dealings with Homer and Ovid, it is worth remembering that the poet's classical repertoire is wider than this: while the Greek epic poet and the Latin author of the *Metamorphoses* have taken centre stage since *Gorse Fires* (1991), earlier classical strata in Longley's writing contain elements of Latin elegy, especially poets like Catullus and Sextus Propertius. A more comprehensive study of Longley's classical connections would be obliged to spend much time with these Latin poets, and they would prove central, also, to any adequate engagement with Longley's notions of love poetry in general. Longley has recalled his fondness for the Latin love-elegists in the earlier years of his career, and their presences can be felt in his first books of poetry. Indeed, such writers are nothing if not 'secular', and it might be argued that, for the early Longley, the inspirational value of love-poetry itself is in part dependent upon its celebratory dissent from the sombre (but palpable) proprieties of what, for want of a better word, we might call 'religion'. The powers to which the young poet was especially responsive are essentially those of *lyric* poetry, and the notion of lyric as tender subversion was to have important consequences for Longley's future work.

'Altera Cithera', from *An Exploded View*, asks a revealing question in its first stanza:

> A change of tune, then,
> On another zither,
> A new aesthetic, or
> The same old songs
> That are out of key,
> Unwashed by epic oceans
> And dipped by love
> In lyric waters only?
>
> (P 102)

Love and lyric are here the alternatives to 'epic oceans' and what Longley calls at the end of the poem 'Soldiers, politicians / And all the dreary / Epics of the muscle-bound'. The figure who is enlisted to help with this act of re-direction is 'Gaius / Sextus Propertius, / An old friend'. The complex resonances of 'love' in Longley's poetry are matters for a study in themselves; but it is interesting that 'love''s challenge to the 'muscle-bound' is made also in the name of lyric as against epic. There are poetic advantages for Longley in having Cupid outface the sterner deities, and a very early (1962) translation from Propertius might be seen as clearing a space for the erotic and aesthetic manoeuvres that were still to come in the poet's mature writing. Since Longley has printed this early poem in recent years, it can perhaps be quoted here without appearing to disturb juvenilia better left alone; in fact, it is an accomplished and individual poem, one of which many poets older than twenty-three would be proud:

Cupid
after Sextus Propertius

Whoever he was who painted Love as a boy
    Had a marvellous touch, don't you think?
    He understood the way our hearts sink
Over little things, that we lovers can't enjoy

The good times because we never have the sense to.
    And he gave the boy a pair of wings
    To fan our pulses with his blowings
Hot and blowings cold. Running away will do

No good for he carries arrows, barbed of course –
    A quiverful dangles from his back.
    No one anticipates the attack
And no one gets away unhurt. My case is worse –

He's lost his wings for sure and never leaves my breast
    Where with his arrows he remains
    To battle continually through my veins.
Oh, why can't new blood claim his deadly interest?

Or do my dried-up bones have such appeal that he
    Enjoys his battered lodgings in
    Half a man? And should he ruin
The poor poet who can bring him fame, and with me

The little genius which is all I have to show,
    Who will celebrate the face and curls,
    The fingers and dark eyes of my girl,
And who will sing of how softly her footsteps go?[3]

With hindsight, we can see that this material was always, as it were, meant for Michael Longley; the extremely delicate balance in the English poem's tone, in which Cupid's menaces must seem simultaneously more and less threatening than those his methods imitate, is maintained in a supple and delicate metrical arrangement. In fact, we can understand that it was in undertaking translations like these (and, of course, in the sensitive reading that lies behind them) that Longley began to discover those possible paths along which his imagination and technique could start to develop. The seriousness of a poem like 'Cupid' consists in the very fragility and delicacy of its internal ironies and balances; learning this early made a difference to Longley's writing, and was to serve him crucially in later years, when such senses of precision were sorely necessary.

In the 1970s, Longley found Tibullus (a newer classical 'friend') providing the medium for a poem where the matter of domesticity, love and 'little things' was indeed to be (in the phraseology of 'Altera Cithera') put in a sling and aimed at history. In a way, the poem marks the culmination of Longley's involvement with the Latin love elegists, as well as putting on display a whole vision of settled life and prosperity which dares the reader to imagine its translation from idea into reality:

> I want to live until the white hairs shine above
> A pensioner's memories of better days. Meanwhile
> I would like peace to be my partner on the farm,
> Peace personified: oxen under the curved yoke;
> Compost for the vines, grape-juice turning into wine,
> Vintage years handed down from father to son;
> Hoe and ploughshare gleaming, while in some dark corner
> Rust keeps the soldier's grisly weapons in their place;
> The labourer steering his wife and children home
> In a hay cart from the fields, a trifle sozzled.
>
> (P 170)

While Longley, as the poet, translates Tibullus into English, the English poetry here asks to be translated into Northern Ireland in the 1970s, and this daring strategy is perhaps the culmination of Longley's involvement with the subversive, or designedly mischievous and unsettling, possibilities of love-elegy. The challenge here is to things as they are, and the alternative offered (or rather, the alternative which this translation shows to be there and waiting) is expressed in terms of love: 'if there are skirmishes, guerilla tactics, / It's only lovers quarrelling'. The vision of peace on offer in the poem comes at times to within a hair's breadth of the sentimental: in this respect, perhaps, it is only its Latin underpinning which keeps things together. Nevertheless, the locations of the poem once again prefigure a phase of Longley's writing which was still to come; the pastoral images, which have not been fully 'translated' out of the Latin into a contemporary idiom, are ones which the poet's later classical endeavours revisit.

There are certain dangers in an apparently uncontentious term like 'classical', and they can make it more difficult to understand and critically evaluate a poet like Longley, as well as making more problematic his ambitions to be 'musarum sacerdos'. In the critical language of our own century, 'classical' has gone all the way from being a term loaded with contention and confrontational energy, as it was in the 1920s, to its present condition of comparative intellectual torpor. When T.S. Eliot played with the term in his prose essays and in the frequently acidic journalism of *The Criterion*, 'classic' (especially in opposition to 'romantic') was at the height of its vogue, and carried certain clear connotations: principally, these were of literary eclecticism, political conservatism, and religious orthodoxy. In so far as such a fashion touched on ancient literature at all, its poet was Virgil. Now, at the other end of the century, 'classicism' is more likely to be a blandly descriptive term: it may indicate some measure of self-imposed restraint on the level of personal expression, or even a vague (and, at all events, a vaguely comprehended) habit of allusion to old literature. Between these points, of course, is the steady but definite decline of the words 'classical' and 'classic' into meaninglessness: to recordings of favourite classics, to classic cars, to slightly out of date paperbacks repackaged as 'modern classics'. In the midst of all this semantic noise, a classicist, or one who reads the classics, is likely to be ignorable, and is seldom heard above the racket.

In this context, Longley's profession of lapsed classicism is likely to be either misinterpreted or underinterpreted. In a revealing aside (in the course of an otherwise alert and intelligent book), the critic Bernard O'Donoghue compared Seamus Heaney's ability to learn from 'a freestyle poetic' with Longley and Derek Mahon, and their 'classicism [. . .] which can seem unbending'.[4] The term 'unbending' here is lazy, for it assumes that there is something which ought to give, and colludes with a received notion of classicism as a refuge in form from the riskier and freer realms of the emancipated imagination. Such assumptions may colour even little mistakes, as that in the *Oxford Companion to Irish Literature* which has Derek Mahon study Classics at Trinity (Mahon being, presumably, the *kind* of poet who might be supposed to have studied a subject like this).[5] At the same time, the classics can be treated not as paths of withdrawal into allusion and constricting form, but as a common heritage, one which is all too unproblematically available to writers and readers. In Ireland, this is again a habit with a history, one which might perhaps be seen as culminating in the promiscuous 'translations' of Greek drama by Irish poets in the 1980s, with a theoretical basis in Brian

Friel's too-celebrated *Translations*.⁶ But neither the 'unbending' nor the 'available' model of classicism fits Longley, whose elements of classicism are not, after all, strategies but parts of an idiom; his work in classical modes is not an intricate maze of obscurities and tight-lipped reticence, nor is it a laying bare of literary properties suddenly revealed to have some burning, and instantly accessible, contemporary relevance. His classicism is something other than this; yet the coarsening of critical language (which is necessarily the coarsening of critical thought) means that it is increasingly difficult for critics to describe and even (perhaps) for readers to appreciate. The dark tones of ruminations like these may be more in tune with the asperities of 'classicism' in criticism earlier in the century; if so, it may be worth bringing back into play classicism's old opponent, romanticism, as a tendency with which to reckon. How do Longley's lapsed classics stand in relation to this? Is an aspiration to be 'musarum sacerdos' 'classic' or 'romantic'? Do such things matter? And, if they do, how, and to whom?

II

Between Homer and Ovid there is more than a difference in languages: where the Greek epic poet stands as far back into the past (and in oral poetic tradition) as we can reach, the Latin author is historically located, and his various works exist in the context of an already rich and complex poetic tradition. Ovid's *Metamorphoses* is not like Homer's *Iliad* or *Odyssey*, since it combines, splices and cross-fades a multiplicity of narrative fragments, concentrating its energies on sheer style, for which its stories of transformation provide ready opportunities. Homeric style is an altogether different affair, for it is a consequence of Homeric narrative, and not readily to be divorced from that narrative; in Ovid, overall narrative intent and direction are, at best, sketchy affairs. Longley's involvement with these two kinds of classical poetry comes in *Gorse Fires*, with its seven poems from the *Odyssey*, and in *The Ghost Orchid* (1995), with further *Odyssey*-derived poems, poems taken also from sources in the *Iliad*, and poems adapted from the *Metamorphoses*. In the context of two volumes of the usual slimness, this can fairly be called a burst of translation-related activity for the poet, and suggests a new turn in his classical practice. It may also, however, help to make a little clearer the degree to which Longley's classicism shades into, or out of, more sacerdotal concerns and, indeed, the extent to which it has dealings with more apparently 'romantic' orientations.

Lapsed Classics: Homer, Ovid, and Michael Longley's Poetry 41

The poems derived from the *Odyssey* in *Gorse Fires* are among Longley's most powerful performances, and set the standard for the kind of classicism in contemporary poetic practice which makes notions of an 'unbending' stance, or of simple and unproblematic contemporary 'relevance', redundant. The poems are best characterised as transformations into lyric of narrative material; they condense Homeric episodes, employing long lines and a syntax which maintains a degree of complexity without falling into convolutedness. It is noteworthy, too, that Longley's practice as a translator in these poems is in many ways to be literally faithful to his sources. While he arranges lines, joining passages from different Books on occasion, and acts as a kind of editor, he *adds* very little to most of these poems. This seems a modest enough description, but it should be qualified by saying that Longley does, of course, *make* these passages from the Homeric narratives into distinct poems in their own right. In that sense, at least, the apparent authorial absence is illusory.

Gorse Fires is an extremely carefully arranged collection, and the Homeric poems are deployed as parts in an intricate and subtle pattern. The narrative of which they are components is that of Odysseus's return to the island of Ithaca, his encounter with the ghost of his mother, his landing on the island itself, his meetings with his old nurse, his father and his still-faithful dog, and finally his massacre (with his son Telemachus) of the suitors in the palace. However, what Longley does with these narrative elements is not exactly to construct (or re-construct) a narrative; rather, he inserts the poems as lyrics in the sequence of the book's other lyrics, thus building over their original narrative foundations delicate structures of his own. In one of the versions, 'Eurycleia', this takes the form of an explicit departure from Homer, where the old woman crosses over to the poet's own remembered nurse:

> I began like Odysseus by loving the wrong woman
> Who has disappeared among the skyscrapers of New York
> After wandering for thousands of years from Ithaca.
>
> (*GF* 31)

The first line's allusion here is to the opening of Longley's autobiographical prose piece 'Tuppenny Stung', where memories of the infant poet's nurse Lena are prefaced with the remark that 'I began by loving the wrong woman'.[7] Yet this moment of autobiographical imposition is very rare in Longley's Homeric poems, and even here it is formally segregated from the rest of the poem; indeed, the degree of authorial 'interference' is higher here than usual, since Longley distils his lyric from the episode of Eurycleia's recognition of her former charge and master without including Odysseus's reaction to that recognition. The poem 'Eurycleia' is a lyric of recovery, love, and joy; Longley builds to a climax as he ends the first section with the nurse's speech:

> Such pain and happiness, her eyes filling with tears,
> Her old voice cracking as she stroked his beard and whispered
> 'You are my baby boy for sure and I didn't know you
> Until I had fondled my master's body all over.'
>
> (*GF* 31)

Like 'Laertes' and 'Anticleia' elsewhere in the volume, this serves to crystallize an epiphanic moment in Longley's developing lyric meditations and their accretion. After this point, the first-person, autobiographical voice can speak, however briefly, leaving Homer's narrative behind. It is worth remembering what *does* happen just after this in the *Odyssey* itself, when Odysseus's 'right hand sought and gripped the old woman's throat':

'Nurse', he said, 'do you wish to ruin me, you who reared me at your own breast? I am indeed home after nineteen years of hard adventure. But since by some unlucky chance you have lit on the fact, keep your mouth shut and let not a soul in the house learn the truth. Otherwise I tell you plainly – and you know I make no idle threats – that if I am lucky enough to defeat these love-sick noblemen, I won't spare you, though you're my own nurse, on the day when I put the rest of the maids in my palace to death'.[8]

This is hardly the stuff of love lyric, and Longley's transformation of Homer from narrative into lyric moments means that it will not be accommodated. Although the darker side of the story of Odysseus's return to Ithaca is of pressing importance to *Gorse Fires* (and later, to a lesser extent, to *The Ghost Orchid*), the integrity of lyric, in Longley's poetics, means that the lyric 'I' must not be polluted by the violence of its surroundings. In a way, this is a logical consequence (and, of course, a triumphant maturing) of the jealously guarded spaces for love and the lyric voice in Longley's poetry of the 1970s.

Gorse Fires ends with a Homeric poem, one condensed from episodes in the aftermath of the slaughter of the suitors. Longley's title for this, 'The Butchers', courts (but does not exactly lay claim to) parallels with the shorthand of Northern Irish atrocities. Apart from this, the poet's authorial interventions in the material are nowhere to be found, and yet they seem to be somehow everywhere in evidence. If Homer has functioned as a lens, so to speak, through which to regard the most painful, private, and tender things elsewhere in the volume, here at the book's conclusion he is a means of bringing into focus the most appalling things, without commentary or overt interpretation. One of the significant contexts for the poem is the sequence 'Ghetto', where Longley's lyric voice finds a space for itself in matter of terrible (and perhaps overpowering) bearing: properly, that sequence does not affect to look into the gas-chambers, and its integrity resides in its own awareness of the avertedness of its gaze. When, shortly afterwards, 'The Butchers' concludes the volume, it balances direct observation of brutality with another passage, from Book XXIV of the *Odyssey*, in which the souls of the dead are shepherded away by Hermes. In an extraordinary feat of syntactical suppleness, Longley joins his two source passages together without a moment's sign of the surgery: the 28 long lines of the poem as a whole constitute one complete sentence, and the slaughter is made literally of a piece with its supernatural sequel. Hermes leads the souls of the killed into a 'dreamy region', a place which the reader of *Gorse Fires* has already, in some senses, come to identify with Longley's own lyric territory:

> . . . so their souls were batsqueaks
> As they flittered after Hermes, their deliverer, who led them
> Along the clammy sheughs, then past the oceanic streams
> And the white rock, the sun's gatepost in that dreamy region,
> Until they came to a bog-meadow full of bog-asphodels
> Where the residents are ghosts or images of the dead.
>
> (*GF* 51)

It is an extraordinary moment, and it relies on an extraordinary mastery of syntax and pace on Longley's part. If the conclusion of 'The Butchers' is one of pastoral calm, it is a calm which carries within it, like 'batsqueaks', the enduring echoes of massacre and distress. Plainly, Longley's sense of pastoral in *Gorse Fires* is similarly haunted; the loaded silences and absences are those of section VII of 'Ghetto':

> Fingers leave shadows on a violin, harmonics,
> A blackbird fluttering between electrified fences.
>
> (*GF* 43)

These 'shadows', which congregate around both personal experience, the family dead, and more public histories, with their dead in millions, are absorbed finally into the Homeric 'eidōla kamontōn', 'ghosts or images of the dead'.

In so far as this is understood as a discipline on the poet's part, a habit of restraint, it is a conventionally 'classical' strategy for a modern poet to adopt. But such restraint is more readily celebrated than practised in habits of reading and interpretation, and the temptation to see Longley's versions of Homer as beautiful and elaborate systems of parallels between classical source and contemporary personal 'theme' is likely to be strong. It may be, indeed, that such a temptation can beset the poet himself, and to some extent this happens in the Homeric poems in *The Ghost Orchid*, where Longley extends the range of his source material into the *Iliad*. The poet's techniques of lyric distillation remain the same here, and are in some ways much more thoroughgoing (the parting of Hector and Andromache in Book VI of the *Iliad* is reduced to a single couplet (*GO* 38)) while his interest in parallels comes closer to the surface. Where 'The Butchers' had kept contemporary resonances at arm's length, the poem 'Phemios and Medon', also drawn from the massacre of the suitors in the *Odyssey*, becomes an exercise in Ulster-Scots narrative poetry and, in its portrait of the court-poet, sets up a caricature of 'classical' restraint and impersonality:

> 'I ask for pity and respect. How could you condemn
> A poet who writes for his people and Parnassus,
> Autodidact, his repertoire god-given? I beg you
> Not to be precipitate and cut off my head. Spare me
> And I'll immortalise you in an ode. Telemachos
> Your own dear son will vouch that I was no party-hack
> At the suitors' dinner-parties. Overwhelmed and out-
> Numbered, I gave poetry readings against my will'.

(*GO* 44)

This is set up as 'highfalutin blether', and Telemachos's declaration that Phemios is innocent is rendered in the poem's dialect as 'He's only a harmless crayter'. Clearly, the diction of Phemios is part and parcel of his claim to integrity, but Longley's poem insists on its essentially pompous sense of elevation. In a way, this is Longley's joke at his own expense, or at the expense of a critical caricature from which, in superficial ways, his critical image has suffered; but it is a joke *with* its own expense too, since it allows the poem to inhabit the mode of translation as parallel, with personal and contemporary resonances becoming the prime concern and point of the enterprise. In its portrait of the 'classical' stance, and its use for classical material, it adopts a satirical position that is, it could be argued, essentially 'romantic' in character. Interestingly, this makes Odysseus and Telemachos the centres of sympathy: a tactic which would unbalance a poem like 'The Butchers' altogether.

A central exhibit in any discussion of Longley's Homeric versions must be the poem 'Ceasefire' from *The Ghost Orchid*, which takes its material from the meeting of Achilles and King Priam in the *Iliad*. Here again the poet's ability to keep at a distance from the parallels which his material suggests is crucial to the poem's success. The distillation process is effective, producing a sonnet, in which each stage of the developing narrative has a section to itself, and a final plea takes up the concluding couplet. As with 'The Butchers', Longley's title establishes a contemporary resonance, while the poem goes on not to elaborate explicitly upon this:

I
Put in mind of his own father and moved to tears
Achilles took him by the hand and pushed the old king
Gently away, but Priam curled up at his feet and
Wept with him until their sadness filled the building.

II
Taking Hector's corpse into his own hands Achilles
Made sure it was washed and, for the old king's sake,
Laid out in uniform, ready for Priam to carry
Wrapped like a present home to Troy at daybreak.

III
When they had eaten together, it pleased them both
To stare at each other's beauty as lovers might,
Achilles built like a god, Priam good-looking still
And full of conversation, who earlier had sighed:

IV
'I get down on my knees and do what must be done
And kiss Achilles' hand, the killer of my son'.

(GO 39)

The poem's economy and structured progression are remarkable, and it marks the most successful point in Longley's distillation process of Homer from narrative into contained and self-sufficient lyric form. Now, all the narrative matter is matter for concentration, and the containing force of poetic form (here the sonnet shape, combined with the fully individual and controlled cadences of Longley's lines) takes the measure of seemingly unstoppable emotions. If we wish to reach back to earlier notions of the 'classical' in poetic style, we could do worse than settle on the term 'impersonal' to characterise Longley's writing here. Like another *Iliad*-derived poem in *The Ghost Orchid*, 'The Scales', it provides an excellent example of what a fully original, fully achieved 'classical' poem can be; even so, its status as a lyric, as narrative made into lyric, carries implications for reading which may still be at odds with such an assessment.

In a talk given in 1995, Longley himself accounted for the poem in terms of its occasion, or occasions, telling the story of the Homeric incidents, then reflecting on his own use of them:

I concentrated into a sonnet all that I wanted to borrow from this episode. Because at that time we were praying for an IRA ceasefire, I called the poem 'Ceasefire' and, hoping to make my own minute contribution, sent it to the *Irish Times*. It was the poem's good luck to be published two days after the IRA's declaration. Almost always a poem makes its own occasion in private. This was an exception, and I still find warming the response of several readers, some of them damaged or bereaved in the Troubles.[9]

Where the poem's strength resides in its capacity to keep the sense of parallel at bay, as something present but contained, this reading's weakness is its willingness to see the occasion as an integral (and perhaps primary) part of the poem's meaning. But here Longley is speaking in a mode quite distinct from that of the poem (and, indeed, from that of his poetry in general), trying to articulate his own sense of poetry's possible power of ministration in particular sorrowful circumstances. He may be right in and about these circumstances; yet his reading is at bottom a romantic one, and is a more contingent thing than the poem – even a lesser thing. The role adopted by Longley here (and *not*, one might contend, adopted by or in the poem) is that of 'musarum sacerdos', the priest of the muses, and it brings to the surface tensions between the classicist and the lapsed classicist, the impersonal and the religious, which run through *The Ghost Orchid* as a whole.

III

Longley's involvement with Ovid's *Metamorphoses* comes in *The Ghost Orchid*, and it develops from the various successes in dealing with Homer which had been so important a feature of *Gorse Fires*.

A technique learned on Homer, so to speak, is subsequently applied to Ovid. Longley comes to Ovid with a degree of confidence in his abilities to transform narrative into lyric; but the material now is not Homeric narrative, and is, indeed, already a species of narrative intent on lyrical effects and possibilities. There is another, 'external' influence on the recourse to Ovid, which Longley's note at the end of his volume acknowledges; this is the project set up by Michael Hofmann and James Lasdun, for translations of portions of the *Metamorphoses* by a wide array of British and American poets, which was to issue in the 1994 miscellany *After Ovid: New Metamorphoses* and, later, in Ted Hughes's hefty *Tales from Ovid* (1997). The Hofmann and Lasdun volume's preface voices an attitude to Ovid in which the Latin poet comes to seem the natural companion for postmodern writers and readers, and its tone is an excited one, tickled perhaps by what seems so new, immediate and contemporary in the ancient material:

There are many reasons for Ovid's renewed appeal. Such qualities as his mischief and cleverness, his deliberate use of shock – not always relished in the past – are contemporary values. Then, too, the stories have direct, obvious and powerful affinities with contemporary reality. They offer a mythical key to most of the more extreme forms of human behaviour and suffering, especially ones we think of as peculiarly modern: holocaust, plague, sexual harassment, rape, incest, seduction, pollution, sex-change, suicide, hetero- and homosexual love, torture, war, child-battering, depression and intoxication form the bulk of the themes.[10]

It would be difficult to find a better example of the meaninglessness of 'classical' understanding in the kind of sensibility for which (and out of and to which) Hofmann and Lasdun are speaking here. The complacency of the 'contemporary', and of 'we' who value it, turns Ovid into a contemporary poet who has waited all these centuries for his moment to come: a New Generation Poet of the Augustan age. Whatever writing like this describes, it is not the kind of poetic theme or practice in which Longley makes himself at home. In fact, Longley's work has tended more often towards the static rather than the metamorphic; his lyric energies have their strength in the deep conservative pull they exert on perception and experience, and not in their propulsion towards breakneck change and astounding transformation. It is a sense for this which leads John Lyon to note (in relation to the Ovidian poems) that 'Longley seems to be impelled to write against the facts of metamorphosis and mutability and in resistance to shape-shifting, and, indeed, narrative'.[11]

The version of Ovid's story of 'Baucis and Philemon' which Longley contributes to the *After Ovid* volume, and which subsequently goes on to become a central piece in *The Ghost Orchid*, is an interesting (and successful) instance of close translation in contemporary poetry. Longley follows his source faithfully, and thus devotes a lot of the poem to precise descriptions of the old couple's cottage and their catering arrangements: the scene of frugal hospitality, peace and generosity of course both sets up and benefits from echoes within the Longley *oeuvre*, recalling the Tibullus of 'Peace', while it also engages with themes of conjugal love and domesticity on which the poet focuses his lyrics elsewhere. While the episode culminates in a transformation, it is a transformation which functions to preserve a state of married love in perpetuity:

> At the end of their days when they were very old and bowed
> And living on their memories, outside the chapel door
> Baucis who was leafy too watched Philemon sprouting leaves.
> As tree-tops overgrew their smiles they called in unison
> 'Goodbye, my dear'. Then the bark knitted and hid their lips.
>
> (*GO* 25)

Longley's achievement is not the same here as in the Homeric poems, for he remains faithful to a passage of narrative *as narrative*: there is no attempt at lyric distillation in the piece. On the other hand, there is here the achievement of lyric architecture, with the Ovidian narrative finding its form in beautifully crafted and balanced five-line stanzas. The poetry which is being translated is also, in fact, that of an Ovid who is amenable to Longley's imagination, and not the Ovid described in Hofmann and Lasdun's preface.

In a series of much shorter poems, Longley does attempt to practise his own metamorphoses on Ovidian sources. To do this, the poet ventures out on a course which takes him away from the classicism of his Homeric poems, and their instinct for withdrawal and restraint, towards something much more explicit in its procedures. The authorial voice introduces itself alongside its mythic subject-matter, with Ovid supplying the shapes of narrative, so that a poem like 'Spiderwoman' is prefaced with 'Arachne starts with Ovid and finishes with me' (*GO* 13). While this technique works wonderfully in 'Phoenix', where Ovid's account of the mythical bird is framed within a simple anecdotal motif which begins and ends the one-sentence poem, it shows liabilities elsewhere in the volume. The humorous and alert scepticism which Longley directs at the idea of postmodernism in 'After Horace' does not always inoculate him against certain effects in the Ovidian poems where he attempts to encompass and celebrate patterns of multiplicity, change, and flux with which the foundations of his lyric poetry are more generally at odds. Where the Homeric poems refract elements of personal experience, projecting them in a new lyric medium, poems like 'A Flowering' try to combine free translation with a self-regard that, perhaps too freely, takes tonal risks.

It would be an over-simplification to propose that, while Homer brings out the 'classical' in Longley, Ovid draws him towards the 'romantic'. In fact, we need to be extremely cautious about the use of both terms; nevertheless, the balance of the artistic success for Longley does, on the whole, incline on the side of Homer. It is perhaps significant that one of the best classically-founded poems in *The Ghost Orchid* is 'The Oar', where Odysseus's future is beautifully prophesied:

> I am meant to wander inland with a well-balanced oar
> Until I meet people who know nothing about the sea
> – Salty food, prows painted purple, oars that are ships'
> Wings – and somebody mistakes the oar on my shoulder
> For a winnowing fan:
>   the signal to plant it in the ground
> And start saying my prayers, to go on saying my prayers
> Once I'm home, weary but well looked after in old age
> By my family and friends and other happy islanders,
> And death will come to me, a gentle sea-breeze, no more than
> An exhalation, the waft from a winnowing fan or oar.
>
> (GO 58)

The voice of Odysseus suits Longley better than the first-person voice of a poet jumping headlong into the *Metamorphoses*, and results in better poetry. The 'oars that are ships' / Wings' here, like the 'winnowing fan', set up resonances with other lyrics in *The Ghost Orchid*, and Longley lights upon an inspired phrase for Odysseus's death, 'no more than / An exhalation', in which his English sounds an echo of the mysterious phrase in the Greek 'ex halos' [literally, out of (or far from) the sea].[12] With poetry like this, discussions of the poet's degrees of 'personality' and 'impersonality' become critically redundant; rather, Longley creates a durable lyric out of classical material and out of the material of his volume as a whole. Like much of his best writing, it has an achieved poise and stasis which work potently (and permanently) against change.

To praise this aspect of Longley's classicism is not, in the end, to give unqualified assent to the poet as 'musarum sacerdos'. There is a degree of overlap between this notion of the poet as one with a priestly calling in a secular world, and the idea of the poet as a personality gifted with a burning, unique vision, and equipped with an equally individual power of inspired expression. The 'religious' and the 'romantic' are not always distinct, and they can be combined in some of Longley's more extravagant registers. Religion, even (or especially) 'secular' religion and poetry are not the same thing; one is not a satisfactory substitute for the other, however tempting it may be to allow these things to blur. If a contemporary classicism in poetry can be defined, however, it will be partly with reference to the best of Longley's writing; the value which this might represent will not be 'sacerdotal', but it will be secure.

MICHAEL LONGLEY AND THE WEST

ROBERT WELCH

> When working at Zen, the important
> thing is to generate the *i ching*,
> the 'doubt-sensation'.
>
> When working at Zen, it is important
> not to lose the right thought. This
> is the thought of *tsan*, meaning
> 'to bore into'.
>
> From the *Discourses of Master Po Shan*

These Zen masters are hard cases. When Han Shan was reluctant to return to school as a little boy his mother dragged him by the hair of his head to the river and threw him in. No softness there. There's no softness either in the poetry of Michael Longley: gentleness, yes, but that's a different matter entirely. Gentleness and courtesy are qualities that depend for their exercise upon force of character and moral courage. I'm not talking here about 'gentleness' and 'courage' as they often parade themselves in society – simulacra of decency – I'm talking about that harder more durable functioning that isn't masquerade, but a wholeness of personality engaged in the bewildering circumstance of moral, political, and social flux that is daily experience. It may strike some as a little odd to have such a vocabulary of moral action used in relation to the operations of poetry, frequently regarded as amongst the least 'utile' of the arts. We don't normally think of poetry as allied in any way to practical morality.

However such a distinction is relatively recent. There is very little question that writers as different as Milton, Dryden, Blake, Wordsworth, Shelley and Arnold all considered poetry as deeply allied not only with the strengthening of instinct but also as having a crucial function in enabling and fortifying the capacity for moral discrimination. Good taste was linked to goodness as much as to taste. The list of writers cited above (with the partial exception of Dryden) also points to another factor in the development of the moral poetics of modern Europe: they are all Protestant as well as being English. One of the reasons for the energy and force of realization in modern English poetry (that is poetry since the Renaissance) is precisely this alliance between an earthed imagination and a preoccupation with questions of right and wrong as they impinge upon the individual imagination. All of the writers cited, from Milton through to Arnold and even Lawrence (we could go further and extend the line to William Empson, Ted Hughes, Peter Reading) are concerned to bring the reader to a participation in a moral realization that is active on both the emotional and intellectual fronts. Poetry, Swift (also, to some extent, in this line) wrote: 'is a court of judgement in the soul',[1] a court in which the reader is both accused and prosecutor, judge and jury, while the poetry conducts the case.

The realizations that come about through this poetic are not mere momentary thrills: they are meant to influence judgement in practical affairs and to increase the arenas of civilized discourse. It is not an accident that Leavis (also in this line) argued so forcefully for the efficacy of poetry in inculcating practices of moral and social discipline. If Milton or Blake or Shelley thought that they could ever be read as an aesthetic delectation, freed from all requirements of social delivery, or as a self-contained discourse illustrating the relativity of all judgement, they would be appalled. They thought that poetry was a means of cleansing perception and of improving the will by dint of the effort of complex understanding. Poetry is a labour in which a new personality may be fashioned through the exercise of restraint, judgement, courtesy, wholeness of response – the kind of things Leavis sought to enthuse his pupils with in the Cambridge of the 1930s, '40s and '50s.

It will be now apparent where I am heading to: the signal predominant absence at the head of this line, and the most influential figure (apart from Shakespeare, a different and not unrelated presence) in the history of English poetry and poetry in English. I refer to that fashioner of this vital interanimation in English tradition – that between the imagination and moral inquiry – the great Protestant poet, Edmund Spenser. He put it quite bluntly (all those poets, by the way, are amazingly blunt and direct, a quality noticed by George Mackay Brown in Longley): Spenser declares with insouciant and bare-faced confidence that the intent of his poem *The Faerie Queene* is to 'fashion' a 'gentleman or noble person in vertuous and gentle discipline'.[2] Every rhyme, every loaded pun, every salacious piece of illusory trickery, every woeful incarceration, every brutal exercise of savage triumph is there to call the entire personality, the 'whole soul' in Sidney's (his friend and mentor) phrase, into activity, so that the reader may become his own confessor and take control of the direction of his own spirit in a new order of spiritualized realization. Each man is his own resurrection in the trying circumstances of Spenser's text which both informs the reader disposed to unlearn falsehood and duplicity while also fortifying, by means of ever subtler discriminations, his 'skill to read'. By hindsight (or Merlin-like foresight) not at all unlike Leavis.

As C. S. Lewis (yet another practitioner of moralized aesthetics) pointed out ages ago, Spenser's metaphor for this arena of spiritual exploration and experimental testing is the forest, the forest of legend, fairy-tale, and myth, where adventures happen, where the Christian soul encounters its multi-faceted fate.[3] It is also, however, the forest of Ireland, where Spenser encountered the apparent wildness of a different civilization and the certain enmity of an opposed ideology, faith, and polity. Spenser's Ireland is the West that lies outside and beyond the pale of civilized discourse. It is the realm of error, but it is also the testing ground where resolve may flourish and consolidate itself. It is a place of trial and always possible failure, but it is the ground which the reformation must win if the perversions and monstrosities of Duessa and her troop of errant (papist) followers are to be checked. English poetry (and poetry in English) cannot but be deeply informed by this Protestant resolution: that the world is a place of trial and of error and that the effort and discipline of ordered language (the word) has a key function in bringing the inchoate wildness of superstition, hocus-pocus, and anarchy to some form of order.

English poetry is entirely implicated in the economics and politics of the development of the British Empire over the last hundreds of years. This is not said in any mood of accusation, it is simply to register a fact and to recognize a major source of the power of English writing (especially poetry) since the sixteenth century: its Protestant, reforming impulse, based upon the efficacy of the individual conscience, under the direction and stimulus of a capacious imagination, to come into possession of its own power and liberty. This impulse, its irremissive urgings, and its inevitable thwarting, is the core-theme of another great Protestant (and Irish) writer: Joyce Cary.

How does all of this refer to Longley? My contention is that Longley is an Irish poet engaged, by virtue of language and background, upon an exploration of the world as a place of trial and error, a perspective which comes to us from the moralist aesthetic of English Protestant poetic tradition. All Irish poets who write in English are, to a significant degree, sharers of this inheritance – it is part of the linguistic air they breathe – but Longley's fidelity to certain moods of conditionality, a sense that the conscience is a lonely hunter, that it is best to face the hard road of effort and duty rather than submit to the allure of emotion or sentiment – all these ally him to a Protestant, indeed puritan, line of thinking and moral persuasion such as we associate with Spenser and Marvell, and find in the fiction of George Eliot. That Protestant resolve tested itself by turning westward, towards Ireland and the new world: the cannibals of Book VI of *The Faerie Queene* are both Irish woodkerns and Virginian savages. The west is the frontier which tests the Christian warrior's fortitude and resolve. He must expand further if the destiny of Britain, to be the founder of a new Troy (Troynovant), is to be accomplished. That expansion was a linguistic as well as an economic and social one, and this not simply in the sense that English was to become the language spoken in Ireland and in the new worlds to the West and South. This expansion, as we observe it in the history of English literature, especially poetry, was an interior one as well: as Seamus Heaney has it, 'Our pioneers keep striking / Inwards and downwards'.[4] In Spenser, Shakespeare, Milton, Blake, and Wordsworth (to name only those most powerful exponents of the affective and moral resources of English) poetry realizes a complex and dangerous inner world where are opened to our view the landscapes and corridors, the voices and silences, hesitancies and dynamics, of modern consciousness. This inner exploration is, I believe, profoundly annexed to the outer one in the realms of politics, money, and power, and the drive animating both is that of the Protestant will and its ethic.

It is this rich field of linguistic energy, with all its subtle and risky contours, its difficult buried strata, its recollections of triumph and victory as well as its cruelties and remorse, to which Longley immediately connected in his (resonantly titled: was Troy ever rebuilt?) first collection *No Continuing City* (1969). I remember my professor at UCC, Seán Lucy, who had this book for review, coming in to our third-year lecture theatre with the black-jacketed volume; I remember him opening it and running his index finger down the spine and, before reading, telling us that here was elegance, but more than that, he said. There was also an extraordinary ability to connect with the resources of some of the finest poetry in English: I remember he spoke of Marvell and of 'tough reasonableness', an utterly contemporary sensibility linked to a resonant and scrupulous intelligence.

Longley has carried forward aspects of seventeenth century English poetic tradition, but it does not seem appropriate to use the term 'metaphysical wit', familiar to us from T.S. Eliot's and Helen Gardner's commentaries on this poetry, to describe the kind of awakening intelligence we observe at work in Longley. There is wit there all right, a kind of sudden alacrity capable of swift turns and dizzy excitements, but there is also a kind of languor, a slow meditative peacefulness. This latter quality brings him into touch with a pastoral mood, in itself, as practised by the English poets, a convention imbued with strong puritan persuasions. Marvell, for example, when he writes of gardens, rivers, houses and their environs, is also often creating sweet and just places for the soul to rest in, havens in which everything accords, where all secrets are opened, where all is at-one. These are places of at-one-ment, atonement; strife is quelled, no differing vantages appear:

> The Nectaren, and curious Peach,
> Into my hands themselves do reach...
>
> ('The Garden')[5]

or in 'Upon Appleton House, to my Lord Fairfax':

> The Nightingale does here make choice
> To sing the Tryals of her Voice.
> Low Shrubs she sits in, and adorns
> With Musick high the squatted Thorns.
> But highest Oakes stoop down to hear,
> And listning Elders prick the Ear.
> The Thorn, lest it should hurt her, draws
> Within the Skin its shrunken claws.[6]

This trope, of commutual yielding, of nature purged of its fallen striving, is taken up in Longley's early 'Camouflage', but given a troublesome slant (needless to say, Marvell himself frequently exploits the dangers that lurk in apparently sweet and mossy places). Longley's method in this poem is to create a scene in which animals and their habitat are at one, but very steadfastly to keep his distance. He refuses to be a clamorous celebrant of a pastoral at-one-ment, slowing down, to an almost secretive watchfulness, his own contemplation of the witty and swiftly changing scenes he imagines. There are, also, mixed in with this steady unruffled appraisal, touches of comedy. In the following stanza, for example, note the comic finesse evident in the verb 'presume' to convey the absurdly lengthened necks of giraffes. There is something brilliantly effective in that word to convey the slightly baffled clumsiness of the giraffe, tiny head on huge flexile neck, big ears, dots, the lot – they're all there in that verb 'presume'. And this also demonstrates Longley's 'secret' Protestant, indeed puritan, wit: a scrupulous distrust of language and its imaginings, which compels him to appraise, investigate, and try each syllable, thereby alerting the reader (as Spenser does continually) to his/her own need to subject words to ceaseless and unremitting scrutiny:

> The leopard's coat accepting light through leaves,
> Giraffes whose necks presume that certain trees
> Are tall, whose elongated stance relieves
> Those boughs of height's responsibilities –
> Such attributes a balanced world conceives,
> Itself reflected, its streams reflecting these.
>
> (P 23)

The inter-involving meanings of these lines, the ways in which the mind criss-crosses itself as it follows the reflections and refractions, raise excitement and doubt. As Po Shan said, the important thing, when working at Zen, is 'to generate the *i ching*', the 'doubt-sensation'. There is an at-one-ment here in these lines – the giraffes' presumptuous necks relieve the trees of the responsibilities of height – but the wholeness is gloriously fuddled by a searching dubiety, a puritan wit, a zen-like nonsensicality. The 'balanced world' is very precariously held in equilibrium. Beneath the criss-cross of witty exertion there is risk and danger. In 'A Personal Statement', dedicated to Seamus Heaney, Longley describes this troubled equilibrium as it subsists in the personality. Here the presiding genius is George Herbert:

> My person is
> A chamber where the elements postpone
> In lively synthesis,
> In peace on loan,
>
> Old wars of flood and earthquake, storm
> And holocaust . . .
>
> (P 27)

A 'lively synthesis' indeed in which history is impacted. Poetry, for Longley, is a raising of the 'doubt-sensation' in regard to everything that history remits. It involves the kind of thinking, characterized by Po Shan, as *tsan*, 'boring into'; Longley's 'Zen' is *tsan Zen*, a meditation that 'bores into' the materials of history, memory, thought. The synthesis of at-one-ment, so longed-for in the puritan ache for the recovery of peace, is precarious and *constantly moving*. There is 'no continuing city'. All balance resides in the interplay of opposing forces, their dynamics precariously stilled. Balance is, as Longley recalls W.B. Stanford pointing out in TCD, 'a tension', not a static moribund.

In the (brief) note to *Gorse Fires* (1991) Longley, in the course of some glossary explications of Irish or Hiberno-English words, refers to usages in 'my part of Mayo'. We can be dead certain that this is no slack familiar usage: some kind of fidelity and belonging is most seriously implicated. And of course the imagery of Mayo and the west – its topography, flora, fauna; the loving and specialized naming of its rare species of flower and weed; the trance-like absorption in the particulars of light on stone or in the sky; the intimacy with neighbours involving keeping a distance – all these form clusters of interrelated materials that constitute a major centre of gravity in the Longley system of checks and balancings. Carrigskeewaun comes in explicitly from *An Exploded View* (1973) on, but the western gravity-cluster is there from *No Continuing City*, especially in that brilliant and ambitious poem 'The Hebrides', which mixes the intellectual forensics of Marvell with the Romantic meditative odes as practised by William Collins and Thomas Gray, save that Longley keeps his distance from the ready allures and vertigo that Gray, for example, revelled in in 'The Bard'. He concludes the poem by saying that though he'd love the free-fall exhilaration of romantic vertigo, he fights always to keep his balance:

> Granting the trawlers far below their stance,
> Their anchorage,
> I fight all the way for balance –
> In the mountain's shadow
> Losing foothold, covet the privilege
> Of vertigo.

(P 43)

He refuses this privilege; as much as to say: I know the allure of romanticism, there are times when it may be a relief to let go, but no – the fight is for the tension of balance, the strenuous exertion required to keep on investigating the mind-traps of language, held in place by the lethal springs of certainty and emotion.

The west in Irish literature and culture is seen as a repository of authentic value. We recall Yeats's declamation to Synge in Paris – enjoining him to go to Aran and give expression to a life as yet unexpressed. Or earlier, there were the self-accusations of J.J. Callanan when he felt he could not adequately translate the energy of the Gaelic poetry he encountered in Gougane Barra and Millstreet in West Cork. Or there is MacNeice, whose evocations of the west become part of his non-aligned evaluation of the variant elements that constitute his mind-set and sensibility. Longley, although closer to MacNeice than any of the other writers who have been drawn to the west as inspiration and locale, has his own very specific reading of this not unproblematic gravity-cluster with its associations of romance (Flora Mac-Ivor leaning over the trembling structure of a ramshackle bridge in Sir Walter Scott's *Waverley*), sentiment (John Ford's *The Quiet Man*), menace (Mulrennan in Joyce's *Portrait*), or sadness and treachery ('the mutinous Shannon waves' in Joyce's 'The Dead'). The west in Longley is linked to the puritan attitude to landscape, which has two aspects. On the one hand there is the 'good place', the *locus amoenus* where human and natural worlds are in accord (we've seen this in Marvell and it also surfaces in Samuel Ferguson's dreams of the valley of Six Mile Water transformed by the light of rectitude and justice). On the other hand there is the sense that landscapes, even beautiful ones, may be false, lures to trap the sensitive mind, weakly seeking rest, relief from tension. This suspicion is everywhere alive in Spenser and Milton, and it is the distrust that fuels the poetic inquiry. One needs an internal system of checks and balances, a moral Geiger-counter, to read what the eye thinks it sees. This suspicion of what appears to be beautiful gives its moral acerbity and edge to English poetry and (if I may take the opportunity to offer this momentary observation) it is not impossible that this doubting, this doubt-sensation, owes not a little to the fact that the presiding intelligence in the tradition, Edmund Spenser, was always mindful to doubt the security of what was before his eyes on his lands in Ireland. To the true Christian, the true knight of holiness or temperance, there is no earthly home; the fact of living in Ireland, as a colonial or a landed settler, would have given that maxim the force of lived reality. Of course you could never entirely believe what you saw.

Longley embraces this double vision. The west, a gravity-cluster, enters the poetry with all its spacious skies and minute particulars, but not without the rueful and doubting associations of his particular brand of Zen Protestantism. The entrance is magnificent, a release, as fresh complexity, new perspectives, are engaged:

> The winds' enclosure, Atlantic's premises,
>   Last balconies
> Above the waves, the Hebrides –
>   Too long did I postpone
> Presbyterian granite and the lack of trees,
>   This orphaned stone
>
> Day in, day out colliding with the sea.
>
> (P 40)

But he is in two minds. He is drawn back to the city, Belfast, which to some extent continues in him, drawn back to:

> Dry dock, gantries,
> Dykes of apparatus...

The poem is not *about* the Hebrides. It is a linguistic testing-ground in which different locations – the elemental and the technological – are worked through. Its enigmatic lack of a theme, in the sense of something pursued and engaged and concluded (upon) is a characteristic of the way in which Longley's method proceeds. It is process more than product, a meditation that works into the moving and changing realizations of a mind that seeks no rest from weariness, but rather the fully-focussed coordinates of a tension that never recedes. It is, again, a kind of *tsan Zen*. And yet Longley's poetry, while full of tension, is not a poetry of anxiety. It doesn't dwell on things or ransack them for their essence (perhaps a Catholic tradition in modern poetry deriving its inspiration from Hopkins); it keeps the mind mobile, the intelligence alert, the spaces wide-open between the images for the reader to fill. It is a poetry in which the depth is always implied and it is utterly unpretentious. That is not to say that it cannot be tricksy and baffling, as all good Zen practitioners tend to be. 'Kingfisher' in the small sequence called 'The Corner of the Eye' in *An Exploded View* creates a whole landscape, but from a very unusual and strange set of vantages. This tries out new ways of looking, and invites the reader to divest him/herself of the form and formality of what we normally think of as seeing. Again, this is a raising of the doubt-sensation (*i ching*), a sense (shared with MacNeice) that the world is utterly various and manifold:

> a knife-thrower
> hurling himself, a rainbow

> fractured against
> the plate glass of winter: [. . .]
>
> (P 72)

Suddenness, violence, the shock of vividness, the mind is enlivened with the (silent) smash of glass, the frost, the agitation of every colour. And now, after the colon's pause, like a breath taken in meditation, we move inside the bird's eye where we see a baffling, strange, and compelling open:

> his eye a water bead,
> lens and meniscus where
> the dragonfly drowns,
> the water-boatman crawls.

This is an experience rather than a piece of knowledge or a conclusion. It cannot, like all the finest poetry, be intellectualized; it just is. The strangeness of the angle taken here, which is very characteristic of Longley's poetry, occurs in another Irish work, to my knowledge. It happens in *The Real Charlotte* (1894) by Somerville and Ross, during the picnic on the lake-island when suddenly, and with a cold shock, the picnic-scene (lovers, fussy parents, dogs, basket, food) are all looked at from the angle of the trout's eye in a pool nearby. Somerville and Ross, like Longley, carry with them a deep distrust of appearance, what people say they will do, gesture, attitude, poise. This gives the two women their humour (people used to hear them howling with laughter in their study as they composed); it gives Longley his angular wit and enigmatic daring as he traverses the stepping stones of his imagining.

This angular vision is part of Longley's method, his discipline, technique. From 'The Hebrides' onwards the west becomes an integral part of his *modus operandi* as a poet. It is not an escape, or a dream-place where all is in harmony: it is a key-element in the intellectual and aesthetic apparatus he brings to bear upon language and experience, all the more germane to the operations of that apparatus for being somewhat 'out there', off-centre, angled. It is a means by which a strangeness becomes part of the way the poetry happens. The last poem in *The Ghost Orchid* (1995), 'Out There', describes this discipline and also to some extent enacts it in the 'outer' music it conjures:

> Do they ever meet out there,
> The dolphins I counted,
> The otter I wait for?

> I should have spent my life
> Listening to the waves.
>
> (GO 60)

The question ('Do they ever meet out there?') is baffling, but it invites us to consider things out of their 'thereness'. It extends the perspective so that what is seen is qualified by the motes travelling to the corner of the eye. The question is, at once, both estranging and intimate. The mind opens to receive, not an answer but a statement, full of a mixture of confidence and remorse, self-knowledge and self-criticism:

> I should have spent my life
> Listening to the waves.

The question (like some Mayo *koan*) raises the doubt-sensation (*i ching*) in order to allow the poem to become a space for lucent calm attentiveness to the relationships and distances between words, mind, and things. The peculiar especial music of Longley's mature verse includes this distance. It is a kind of openwork, a lace-making, in which the separations between things are part of the fabricated shape.

It is part of the Catholic mind to sacramentalize experience and reality. Catholicism imbues the particulars of creation with a potential for miracle; or turning it around the other way, the divine can enter into the actual texture of things, the material world can be infused with divinity, as in the doctrine of the Real Presence, where Christ is actually existent under the form of bread and wine in the Eucharist. Protestant doctrine holds the divine and the human in separation, and puritanism (the energy which, it is my belief, fuels so much of the excellence of English poetry) insists upon that distance with a greater degree of emphasis than is the case within the more accommodating tenets of Anglican settlement and compromise. That distance has its coldness but it allows each consistent element of perception its own valid space: it involves a kind of democracy of the intellect, a free space in which things co-exist. This open-work lattice is the structural principle of Longley's verse, and it is the source of his particular music, a lovely threnody flowing between and across the interstices of his open spaces, spaces retained by a watchful regard originating in that western 'gravity-cluster'. But let us hear some of this watchful music, a kind of Satie-like loneliness operating between parts of speech. Here are two quatrains from 'In Mayo' in *Man Lying on a Wall* (1976):

> When it is time for her to fall asleep
> And I touch her eyelids, may night itself,
> By my rule of thumb, be no profounder
> Than the grassy well among irises
>
> Where wild duck shelter their candid eggs:
> No more beguiling than a gull's feather
> In whose manifold gradations of light
> I clothe her now and erase the scene.
>
> (P 118)

This is a magical lyricism, but when looked at closely it becomes clear that there is no blurring of clear distinctions to evoke a rhapsodic blur. It is an epithalamium (with, incidentally, a memory of Spenser in the – human – blessing invoked) in which a world comes into shape, all its distinct particulars intact. The lyric focus even registers the different qualities of light in a gull's feather, light which clothes the lover as the poem decently cancels itself, leaving the candid eggs among the irises near the grassy well. In Donne, Dr Johnson has told us, 'heterogeneous ideas are yoked by violence together'; here Longley is connecting a heterogeneity of realization in a free and open fluidity of motion, where the rhythm and grammatical pulse of the syntax carry one strangeness into another with all the force and immediacy of nature itself. Surprise follows surprise: by this 'rule of thumb' a complete emotional curve is inscribed. Each element is graphically registered in the musical impulse, but the relations between them and the scene itself retain an integral strangeness: something is half-hidden, not out of secrecy but because it is not appropriate to speak of what must essentially remain mysterious. And the verbal music has that Satie-like calm and collectedness. It is content to register 'manifold gradations' and to let it at that. God knows, it's enough.

This 'open work' or patch work – see 'An Amish Rug' in *Gorse Fires* (1991) – coming out of Longley's angular vision in which the west provides a necessary 'gravity-cluster' gives his lyric and erotic verse its suddenness and fluidity: the poetry becomes a dynamic animation between materials held distinct in a chaste appraisal. The mental and moral disposition becomes the motor of the style.

But this Satie-like caution and finesse, this Protestant resolve to refrain from too rapid a foreclosure on the manifold gradations inherent in things, has other manifestations also, especially in the later work. In *Gorse Fires*, for example, there is a little suite in homage to Satie, 'The Velocipede' and 'Halley's Comet'. In 'The

Velocipede' (a title silently taken from Satie) we have a brilliant and witty Mayo sketch, although to call it a sketch is something of a misnomer. It is a series of mobilizations in which present and past interanimate; clumsiness and activity inhabit the same ground; and the reader is kept guessing in the evolving set of mutations:

> He walks past my bedroom window carrying a spade.
> That Joseph Murphy, father of four sets of twins,
> Jockey, lover of horses, the gun club's secretary,
> Should hide in his cottage a ledger full of poems
> Is hardly surprising: consider his grandfather
> Who beachcombed from the strand barrels and spars
> And built the first velocipede in Thallabaun.
>
> (GF 14)

Take a breath. We are now adjusting our perspectives, to take in as part of the same act of realization a Mayo countryside and strange gents cycling about on elaborate pedalling contrivances. Longley is raising the anti, the *i ching*, the doubt-sensation; the realizing process is lustrously at play as he re-assembles our perceptions. The grandfather of the poem doesn't rest content with a velocipede:

> Out of an umbrella and old sheets he improvised
> A parachute, launched himself from the byre roof
> And after a brief flight was taken to hospital.

No assumptions here, no crazy air-lifts. But wait a minute:

> On home-made crutches and slipping all the tethers
> Joseph Murphy's grandfather swings past my window.

This little 'gymnopaede' derives its animation from the unsettling energy continually alive in things and in our strange and distant relations with them. The style registers that, in its witty and surprising juxtapositions, and the juxtapositions themselves recall to the reader how little he or she knows of baffling variety all around. The present is mysterious, as is the past. The labour and effort of poetry, the exercise of the focussed but undetermining will, is to free the past from the captious needs of the present, the present from the insistent rhetorics of the past. Poetry is the midpoint of consciousness, the actuality of conscience, the 'breath and finer spirit of all knowledge'. So that when Longley turns to Homer or Ovid he does so as much to set them free of us, as to free us from the harsh and doctrinal uses to which we put myth and history. Part of that animation of the conscience is Mayo and the west, a testing ground of perception:

> All night crackling camp-fires boosted their morale
> As they dozed in no man's land and the killing fields.
> (There are balmy nights – not a breath, constellations
> Resplendent in the sky around a dazzling moon –
> When a clearance high in the atmosphere unveils
> The boundlessness of space, and all the stars are out
> Lighting up hill-tops, glens, headlands, vantage
> Points like Tonakeera and Allaran where the tide
> Turns into Killary, where salmon run from the sea,
> Where the shepherd smiles on his luminous townland.
> That many camp-fires sparkled in front of Ilium
> Between the river and the ships, a thousand fires,
> Round each one fifty men relaxing in the fire-light.)
> Shuffling next to the chariots, munching shiny oats
> And barley, their horses waited for the sunrise.
>
> (*GO* 37)

The Somme, Vietnam, Troy; the stars, the fires, the shiny oats, and barley: all registered in a process of awe and awakening. The doubt-sensation spilling over back into what is there before us, just there. No more to be said. Tomorrow brings we know not what.

Gathering Mushrooms

Pushed up between the masses of the night,
Exhaled at dawn with the cattle's breath —
A dim harvest had come to light
Out of the reticent ill-fitting earth.

Across those acres where mushrooms grew
Among fallen leaves and dung like emblems
— Bonus and bounty rocketed asleep,
Regalia of decay, ~~acute blooms~~ —
                    glib emblems

We moved, each of us a somnambulist,
Out of touch, in the distance turning,
Stooping down to an infinite arrest
~~In that wide meadow that summer morning~~

We moved, each of us a somnambulist
Out of touch, in the distance turning,
In the wide meadow that summer morning
Stooping down to ~~an~~ infinite arrest.
                    perpetual

Bonus as
Across those acres where mushrooms grew

SWANS MATING

Even now I wish that you had been there
Sitting beside me on the riverbank:
The cob and his pen sailing in rhythm
Slowly, till their heads met and the final
Heraldic moment dissolved the ripples.

Swans Mating   The
                 sidedown
                 as into an sidedown

Even now I wish that you had been there
Sitting beside me on the riverbank
When the two ~~swans~~ glided
The cob and his hen   a final
Heraldic moment dissolved in ripples

Her feathers full of water and her neck
Under the water like a bar of light.

Until their small heads met and the final

This was a marriage and a baptism,
A holding of the breath

His wings spread wide for balance

A holding of breath, nearly a drowning,

This was a marriage and a baptism,
A holding of breath, nearly a drowning,
His wings spread wide for balance as he trod

This was a marriage and a baptism,
A holding of breath, nearly a drowning,
Wings spread wide for balance where he trod,
Her feathers full of water and her neck
Under the water like a bar of light.

Even now I wish that you had been there
Sitting beside me on the riverbank:
The cob and his hen ~~floating~~ sailing in rhythm,
~~their heads~~   until the final
Heraldic moment dissolved in ripples,
Slowly, until their heads met and the final

AND NO MORE SINGING

On Reading Edward Thomas's Diary

<u>And no more singing for the bird</u>

One night in the trenches
You dreamnt you were at home
And couldn't stay for tea,
Then woke where shell holes
Filled with bloodstained water,

You received larks singing
Like a letter from home
Posted in No Man's Land
Where a frantic bat seemed
A piece of burnt paper.

THE LINEN INDUSTRY

Pulling up flax after the blue flowers have fallen
And laying our handfuls in the peaty water
To rot those grasses to the bone, or building stocks
That recall the skirts of an invisible dancer,

We become a part of the linen industry
And follow its processes to the grubby town
Where fields are compacted into window-boxes
And there is little room among the big machines.

But even in our attic under the skylight
We make love on a bleach green, the whole meadow
Draped with material turning white in the sun
As though snow reluctant to melt were our attire.

We are employed a battering of stubborn stalks,
Then a gentle combing out of fibres like hair
And a weaving of these into christening robes,
Into garments for a marriage or funerals.

bereavement once the labour's done
To find ourselves last workers in a dying trade.
flax our matchmaker, our undertaker,
The provider of sheets for whatever the bed.

shy of your breasts in the presence of death
that you look more beautiful in linen
Wearing white petticoats, the bow on your bodice
A butterfly attending the embroidered flowers.

DETOUR

I want my ~~last journey~~ General to include ~~a~~ The detour
Down the single street of a small country town,   ? maker
On either side of the procession such names as
~~Darley, Lacy,~~ MacNamara, Phibbin, Keane.
A reverend pause to let a herd of milkers pass
Will bring me face to face with parsnips, carrots
A ~~light rain~~ ~~is rinsing~~ ~~down on the pavement,~~
~~Now,~~ hay rakes, broom handles, gas cylinders.
Reflected in the slow sequence of shop windows
I shall ~~be~~ part of the action when his wife
Draining the potatoes into a steamy sink
Calls to the grocer to get ready for dinner
~~Than~~ the publican descends to change a barrel.
From behind the one ~~locked~~ door for miles around
I shall ~~hold a confidential~~ conversation
With the man in the concrete telephone kiosk
About ~~yesterday's crumpled starting prices~~
Or the riddle on a discarded ice-lolly stick.
About where my funeral will be going next.
                          night

Hanging above the pavement in a rainstorm
And carrots hanging out in a rainshower
so Phibbin, O'Malley, MacNamara, Keane

From April to April it has been one long
drain, slowly between the same embankments
~~Streams~~
Cattle are dungy still, smudged by winter, lambs
But the lambs seem to be wearing may blossom
Since the lambs have skipped ~~from last year wearing may.~~
Have skipped from last year into enclosures
Three or four men circle a rusty tractor
Before going to work in separate fields

Though smoke from the peat fires primroses burn
and may and celandines and gorse flowers

~~From April to April it has been one long~~
~~Drain, slowly between the same embankments.~~
Cattle are dungy still, smudged by winter, lambs
Have skipped from last ~~year~~ as far as enclosures.
~~Three or~~ four men gather at a rusty tractor
~~Before going with~~ their implements to separate fields.
~~Smoke from peat fires~~, but the primroses burn
And may and celandines and gorse flowers
Where fires are smoking, but the primroses burn
And with the may and celandines the gorse flowers

From April to April I have walked to you
~~From April to April I have been walking towards you.~~
~~At the same rain flowing between~~ the two embankments.
And the same rain between the old embankments
Where fires are smoking, out the primroses burn
And the white may and celandines and gorse flowers
I have been walking from April towards April.
It is the same rain between the embankments.

THE ICE-CREAM MAN

Rum and raisin, vanilla, butter-scotch, walnut, peach:
You would rhyme off the flavours. That was before
They murdered the ice-cream man on the Lisburn Road
And you bought carnations to lay outside his shop.
I named for you all the wild flowers of the Burren
I had seen in one day: valerian, thyme, loosestrife,
crowfoot, meadowsweet, ling, angelica,
Loosestrife, herb robert, marjoram, cow parsley, vetch,
Mountain avens, wood sage, ragged robin, bindweed,
Yarrow, lady's bedstraw, stitchwort, bog pimpernel.

CONFLICT, VIOLENCE AND 'THE FUNDAMENTAL INTERRELATEDNESS OF ALL THINGS' IN THE POETRY OF MICHAEL LONGLEY

ELMER KENNEDY-ANDREWS

Unlike fellow poets from the North of Ireland such as Heaney, Mahon and Muldoon, Longley has remained in the North throughout his career, and it would indeed be a surprise if the experience of almost thirty years of civil unrest, political violence and sectarian bloodletting did not impinge upon his work. Yet only a relatively small number of his poems represent direct responses to the 'Troubles' (as the civil turmoil and paramilitary violence have euphemistically come to be called). Politically minded critics have accused him of refusing to enter history. Stan Smith, for example, criticises him for standing 'at one remove' from the Troubles, denying 'complicity' in the massacre, and washing his hands in 'sanctimonious disdain'.[1] Smith favours a poetry of 'anger and ferocity', of direct engagement with history, and dismisses Longley's and Mahon's poetry as 'equivocal toyings' with their 'ambiguous' identities. Smith concludes that 'the middle ground and the middle distance are not the place where thought may grow, or wisdom flourish'.

This represents a remarkably prescriptive and reductive view of what good poetry might be. Smith sneers at a poetry of 'urbane tolerance' when, more than anything, it might be argued, it is precisely the lack of tolerance — the entrenchment, distrust and intransigence on both sides of the sectarian divide — that is the root cause of the present conflict, and that must be confronted if there is ever to be peace. It is true that Longley refuses to take sides, but that is because he believes the 'middle ground' is the only ground where accommodation can take place and mutual respect and understanding develop. To map that ground, far from being an evasion or withdrawal, may yet be the most socially and politically beneficial act the poet can perform. Identity need not be constructed in narrow political terms: there are other ways, which Longley's poetry helps to suggest. To contemplate these alternative modes of being is perhaps all the more necessary since the politicians have so conspicuously failed to escape the dead hand of the past. As poems such as 'Peace: after Tibullus' and 'Ceasefire' would attest, Longley is interested in exploring alternative possibilities to the present situation, but that does not mean he simply washes his hands of the violence. He insists that we all recognise our propensity to savagery. Poems such as 'Casualty' and 'The Goose' are little dramas of 'complicity'. In poems dealing directly with acts of terrorist atrocity such as the well-known 'Wounds' or 'Wreaths', the detached stance is not one adopted in a spirit of 'sanctimonious disdain'. The use of understatement in these poems, far from implying 'indifference' as Smith says, conveys an ironic and unsettling sense of the hideous and grotesque normality of the violence. Longley stands back from the contingent world to create a space for himself, an artistic distance, where he can view the local and immediate atrocity with a broad cultural and historical inclusiveness, and deliberately avoid partisanship. It is a stance which enables him to maintain balance in the face of a potentially demoralising violence. For Heaney, contemplation of the ancient bog victims was a way of understanding the contemporary horror in Ulster as part of a timeless continuum. Longley, too, interrogates the past in order to comprehend the present, though his poetry has none of Heaney's religious or tribal watermarking, and evinces none of Heaney's elaborate mythicising tendencies. Rather, Longley continues a tradition of unaligned, liberal scepticism in modern Irish poetry, especially associated with Louis MacNeice.

Underlying Longley's approach to violence, and to life in general, is a notion of what he calls in a recent poem 'According to Pythagoras' (*The Ghost Orchid*) 'the fundamental interconnectedness of all things'. In a context of social conflict and violence, this Whitmanesque idea of the unity of all creation can have a powerfully steadying and reassuring effect. As a tenet of faith it can help ensure against demoralisation and defeat, as it can against dogmatism and partisanship. As we shall see, Longley's aesthetic – his use of metaphor, his techniques of fusion, juxtaposition and parallelism, his fluid handling of time, place and identity, his self-conscious intertextuality – has been specifically designed to express this idea of interconnectedness. In the poem already referred to, 'According to Pythagoras', a free working of a passage from Ovid's *Metamorphoses*, the theme is the flux of life. The idea of 'the fundamental interconnectedness of all things' is presented in biological and physical terms, as a basic fact of life: life is generated out of the putrefaction of death, the shore-crab's claw grows into a scorpion, worms into butterflies, germs into frogs, larvae into bees, eggs into birds, rotting spines into snakes; hyenas change sex, chameleons change colour, lynxes' urine becomes stones. Formally, the notion of universal interconnectedness is acted out in the links that Longley establishes with Pythagoras and Ovid, in the fusion of classical and contemporary worlds, in the play of a powerful colloquial freedom within the formal framework of a traditional iambic line.

This idea of 'the fundamental interconnectedness of all things' has not only shaped Longley's poetry but informed his whole cultural project as Combined Arts Director for the Arts Council of Northern Ireland until his retirement in 1991. As man and poet, he has always felt compelled to break down and cross the usual (social, political and cultural) boundaries. In *Tuppeny Stung: Autobiographical Chapters* (1994) he tells of his efforts to bring traditional Irish music to the UDA, and government funding to the Glor-na-nGael language-group in West Belfast. In joining the Cultural Traditions Group, which had just been set up in 1988, he wanted to be part of the effort 'to encourage in Northern Ireland the acceptance and understanding of cultural diversity; to replace political belligerence with cultural pride'. His whole cultural outlook, as he explains in *Tuppeny Stung*, is based on a view of cultural difference as enriching rather than threatening:

In Ulster cultural apartheid is sustained to their mutual impoverishment by both communities. W.R. Rodgers referred to the 'creative wave of self-consciousness' which can result from a confluence of cultures. In Ulster this confluence pools historical contributions from the Irish, the Scots, the English and the Anglo-Irish. Reconciliation does not mean all the colours of the spectrum running so wetly together that they blur into muddy uniformity. Nor does it mean denying political differences . . . But reconstructing the past or constructing identities has too frequently been a purely propagandist activity in Northern Ireland. The Cultural Traditions approach involves a mixture of affirmation, self-interrogation and mutual curiosity. To bring to light all that has been repressed can be a painful process; but, to quote the American theologian Don Shriver:

'The cure and the remembrance are co-terminous'.²

Terry Eagleton believes that liberal humanist idealism is simply a recipe for inertia, and thus submission to the status quo. Longley's statement is clearly not acquiescence in the status quo or evidence of 'shell-shocked' passivity or 'indifference' (Smith's terms) in the face of division and violence. Rather, Longley describes a programme for creating new conditions of life, new identities, relationships and structures. *Tuppeny Song* is, in fact, a fascinating account of an administrator's struggle to bring about in practical ways the vision of wholeness and healing that his poetry explores. Despite what Smith says, Longley's poetry does not exist in some detached aesthetic realm cut off from the realities of the everyday world: Longley's idea of interconnectedness includes the inseparability of the aesthetic and the ethical. His work as both man and poet is based on an ideal of liberal, pluralist accommodation which refuses to buy into a culture of guilt and blame, and seeks to break the vicious circle of violence through encouraging mutual understanding, respect and forgiveness.

2

Violence has always been a central theme in Longley's poetry. In his first volume, *No Continuing City*, he explores the violence in nature. It is incarnated in the predatory figures of 'the weasel and ferret, the stoat and fox' which traverse the winter landscape in 'Persephone'. However, Longley's picture of the natural world is balanced and complex. He alludes to winter's 'delirium' of chaos and destruction, and describes nature's creatures as 'straightjacketed' by the cold, but the references to the mole's 'buildings' and the swallows' 'home' evoke a notion of natural order. The bat and squirrel know how to adapt to difficult conditions – they are 'the welladjusted and the skilled'. The silent predators are also graceful, beautiful creatures. Persephone, the corn-goddess, returns from the underworld for six months of every year to restore the fertility of the land. The poem, in fact, suggests a basic duality in nature. This tension is subtly enacted in the carefully disordered iambic pentameter, and in the tendency of the rhyming couplets to relax to half-rhyme.

In exploring the violence of the natural order in his poetry, Longley seeks to locate man within that order. He probes the elemental life behind politics and rationality: 'My brain-child, help me find my own way back / To fire, air, water, earth' ('A Personal

Statement'). 'Casualty' at first seems to be a poem about violence out there, in the world of nature. It describes in minute detail 'other animals' scavenging the carcass of a ram. However, the passive observation of natural violence is not entirely dispassionate and detached, the central lines of the poem – 'more and more / I wanted to get closer to it' – declaring the speaker's fascination with, and implication in, the activity that is taking place before him. In 'The Goose', this passive observation develops into an active, socially acceptable desecration.

Longley's presentation of the desecration of the dead animal in 'Casualty' is, like the act itself, gradual and exact, a mimicking of the sinister process of dismemberment. This primeval, repulsive destruction is depicted as a sacrificial ritual: the act is 'ceremonious', the ram's hooves 'immaculate'. Violence is purifying. The poet, acting as 'priest at hand' (as he describes himself in 'A Personal Statement'), contemplates the body's dissolution with religious concentration. Watching the process of decay, it was

> As though something that had followed
> Fox and crow was desperate for
> A last morsel and was
> Other than wind or rain.
>
> (P 74)

That use of 'something' is significant, suggesting the difficulty of clearly identifying the uncontrollable, destructive force at work in nature and in man.

That 'something' is present in 'The Goose' too, where the goose, proverbial creature of dumb innocence, is subjected to a slow, deliberate, ceremonious *human* depredation. There are obvious similarities between the two poems – the verse form that is used, the clinical approach to the subject, the matter-of-factness in the description of process, the close objective rendering of sensuous detail. The speaker performs his ritual preparations of the goose for the oven with an almost erotic thrill, delighting in the total power he enjoys:

> It was right to hesitate before
> I punctured the skin, made incisions
> And broached with my reluctant fingers
> The chill of its intestines . . .
>
> (P 113)

The last stanza unmasks the primal, violent impulses that lie behind the civilised facade of sophistication, complacency and control:

> I would boil the egg for your breakfast,
> Conserve for weeks the delicate fats
> As in the old days. In the meantime
> We dismantled it, limb by limb.

Complicit with the male speaker is his female partner. He presents himself as active, strong, bold, proud: she is passive and weak. He protects her from horror: 'Much else followed which, for your sake, / I bundled away, burned on the fire'. Nevertheless, he, too, reveals his sensitivity, covering the goose's head, noting the 'expression of disappointment' in its 'pink eyes', confessing that he thought 'It was right to hesitate' before puncturing the skin, recording the almost poignant discovery of 'the last egg', while she, the supposedly sensitive one, can enjoy eating the sacrificial 'last egg' and help him perform the less squeamish jobs. Clear lines of demarcation between male and female are blurred. Each category is traced through with the other. The poem, we may conclude, presents two complementary aspects of the speaker's own psyche, a characteristic Longley balancing of opposites.

These studies of human fascination with corruption and butchery establish the general human context within which war and terrorism are viewed in well-known poems such as 'Wounds' and 'Wreaths'. Longley recognises in man a primeval compulsion towards violence. There is a continuity of man and nature within which violence is as much a part of the human as the natural world. Longley insists we recognise these dark, destructive forces. 'Birthmarks', in his first volume, speaks of the submerged, transgressive energies in consciousness and in society, personified in the references to 'Thief, murderer and clown' which, as much as the 'lares' (the spirits of hearth and home in ancient Rome), are recognised by the poet as part of what 'makes up the whole': 'These are the poems we cannot write'. In 'Peace: after Tibullus', the speaker good-naturedly ridicules the idea of an idyllic society devoid of violence as mere myth. Humankind, Longley wittily suggests, has been contaminated: 'Murder got into the bloodstream as gene or virus / So that we now give birth to wars, short cuts to death' (P 169). Mankind is possessed of a self-destructive pathology, the strange force that made dismemberment compelling in 'Casualty' and 'The Goose'. The extravagance of the final pastoral image – 'As for me, I want a woman / To come and fondle my ears of wheat and let apples / Overflow between her breasts' –

sounds like self-mocking acknowledgement of the unreality of what he so fervently longs for.

The whole Irish cultural tradition exemplifies this unfortunate pathology. Violence is enshrined in Irish mythology, idolised in myth and poem and song. Poems such as 'Smoke in the Branches' and 'On Slieve Gullion' (P 197–8) reflect the historic Irish fascination with violence. Each of the four short poems that comprise 'Smoke in the Branches' refers to a well-known Celtic legend which resonates with a disturbing contemporary relevance. 'On Slieve Gullion' combines violent images drawn from Irish mythology, history and contemporary events. In choosing Slieve Gullion in South Armagh, he sets his poem in one of the 'hot spots' of the contemporary conflict. It is also the territory of the eighteenth century rapparee, ancient cattle raids and the exploits of Conor Mor. More recently, it is the area in which Robert Nairac, who was officially described as an 'undercover liaison officer' working for the British army, disappeared in 1977. Nairac, a victim of the present Troubles, is linked with the 'severed heads' of the past. Longley himself enters the poem as observer of the violence. Watching a paratrooper out on patrol, the poet first imagines him as a mummer lost in the countryside, then identifies with him – 'Both strangers here'. 'Because of my English connection', Longley explained in a recent interview, 'I am slightly ill at ease in Ireland, and the same applies in England because I am from Ireland. In this community which I am still exploring and trying to understand I still feel a bit of an outsider'.[3] This simultaneous understanding of native tradition and distance from it allows for a kind of complex seeing that Longley valued in the poetry of Louis MacNeice. MacNeice, he believed, was 'a touchstone of what an Ulster (that is to say Irish) poet might be':

Because of his Irish and English and Ulster viewpoints MacNeice was able to respond with flexibility and objectivity to the complexities of Ireland, her 'jumble of opposites', her 'intricacies of gloom and glint'.[4]

Longley, too, specialises in a poetry of multiple viewpoint, a poetry that seeks to acknowledge the 'confluence of cultures'.

In a sequence of powerful poems he acknowledges his own haunting by violence, his own sense of the burden of history. The description of the fairground, in the poem of that title, recalls Muldoon's 'Duffy's Circus', where the narrator, an innocent child, confronts the horror 'beyond the corral'. Similarly, Longley's poem, which becomes increasingly nightmarish and surreal, is concerned with the horror that lies behind the carnival attractions of the fairground. The poem beside 'The Fairground' is 'Nightmare', in which the speaker dreams of carrying a pig which is 'deceptive', coy, highly dangerous, but for which he feels responsible, and to which he is 'indissolubly attached' – even when it bites into his skull, eats his face away and corrodes his memory. Struggling under its weight, he is distracted from 'straight lines and purposes', and carries it 'everywhere / Always, on a dwindling zig-zag' (P 89). In poems such as 'Alibis' and 'Options' the poet can play wittily with the idea of choosing different roles and identities, but in 'The Fairground' and 'Nightmare' he dramatises the profound anxiety which is induced when identity is thrown into jeopardy. Pigs and boars are traditional symbols of Celtic Ireland. Longley's pig is particularly reminiscent of Stephen Dedalus's reference to Ireland in *Portrait of the Artist* as 'the old sow that eats her farrow'. In the poem Longley may thus be considering his own relation to 'the matter of Ireland' and to history. Certainly, his language in the poem is very similar to that which he used in a letter to the *Irish Times* in 1974, where he raised the question of the poet's proper role in time of war:

The artist's first duty . . . is to his imagination. But he has other obligations, surely – and not just as a citizen. He would be inhuman if he didn't respond to tragic events in his own community, and an irresponsible artist if he didn't seek to endorse that response imaginatively. This will probably involve a deflection or zig-zag in the proper quest for imaginative autonomy – an attempt under pressure to absorb what in happier circumstances his imagination might reject as impurities. But, then, who's interested in pure art anyway?[5]

Longley's concern with social conflict pre-dates the outbreak of the Troubles, as a poem such as 'The Centaurs', from his first collection, would indicate. In 'The Centaurs' (P 38–9) we find the characteristic Longley response to conflict and violence in terms of both social attitude and poetic technique. The poem begins on the American frontier with a Hollywood movie image of a 'sergeant, an arrow in his back' bringing word to the settlement of an Indian (?) attack. The speaker implicates himself in the picture – 'He put the idea into *our* heads' [my italics] – which takes on a vaguely Irish colouring with the line about the beleaguered people 'Saying our prayers, fingering our beads', and then a Latin American reference as the narrator, now apparently speaking as a native Indian confronted by the conquistadors, considers his attackers' great advantage: 'their secret weapon is the horse'. In another disorienting shift, those who are routed by the horsemen are referred to as 'squadrons', a term which more appropriately belongs to modern air warfare than to sixteenth century Aztec tribesmen. 'We make on the causeways our last stands' recalls General Custer's 'last stand' against the Indians at the battle of Little Big Horn, and returns us to the opening image of the poem. The reader is situated in a deliberately vague and ever changing vantage point in relation to events which are continually metamorphosing through the language which constructs them. We are unsettled by being denied the basic assumptions of traditional perspective, a reliable view from outside. Longley employs a wide, disparate range of cultural reference, deliberately running together several stories of violent colonial encounter, and deliberately confusing and reversing the identities of the attackers and the attacked. These mergings enact at the formal level a principle which the poem proposes as a social and political potential. Violence is explicitly related to fear of the 'other': resolution of conflict depends not on one side vanquishing the other, but on acceptance of difference as a source of enrichment and renewal, and a stimulus to creativity. When the 'pedestrian' people, as Longley punningly describes them, do manage to break out of the old patterns they can dispel fear and conflict:

> Is our way of life pedestrian?
> Can these be the customs we defend
> Slow aeon after slower aeon?
> But, just as we think THIS IS THE END,
>
> We wake to a world of infantry men.
> We wake from nightmare into reason –
> Of their reins and bridles not a sign.
> We see another sun has risen,
>
> And, our nightmare now a mystery tour,
> At ease along the river's edges
> Each cavalry man becomes a centaur,
> The causeways growing into bridges.

There is a distinctly Irish relevance to all this: 'We wake from nightmare into reason' echoes the Joycean idea of history as a 'nightmare' from which we cannot 'awake'. Longley suggests the possibility of awakening and of progress, a possibility founded on the interrogation of our own past and our willingness to adapt to new circumstances rather than cling to the outmoded forms of the past. When the 'pedestrian' people do this they find they can create a new identity which reconciles self and 'other'. The centaurs are half-man, half-horse. Their creation is a witty transformation of the sergeant's posture of degradation and defeat in the opening stanza: 'on all fours he made his retreat'. Extending his range of references to 1960s pop culture, Longley affirms the possibility of turning Jim Morrison's apocalyptic 'THIS IS THE END' into the Beatles' Magical Mystery Tour. As the series of rhetorical questions in the first of the stanzas quoted would imply, this is a poem about 'options', and it finally, ritually, enacts the choice of life over death, adaptation over extinction, mutual enrichment over endless contestation. The poem echoes something of Yeats's apocalyptic vision in 'The Second Coming', but where in Yeats's poem history gives birth to a monster, a 'shape with lion body and the head of a man', Longley's classical centaurs are symbolic, like Muir's horses, of brave new beginnings, a return to pastoral simplicities. The centaurs symbolise an ideal of positive miscegenation, hybridisation and pluralism, themes which are taken up by Muldoon in poems such as 'The Mixed Marriage', 'Mules' and, more recently, 'Meeting the British'. In Ireland, where colonial myths have been imposed with violence, they have produced equally deforming Nationalist countermythology in which the roles of insider and outsider are rigorously reinforced. Longley demonstrates an imaginative loosening and dissolving of traditional oppositions, a deconstruction of fixed categories, the possibility of reinterpreting old myths so that we need not be bound to attitudes which produce only confrontation, fear and violence.

'The Centaurs' is remarkable for the confidence with which the young poet so early in his career can handle such a wide range of cultural reference, and also for its imaginative boldness and technical ingenuity. The poem also establishes the characteristic Longley response to social conflict and violence in its emphasis on the need for openness to the 'other' as the *sine qua non* of peace, a sentiment which receives its most mature and moving expression in the recent poem 'Ceasefire'. Openness to the 'other' allows for bridge-building and the achievement of a balanced perspective. As the speaker in 'The Centaurs' says: 'Because of the bridge we did not build / Our whole army fights for balance'. In the poem immediately following, 'The Hebrides', the poet confronts his own sense of alienation and the world's 'otherness'. Lost in a wild, harsh landscape, he struggles for 'poise' amid 'flux' – 'I fight all the way for balance'. The poem reflects a young man's desire for mastery, and it contrasts with later poems such as 'Sulpicia' where negotiation of the 'other' is pictured as a seduction, or 'On Mweelrea' where the human profile blends into the landscape. In 'Man Lying on a Wall' the speaker's personal integrity depends on his maintaining balance, remaining steady, prone, passive, 'Above the shoulders of the multitude' (*P* 137). Longley's comment that '"The Man Lying on a Wall" *does* see and feel for both sides, but rejects both a "green" Ireland and an "orange" Ulster as inadequate concepts'[6] recalls Keats's 'negative capability'. Longley values a point of vantage and balance above the main field of action where he is in a position to resist fixed patterns of perception, and can act as an impresario of alternatives, exploring options and aliases, exploring all kinds of mergings and metamorphoses.

The source of this poetic poise is the poet's intuition of the flowing continuous unity of all creation. In the early 'Camouflage' (*P* 23), an unusually discursive and expository poem for Longley, he presents a resonant zoology of harmony, connectedness and adaptability. The animals, unlike humans, seem to be perfectly at ease and at home in their world. They inhabit 'landscapes with which they are in keeping'. The speaker takes this as evidence of 'a balanced world', and this harmonious relationship is reflected in the regularity of the stanza form, iambic measure and rhyme scheme. But it is not a fixed world. The animals live amid 'change' and 'risk' and have learnt how to adapt to altered circumstances in order to survive. They are further examples of 'the welladjusted and the skilled' in 'Persephone'. The four little sketches that comprise 'A Nativity' dramatise the interplay of the natural, the human and the divine, while 'Graffiti' humorously suggests the interconnections between the ideal and the real in a manner that recalls Larkin's 'Sunny Prestatyn'. Some of Longley's most delicate, sensitive and boldly imaginative lyrics – 'Landscape', 'Metamorphosis', 'On Mweelrea', 'View', 'Light Behind the Rain', 'Meniscus', 'Martinmas' – are those which express his sense of the continuity of man and nature. Lovers find themselves absorbed by landscape, finally merging with that landscape ('On Mweelrea'); the human body is viewed as part of the flux of elemental nature ('Meniscus'), human life as part of the large natural cycles of death and rebirth ('Martinmas').

In one of his verse 'Letters', 'To James Simmons', the notion of the 'fundamental interconnectedness of all things' is expressed through the image of the Moebius Band –

> Each gives the other's lines a twist
> Over supper, dinner, breakfast
> To make a sort of Moebius Band,
> Eternal but quotidian . . .
>
> *(P 80)*

The Moebius Band, Longley explains in his notes, 'is an example of a non-orientable surface. It can be illustrated by taking a strip of paper several times longer than it is wide and sticking the two ends together after twisting one of them by a half turn. It is one-sided in the sense that an ant could crawl along the whole length of the strip without crossing the bounding edge and find itself at the starting point on "the other side"'. The image, an unpretentious version of Yeats's 'perning in a gyre', suggests the poet's sense of the oneness of life. It represents a principle of circularity and relatedness which operates at every level of the poem. It may be discerned in the poem's foregrounding of its own intertextuality, its relation to prior texts by Heaney, Mahon and Simmons, and, not least, in Longley's handling of metaphor and verse form. Take the last stanza: poetry, the speaker proclaims, is here

> To exercise in metaphor
> Our knockings at the basement door,
> A ramrod mounted to invade
> The vulva, Hades' palisade,
> The Gates of Horn and Ivory
> Or the Walls of Londonderry.

The richly proliferating metaphors suggest connections between a diverse range of elements, which are nevertheless made to chime harmoniously through the sustained use of rhyming couplets. Longley's listing technique emphasises the teeming possibilities envisioned by the free-wheeling imagination, the conspicuous use of enjambment at the end of stanzas suggesting the running on of one thing into the next in an unbroken flow of signification. The blithely comic yoking together of heterogeneous images and ideas suggests poetry's unpredictable directions and energies, its potential to undercut the hierarchical values of the culture and relativize all structure, order and authority. Life is turned upside down. In the process one finds that 'the great indoors' can be the site of epic adventure, that sex and death are suddenly, shockingly, proximate – as are heaven and hell, the exotic and the quotidian, the far and the near, the high and the low, the mythological and the real. Normal categories of perception are broken down and different orders of experience flow in on one another. The final bathetic reference to the 'Walls of Londonderry' gives ironic emphasis to a view of poetry as a laying siege to a given, fixed reality, a 'knocking' at the door, or an 'invasion', of tabooed knowledges, a penetrating of secret, walled-off places. The poetic imagination knows no boundaries and is continually exceeding the accepted limits: 'Like talking on as the twelfth chime / Ends nineteen hundred and ninety-nine'. The playful erotics of Simmons' poetry seems to Longley to represent an insouciant, witty, irreverent poetic freedom, a radically transgressive impulse which is potentially re-orienting and re-inspiriting, a drive to penetrate and transform old worn-out attitudes and bankrupt mindsets.

Even when he is writing directly about social conflict and violence Longley is implying 'fundamental interconnectedness'. In 'In Memoriam', 'Wounds' and 'The Linen Workers' he approaches the Troubles through the memory of his father who had fought and been wounded on the Somme in 1916, and whose 'old wounds woke / As cancer' in 1959 when Longley was twenty. In 'In Memoriam' it is by reading the 'book' of his father that the poet can all the better read himself into the pity of war and understand the horror, whether in the trenches of the Somme or on the streets of Belfast in the 1970s. The violent images of bodies 'cracked and splintered', the 'death and nightmare' of the battlefield, echo older war poets such as Isaac Rosenberg and Keith Douglas who, as Frank Ormsby says, are Longley's 'adopted fathers'.[7] 'In Memoriam' not only introduces the violent imagery that will be replayed in the context of Ulster's Troubles in later poems, but also establishes the characteristic thrust of Longley's war poetry – the effort to redeem loss and suffering through invoking the power of memory, love and poetry. The whole experience of 'brokenness' is contained within orderly, regularly rhymed stanzas. Death has not demoralised but provoked respectful remembrance, spirited imagining, the demonstration of an urbane and stylish control.

In 'Wounds' (P 86), the link between his father's experiences at the Somme and the contemporary horror of Ulster's conflict is made explicit. The first half ends with a tender, moving image of the poet as 'priest of the muses' assuming a consolatory role, enacting an imaginary ritual of filial love and devotion: 'I touched his hand, his thin head I touched'. This intensely private image is then juxtaposed with more public events: he buries with his father 'Three teenage soldiers, bellies full of / Bullets and Irish beer, their flies undone' and a 'bus-conductor's uniform'. The deaths of these nameless victims of unspeakable violence are conveyed with a disconcerting objectivity and matter-of-factness which make them all the more shocking and pathetic. These diverse horrors are all contemplated under the title 'Wounds' – all wounds are the same. Contemplating his father's wounding has helped the poet to understand the wounds of his own province and the plight of victims of all conflicts. The motives for murder do not concern him, nor does the identity of the murderers. He accords no particular moral approbation or disapproval to any party, allowing the murderer to speak for himself without comment: 'To the children, to a bewildered wife, / I think "Sorry Missus" was what he said'. Even the victims are only scantily particularised. The poem might at first appear to have a more strictly specified historical and social context than, say, the emblematic 'Casualty' or 'The Goose', but though the setting may be the trenches of the Somme in 1916 and then Belfast in the 1970s, the violence is, in fact, deliberately de-historicised, this poem, too, functioning as emblem or paradigm. Through bold linkages of past and present, personal loss and public event, Longley asserts a universal sympathy.

'The Linen Workers' is the third of a suite of poems entitled 'Wreaths' (P 148–9), which presents three progressively more meaningful and comprehensive responses to violence. In the first, the civil servant's wife reacts to her husband's death with an hysterical outburst of hopelessness and despair. In the second, the simple fact of naming the things the greengrocer sells in his shop – 'Dates and chestnuts and tangerines' – has a soothing and reassuring effect. As in 'Wounds', Longley emphasises the way violence breaks in upon the peaceful routines of domestic life, but through his devotion to the small details of ordinary people's everyday lives, he affirms the *lares*, spirits of hearth and home, reasserting the binding force of community and the unquenchable life-force itself. The third poem, 'The Linen Workers', has a more complex allusive field, bringing together a surreal Christ 'fastened for ever / By his exposed canines to a wintry sky', the poet's dead father and the ten linen workers who were massacred at Kingsmill. These deaths merge in the poet's imagination. Through a skilful blending of low and high style, the realistic and the surrealistic, past and present, personal and public, human and divine, Longley explores the complex range of feelings which the deaths evoke. The speaker's feeling for his father teaches him how to feel for the anonymous linen workers. The description of the 'spectacles / Wallets, small change, and a set of dentures: / Blood, food particles, the bread, the wine' strewn beside the dead bodies of the linen workers heightens the pathos but also suggests the sacramental significance of the commonplace. The references to spectacles, money and false teeth remind us of the concentration camps: ultimately, Longley's poem is an elegy to all victims of violence. The last stanza is an image of re-ordering and re-composing, a restoration of balance, a simple ritual of imaginative transformation:

> Before I can bury my father once again
> I must polish the spectacles, balance them
> Upon his nose, fill his pockets with money
> And into his dead mouth slip the set of teeth.

This is a deeply moving image of art's reversal or repair of the 'exploded view'.

Intertextuality confirms literary interconnectedness. In 'Edward Thomas's War Diary', Longley's description of the trenches 'where shell holes / Filled with bloodstained water, / Where empty beer bottles / Littered the barbed wire' echoes closely Thomas's entry for 21 March 1917: 'No Man's Land like Goodwood Racecourse with engineers swarming over it and making a road between shell holes full of blood-stained water and beer bottles among barbed wire'.[8] But it is Longley's affirmation of nature – its beauty and innocence – despite all the destruction and death that most clearly catches the Thomas note:

> Your eye on what remained –
> Light spangling through a hole
> In the cathedral wall
> And the little conical
> Summer house among the trees.
>
> (P 134)

Thomas's diary entry for 25 February 1917 – 'Does a mole ever get hit by a shell?' – is the inspiration and epigraph for 'Mole', the next poem in the book. The mole relates to the soldiers in the trenches and to all innocent victims of man's inhumanity. The subterranean and 'digging' imagery is continued in the next poem, 'Fleance', thus demonstrating another kind of interconnectedness – the intertextual relationships between different parts of the poet's own oeuvre.

In 'Edward Thomas's War Diary' Longley consciously writes out of the English pastoral tradition represented by Thomas. In

'Bog Cotton' (P 167), he seeks to affirm a larger literary and imaginative provenance by combining elements from both English and Irish tradition. He wishes to propose a new commemorative emblem of the Ulster war dead – bog cotton. Bog cotton evokes a distinctively Irish botany, landscape, history and national consciousness. Specifically, it relates to a poetic and cultural discourse that is commonly associated with Seamus Heaney. In his lecture 'Feeling into Words', which he gave at the Royal Society of Literature in October 1974, five years prior to the publication of 'Bog Cotton' in *The Echo Gate*, Heaney proposed the bog as a distinctively 'Irish myth':

bogland . . . is a landscape that has a strange assuaging effect on me, one with associations reaching back into early childhood . . . I began to get an idea of bog as the memory of the landscape . . . I had a tentative unrealized need to make a congruence between memory and bogland and, for the want of a better word, our national consciousness.[9]

However, in proposing the bog cotton as a remembrance of the dead in Ulster's Troubles Longley is conscious of working within an established English tradition of war poetry. His description of the bog cotton is framed by reference to Keith Douglas's 'desert flowers' and Isaac Rosenberg's poppies. Just as Douglas 'saw . . . beyond the thirstier desert flowers' and 'apostrophised' the poppies of Flanders fields that Rosenberg had immortalised in his First World War poem 'Break of Day in the Trenches', Longley sees beyond his own Irish experience, explicitly acknowledging his intertextual relationship to the earlier poets and relating the contemporary Ulster Troubles to both World Wars. He presents his proposal in an extended parenthesis, thereby marking its provisional, tentative nature, its subordinate position within a larger intertextual system. Thus, Longley manages, through the intertextual range of this poem, to express his awareness of the complex cultural forces out of which his own, and Ulster's, identity is composed.

His classical background, of course, enables him to place the contemporary situation in even larger cultural and literary perspectives. In 'Peace: after Tibullus' (P 169–71), written at the request of the Peace People, he adopts the persona of the 1st century B.C. Roman love poet, Tibullus. Longley deftly interweaves ancient and modern elements in his seven 10-line stanzas, lightening the serious purpose with touches of wit and humour, blending a language of 'barricades', 'ghettos', 'kit-bag' and 'goose-step' with classical references to Cerberus and the Styx.

He also invites us to consider the relation between political and sexual violence, and revises the traditional image of Irish woman as the revolutionary muse, Kathleen ni Houlihan, presenting instead a woman who is 'Peace personified', associated with nature's beauty and bounty.

The poem immediately following 'Peace' is 'Sulpicia', named after Tibullus' patron's niece, in which a female persona declares she will 'seduce' Mars from his warlike ways, while in an earlier poem, 'Altera Cithera', Longley takes issue with Propertius's decision to change his tune and write about war, not love. Through his references to Propertius, Tibullus, Sulpicia and, of course, Ovid, Longley wishes to see himself in relation to the ancient tradition of Latin love elegy, which, in defining the individual in terms of *eros* rather than *polis* or *civitas*, ran counter to the prevailing ideology of ancient Rome. The Latin love elegy, which was a private rather than a public poetry, and elevated love and poetry above social obligation, called into question traditional Roman values and virtues, and represented a deliberate challenge to the assumptions of a militaristic society which found expression for the concerns of empire in epic and tragedy. Heaney has uncovered the erotics of Longley's nature poetry, and indeed Longley shares with Ovid and the other Latin love elegists a sense of the creative force of love at a time when the individual is constantly under threat from social and public pressures of all kinds.

3

In the two 1990s collections, *Gorse Fires* (1991) and *The Ghost Orchid* (1995), we can trace the development of Longley's treatment of themes of conflict and violence, the continued refining of touch and tone and lyric craftsmanship, the deepening of feeling, the extending of historical and literary reference. In typical Longley fashion, the arrangement of poems in both books is significant: expressive of a fundamental interconnectedness of poetic vision. Thus, in *Gorse Fires*, a poem about Longley's father ('Northern Lights') faces a poem about Odysseus' father ('Laertes'). 'Northern Lights' presents a moment of great intimacy between father and son, in which both are held in a 'magnetic field' where they feel at one with each other and with the vast, mysterious processes of nature. This lovely moment reverberates against another one, just as tender and intimate, where Odysseus, after his return from the war, is reunited with his father. In 'Laertes', the homely and parochial language enlivens the Homeric universal, the vernacular freedom is contained within a satisfying classical control. These poems are followed by two poems about mothers: first 'The Balloon' a memory of Longley's own mother, then 'Anticleia', a translation of Homer's account of Odysseus' meeting with his mother's ghost in Hades. This poem, in turn, relates to another poem four pages earlier in the book which is a translation of Homer's account of Odysseus' reunion with his old nurse, Eurycleia, after his return from Troy. In the second part of 'Eurycleia' Longley explicitly makes the connection between Odysseus and himself: 'I began like Odysseus by loving the wrong woman' (*GF* 31). Odysseus' feeling for his old nurse parallels Longley's for his childhood nurse and 'surrogate mother'. The personal is linked with the legendary. Time, place and identity are fluid. Eurycleia 'wanders' from Ithaca to Belfast and then among the skyscrapers of New York. Odysseus' scar, 'the key to his identity', is replicated in Longley's wound of maternal rejection, and the more general wounding that he, in common with his fellow Ulster people, has suffered in the Troubles.

The seven Homeric poems in *Gorse Fires* focus on Odysseus' return to home, family, love, nurture – all the sacred concepts of Longley's poetry. Homeric landscapes merge with those of the idyllic west of Ireland, as in the first poem in the book: 'But now from the high ground of Carrigskeewaun / I watch Lesbos rising among the islands' ('Sea Shanty'). However, Odysseus' return is not only the occasion of love and tender reunion, but the eruption of a terrible violence. 'The Butchers', the last poem in the book, is a horrific description of briskly efficient violence carried out without feeling or conscience, the home turned into an abattoir, human life reduced to the level of animals. Even while setting out to rid his home of threat and treachery, Odysseus exacts a retribution that runs to barbarous extremes. A monstrous evil is let loose in the attempt to restore domestic and natural harmony. The language of 'haggard', 'clammy sheughs', 'bog-meadow' and 'bog-asphodels' gives the poem a distinctively Irish inflection, as does the title, with its echo of the 'Shankill Butchers', the infamous Protestant terror gang of the 1970s. Ancient Greece may be the cradle of western civilisation, but western civilisation is also tainted by the ancient Attic bloodlust. In 'The Cairn at Dooaghtry' prehistoric Mayo is ghosted by Nazi atrocity: in the poem facing, 'Argos', Homer and the Holocaust coalesce. Through his techniques of interconnection and interfusion, Longley stresses that the good and evil in these poems are those of anybody, anywhere, at any time.

A sequence of poems in *Gorse Fires* entitled 'Ghetto' provides another kind of perspective on the Ulster situation. 'Ghetto' is a fragmented long poem ('an exploded view') in eight parts or stanzas of varying length, in which Longley elegises the nameless, otherwise forgotten victims of war (as Mahon does in 'A Disused Shed in Co. Wexford'), highlighting the threat to children and to innocence. But while giving full acknowledgement to the violence and horror, he balances these with images of heroically enduring human spirit, affirming the value of the domestic and the commonplace, the indestructibility of the creative and aesthetic instinct, the power of imagination to open up new horizons and alternatives. In the third part a little girl, orphaned, afraid, hungry, surrounded by violence, personifies the spirit of love and hope: 'The little girl without a mother behaves like a mother / With her rag doll to whom she explains fear and anguish' (*GF* 41). In the midst of death and destruction, human feeling and civilisation survive through the child's play. By sustaining eminently rational syntactic and poetic structures in dealing with horror, Longley mirrors the little girl's determination to preserve some concept of home and humanity despite the actions of the 'flame-throwers and dynamiters'.

Part four registers the poet's sense of his irrelevance and ineffectualness when confronted with such terrible human need and misery – a feeling he had confronted in the earlier poem 'Kindertotenlieder' (in *An Exploded View*): 'There can be no songs for dead children / Near the crazy circle of explosions' (*P* 87). It is the feeling which haunted Heaney when he thought of his 'song' as an 'offence' against his people's suffering. Longley resolves the issue by affirming and demonstrating, as best he can, the power of poetry to soothe and reassure. He does so, not with rhetoric or argument, but with a list of names – the names of varieties of potatoes:

> My delivery of Irish Peace, Beauty of Hebron, Home
> Guard, Arran Banners, Kerr's Pinks, resistant to eelworm,
> Resignation, common scab, terror, frost, potato-blight.
>
> (*GF* 42)

'Ghetto' ends by emphasising how the artistic urge can never be completely exterminated – it simply goes underground: 'Lessons were forbidden in that terrible school' – but the prisoners continued to draw. Among the things around them which they drew 'There were drawings of barracks and latrines as well / And the only windows were the windows they drew'. The drawings enabled the prisoners to 'see beyond' their prison, to imagine other worlds, to express hope and possibility. This is the great challenge for the artist: not to be locked into the given order of things as if it were the only order of things, but to be able to envision alternatives and open up new horizons.

Many poems in *Gorse Fires* enact this kind of imaginative transformation. 'The Balloon' (*GF* 34) is a poem about 'seeing things'. It tells of a dream in which the speaker is in a hot air balloon and down below him he sees his mother, who in real life was lame, running and laughing as she looks up at him. The speaker freely admits the unreality of the dream – it is a 'hot air' balloon, the dream can last only as long as he is airborne, the dream balloon 'casts no shadow'. The speaker's excited exhortation to his mother is a comic, affectionate, fantastical command to 'jump over the trees'. But the new perspective where, God-like, he looks down from the sky, and backwards in time to when his mother was a child, produces a sense of exhilarating freedom, the feeling that anything is possible, and Longley, through his skilful handling of syntax and rhythm, conveys this giddy, imaginative excitement very effectively.

Aerial imagery is used again in 'The Velocipede' (*GF* 14) in presenting Joseph Murphy's grandfather's desire to become a sky-walker. The poem celebrates creative freedom and ingenuity, first of Joseph Murphy himself who, amongst his varied attributes, is a poet; then of Joseph's foolhardy grandfather who built a velocipede and ended up in hospital after trying to make it fly. The tone is one of controlled amusement, admiring of the indomitable, adventurous spirit of the swinger, the aerialist, despite his Icarian fall. Further transformations take place in 'Jug Band' (*GF* 16), another poem about the wonderful, comic human potential for improvisation, especially that of children. 'Jug Band' pictures children playing at being a New Orleans marching band in their living-room. This is a poem about play, 'making up'; about the power of imagination to enable us to take on other roles, to enjoy ourselves, to defy the constraints of time, place and fixed identity.

As the many poems in *Gorse Fires* about the deaths of friends and parents, and about the victims of Fascist or terrorist violence, would indicate, Longley never underestimates the dark side of life. The book has a pervasively elegiac structure of feeling: it carries the epigraph 'In Memory of my Parents'. But it is never demoralised or despairing. The elegy is a declaration of faith as well as a formal and sustained lament. The usual impulse behind it is to celebrate and affirm, despite loss and sorrow, and it is this impulse which permeates *Gorse Fires*. Even in the Nazi death camps there was music: 'Fingers leave shadows on a violin, harmonics, / A blackbird fluttering between electrified fences' ('Ghetto').

'The Ice-cream Man' (*GF* 49) remembers the murder of an ice-cream man on Belfast's Lisburn Road. The act of violence itself is referred to only in a simple factual statement in a single line: 'They murdered the ice-cream man on the Lisburn Road' – the poem's central concern being with elaborating an appropriate response to such unspeakable, and unspoken, violence. The poem, as Longley himself has indicated, is addressed to his daughter and, again, affirms nature's beauty and continuance in the face of death and loss. The speaker's daughter, we are told, laid flowers outside the ice-cream man's shop. The rest of the poem consists of an extended list of Burren flowers – another of Longley's 'wreaths' for the dead. The way the listing of ice-cream flavours which opens the poem is echoed in the listing of flowers also helps to unify the poem. The long, pulsing, heavily accented sentence containing the list of flowers acts as a dogged, emphatic affirmation of the life-force, of an innocence that exists despite and beyond the evil occasion. These are flowers with healing powers, the listing of them itself performing a healing function. By resorting to childlike naming, the speaker hopes to restore a child's confidence in the essential goodness of life. No explicit connection is made between the death of the ice-cream man and the incantatory recital of wild flowers. The kind of consolation the poem offers lies at a deeper level than of logical statement. The poem, in fact, is a release from rational mind, from the world of politics, history and ideological conflict. Its comfort lies in the complete devotion to the immediate and the concrete, in the sacred sense of place and nature, in the primitive magic of sounds and words. The poem recognises both horror and delight, death and life, a duality contained in the punning title ('Ice-cream' – 'I scream') and in the connotations of the word ice-cream itself, which relates to the chill and whiteness of death as well as to notions of festive, sensuous, childish delight.

The listing technique which is used so boldly and movingly in 'The Ice-cream Man' is one of the most distinctive features of Longley's mature work. *Gorse Fires* is a book full of names – of places, people, flowers, birds, animals, stars, apples, barges on the Lagan canal, flavours of ice-cream, varieties of potato – and through this precise and loving observation, and the priestly incantation of names, Longley expresses his own grateful, worshipful, sense of the value of life, its wonderful variety and durability, its willingness to offer itself as a home to humankind.

Facing this elegy on the death of the anonymous ice-cream man is another commemorative poem for another victim of violence, Charles Donnelly, the Irish poet and political activist who was killed in action on 27 February, 1937, during the Spanish Civil War, in the Jarama valley, a region noted for its olive trees. Taking the two facing poems together, we see how Longley focuses on the individual tragedy but wants us to view it within larger perspectives. The horror of the Spanish Civil War is juxtaposed with that of the Ulster Troubles: both arenas of conflict are set within the context of the serene and timeless world of nature. In 'In Memory of Charles Donnelly' nature suffers with mankind: Longley quotes Donnelly's famous last words – 'Even the olives are bleeding' – uttered as the soldier-poet picked up a bunch of olives and squeezed them just before he was shot; but Longley movingly transforms Donnelly's perception of suffering nature into a vision of sustaining nature. He dispels the tragedy by imagining Donnelly's dead body merging with the olive tree under which it is buried. The dead poet, and the poems 'you go on not writing' – all the potential that ended with Donnelly's death at the age of twenty-two – are absorbed by deathless nature, wreathed in the eternal circle made by the tree's shadow.

One form that traditionally expressed the close, harmonious relationship between the human and natural worlds was the pastoral elegy, which goes back through Arnold's 'Thyrsis', Shelley's 'Adonais' and Milton's 'Lycidas' in English poetry, to Virgil. Longley develops his own version of this venerable form. Some of the pastoral conventions, although adapted to modern conditions and a non-Christian world view, are particularly evident in poems such as 'The Ice-cream Man' (most notably the list of wild flowers which corresponds to the elaborate description of the flowers which are brought to deck the hearse in 'Lycidas') and 'Between Hovers' (*GF* 5), one of the most powerfully moving poems in *Gorse Fires*. Here, the setting is entirely pastoral and is lovingly recreated and ritually celebrated in the recital of place-names. Like the shepherds of traditional pastoral, the speaker and his friend, Joe O'Toole, are spirits of the rural place. Joe's death is linked, first, to a dead badger they ran over in their car, then to a dying otter the speaker came across some time after his friend's funeral. The poem is haunted by awareness of threat – the cancer that takes Joe's life and the car, symbol of a destructive technological modernity that has invaded the pastoral simplicities of an ancient, vestigially pagan, folkloric, vulnerable landscape. Longley emphasises both the beauty of nature's innocent creatures and the human worth and goodness of the individual who has died.

In many poems, rhythm, sound, image, and a refined, muscular syntax unfolding along the lines are all used to communicate a sense of mysterious energy circulating through the natural and human order, and existing within language itself. In 'Peregrine' (the term itself applicable to bird or human), the speaker expresses the affinity he senses between the natural and human orders: 'I had been waiting for the peregrine falcon / As a way of coming to terms with the silence, / As a way of getting closer to you' (*GF* 9), and he thinks it swoops 'As though to avoid colliding with me'. The peregrine is a gentle, fugitive presence haunting the consciousness of the poem, eluding the poet's efforts to catch it in the net of language. The speaker emphasises the provisionality of the words he uses to describe it: '– an idea / Above the dauch, downy whirlwinds, the wind's / Mother-of-pearl *for instance*, an eddy of bones' [my italics]. The list of images, presented without subordination or comment, but expressive of direct, unmediated concentration on the object of perception, conveys a naive, childlike wonder. A messenger from the spirit of nature, the peregrine occupies the free lyric space that Longley opens up in the historical and material worlds. The poem ends, significantly, with a question: 'wings / Under the road, a blur of spokes and feathers?' So does a companion poem, 'Goldcrest', a couple of pages further on, where the speaker wonders if, in burying the dainty little bird, his 'love' did not release amongst the tree-tops 'The ghost of a bouquet?' The rhetorical questions suggest the speaker's appreciation of the delicacy and wonder of the natural world, and the tentativeness and incompleteness of his efforts to find a form to express these intuitions.

This consciousness of the limitations of the word and the elusiveness and fragility of the world becomes a central feature of *The Ghost Orchid*. It underlies such exquisitely fashioned pieces as the opening poem of the book, with its clever play on the different meanings of the word 'form' –

> Trying to tell it all to you and cover everything
> Is like awakening from its grassy form the hare:
> In that make-shift shelter your hand, then my hand
> Mislays the hare and the warmth it leaves behind –

or the title-poem, which reiterates Longley's perception of the continuity of natural and human. Through personifying the ghost orchid, the poet relates the fragile beauty and vulnerability of the orchid to the human world, invoking the twin notions of mortality and the unity of all creation. With the image of the orchid growing like coral among shadows and leaf-litter, he suggests the Pythagorean interplay of life and death, leavings becoming living things. Placed among other poems that confront violence and atrocity, 'The Ghost Orchid' asserts a residual delicacy and grace, a tenderness which, in 'Ceasefire', the central poetic achievement of the volume, is given wholly human form. 'The Ghost Orchid' is also, of course, a poem about the poet's fragile muse, about that which is secret, delicate, 'bruised into darkness' at the merest approach, the slightest 'touch', the least attempt to bring it into consciousness. The postscript to the volume –

Love poems, elegies: I am losing my place.
Elegies come between me and your face –

expresses with epigrammatic terseness the speaker's pained sense of the continual absence of the desired object, his awareness of displacement and deferment. His words of love and loss attempt to fill the empty space, stand in for the object itself, but also get in the way of the experience of full presence. These are the recognizable concerns of postmodernism, though Longley resists any paralysing Beckettian sense of the artist's impotence, opting instead (in 'After Horace') for gentle ridicule of the postmodernist crisis of confidence.

The poetry of *The Ghost Orchid*, while continuing to register the shock-waves of a nightmarish violence in human life, remains committed to a concept of the interrelatedness of all things and never loses sight of what is life-affirming and life-enhancing. When the poet wants to consider the violence in man, his imagination still turns to the language and images of the First and Second World Wars, to his father's war experiences, and to the classical world. The past is not another country, merely another version of the present. 'I am walking backwards into the future like a Greek' (*GO* 54) is the first line of 'River and Fountain', the last stanza of which refers to the protagonist 'Walking forwards into the past'. The interfusion of past and present, and of the private and public realms, generates the drama of 'The Kilt', one of a series of poems of hallucinatory power. Here, the speaker associates waking his wife out of a nightmare with waking his father out of his nightmare of killing a German soldier. The father's kilt 'unravelled when he was advancing', but, characteristically, the final image is of re-stitching and re-clothing, of the female running to reconstitute what man has 'unravelled':

> You pick up the stitches and with needle and thread
> Accompany him out of the grave and into battle,
> Your arms full of material and his nakedness.
>
> (*GO* 35)

The poem resists closure: the restoration of order, the transformation of both nightmare horror and Chaplinesque absurdity remains a goal, a dream, rather than ever becoming actuality.

Juxtaposed with the images of Second World War battlefields in 'The Kilt' and the poem immediately following, 'Behind a Cloud', are scenes of Homeric battlefields. 'The Camp-Fires ' (*GO* 37), a free translation of part of Book VIII of *The Iliad* describes the ancient battle-scene using the language of the First World War ('no man's land') and the Vietnam War ('killing fields'). Again, Longley seeks to find a proper perspective in which to view man's violent nature. The poem links past and present, classical Greece and parochial Ireland. It begins and ends with a picture of the soldiers waiting around their camp-fires for battle to begin: in between, the speaker, ranging widely in time and space, specifies the context in which the violence takes place. The cosmic imagery and the reference to nature's 'boundlessness' place man's violence under the aspect of eternity, while the loving attention to the small details of everyday life, the fabric of which is shown to remain intact, makes the killing seem all the more unnatural. By emphasising the beauty and innocence of nature, its durability and nurture, Longley makes the human action understandable only as a sacrilege against life. Ironically, these life-affirming observations are relegated to the ghostly status of parenthesis in the historical record.

'The Helmet', which follows, develops another vivid, ironic contrast, this time between Hector's warlike barbarity and his son's childish innocence. Through his use of Ulster dialect ('wean', 'mammy', 'babbie'), Longley is again able to relate Homeric Greece to contemporary Ulster. 'Ceasefire' (*GO* 39) puts 'The Helmet' into perspective: the vainglorious Hector of 'The Helmet' is a corpse in 'Ceasefire', the two poems taken together representing a powerful and moving statement of the futility of war, and a ritual demonstration of the way the vicious circle of violence indicated at the end of 'The Helmet' – where Hector 'Prayed that his son might grow up bloodier than him' – can be broken. The Homeric parallel allows Longley to deal obliquely with the contemporary situation, and without having to identify sides or equate with the defeated Hector or victorious Achilles. The sonnet has a static, emblematic quality, its tender gravitas created from a simple conversational language stripped of ornament, slightly formal, even archaic at times, and a measured, stately movement and finely controlled syntax.

Though there is much in *The Ghost Orchid* that is familiar from earlier collections, the volume has its own distinctive character. As in Heaney's most recent work, there is, first of all, a noticeably more insistent visionary intensity. It is a poetry of ghosts, whispers, fragments; a catching at the elusive, the evanescent and the insubstantial, a poetry of fountains rather than rivers. And, as in Heaney's *Seeing Things*, the search for the transcendent takes place in full awareness of the dangers of illusion. Longley enjoys the excitements of hot air ballooning and the velocipede but, as 'Perdix' emphasises, he also values groundedness as well as flight – a tension that goes back to the early 'The Hebrides', where the speaker fights for balance even while 'coveting' the exhilaration of 'vertigo'. Secondly, *The Ghost Orchid*, again like Heaney's recent work, evinces a loosening up of form and style which produces the supremely relaxed and engaging discursiveness of 'Phemios and Medon', 'Baucis and Philemon' and 'River and Fountain'; and it also produces a developing interest in the poem sequence. 'Chinese Objects' and 'Chinese Occasions' are examples of the Chinese 'linked poem', a form of poetic 'interrelatedness' in which each poem is given its fair play yet also contributes to a larger organic whole. While Longley's habit of linking poems in this, and other collections, is evidence of the effort to achieve unity through variety, he shows none of the epic ambitions of John Montague, and none of Seamus Heaney's increasing interest in the long poem sequence, such as 'Glanmore Sonnets', 'Station Island' or 'Squarings'.

Perhaps the most distinctive feature of the volume is the large proportion of very short poems. More than ever this is poetry of 'the exploded view', the fragmentariness now often explicitly conventionalised in the terms of ancient Chinese and 17th century Japanese poetic forms which, as Chris Agee has pointed out, have striking affinities with early Irish poetry. In the best of his short poems – 'Kestrel', 'Oasis', 'Massive Lovers', 'Chinese Objects', 'The Ghost Orchid' – Longley aims for a miniature perfection reminiscent of Basho. The loosening up is also, paradoxically, a tightening up. This kind of poetry is notable for its economy of means, its water-colour suggestiveness and delicacy, its refined description of nature, its sometimes witty and playful tone, its elegant style, its ritualistic and ceremonial character:

> We are completely out of proportion in the tea-house
> Until we arrange around a single earthenware bowl
> Ourselves, the one life, one meeting, a ribbon of water
> And these makeshift ideograms of wet leaves, green tea.
> ('A Gift of Boxes, II', GO 17)

Longley writes about the tea ceremony and 'the scissors ceremony' (and, in a rather more expansive way, about Baucis and Philemon's ceremony of hospitality, Achilles and Priam's ceremonial reconciliation). 'We pine for ceremony, customary rhythms', Heaney wrote in the teeth of violence and death: and so it is with Longley who, by converting language to incantation and catalogue, and action to ritual, seeks to demonstrate what Agee calls a 'reverential sensibility',[10] the possibility of grace under pressure. In poems such as 'The Ghost Orchid', 'Form', 'Out There', 'Partisans', 'The Eel-Trap', 'Couplet', 'Chinese Objects', 'Chinese Whispers', 'The White Garden', the poet returns to the world of daily experience to discover the truth of beauty, the everlasting self. Relying on the humble and unpretentious imagery of everyday life, he contemplates the water gourd and the length of white silk, the white garden and migrating geese with such intensity that the poem achieves a symbolic resonance without pretending in the least to be symbolic. One is reminded of William Carlos Williams' devotion to the thing itself, and of his motto: 'No ideas but in things'. Like Williams', Longley's perception of the world is one in which subjective preoccupation with self is left behind. He does not impose himself upon the object, but rather the poetry seems to issue from a kind of Whitmanesque universalisation of the self, or Zen-like mergence of self and world. The merit of the best of these poems is not just in their fine phrasing, but in the naturalness of feeling, the sense they convey of the fusion of subject and object, the two in perfect harmony. This seems to be the decisive thrust of *The Ghost Orchid*: the search for the permanent, unchangeable element in poetry, the hidden vital force that shapes it into a meaningful whole: a truly universalised self rather than a subjective counterfeit of the self. 'The Ghost Orchid' is the culminating image of the poet's intuition of eternity in the things that are, by their very own nature, subject to violence and destined to perish.

MY BOTANICAL STUDIES: THE POETRY OF NATURAL HISTORY IN MICHAEL LONGLEY

NEIL CORCORAN

I

In his 1995 book, *The Ghost Orchid*, Michael Longley has a short poem called 'Mr. 10½, *after Robert Mapplethorpe*'. The poem takes off from a 1976 photograph of Mapplethorpe's entitled 'Mark Stevens (Mr 10½)'. It is one of the photographs sealed off by separating red pages in the standard Cape edition of Mapplethorpe's work – one of those erotic or, as Mapplethorpe thought of some of them himself, pornographic images which 'plays with the edge', in the phrase which Arthur C. Danto, in the volume's accompanying essay, tells us Mapplethorpe used.[1] The image is that of a white male torso from neck to upper thigh bent to the right over some sort of table or box. Naked except for a pair of leather chaps, the torso displays on the table a circumcised penis whose astonishing size makes it quite clear how Mark Stevens came by his pseudonym. This is Longley's poem:

> When he lays out as on a market stall or altar
> His penis and testicles in thanksgiving and for sale,
> I find myself considering his first months in the womb
> As a wee girl, and I substitute for his two plums
> Plum-blossom, for his cucumber a yellow flower.

(*GO* 16)

This poem swims buoyantly on what Hugo Williams has called, in a poem, 'the sea / of post-war British photograph poetry',[2] since it behaves so unexpectedly and unpredictably, reading its photographic text with such wayward, oddly-angled intelligence. The photograph might have prompted, after all, a number of responses: a meditation on the particular line or 'edge' which distinguishes the erotic from the pornographic in Mapplethorpe, the kind of meditation Roland Barthes offers in relation to another Mapplethorpe image in his book on photography, *Camera Lucida*;[3] or it might have noticed what Barthes would almost certainly have thought the 'punctum' of the photograph, a tiny tattooed devil on the torso's upper arm, which – given the altar-like nature of the display – might have prompted a meditation on the strange persistence in parodied form of Mapplethorpe's native Catholicism; or it might have given rise, as it does in Danto's essay, to an account of the paradoxical combination in Mapplethorpe of erotic or pornographic content with a chaste classicism of form. These would all be interesting and informative, but in the end obvious critical ways of representing or interpreting the photograph. Michael Longley's way is not like these ways; and in its unlikeness it seems to me entirely characteristic. I want to try to say why.

The poem's sinuous single sentence inspects the image and finds it wanting: it reads the masculine display, this putting of the penis on a pedestal, as an arrogance requiring the correction of deflation. In reading arrogance into the image, Longley is, arguably, moralising it in excess of the facts. There is nothing intrinsic to it to justify his remark that this penis is 'for sale', for instance, unless this implies not prostitution but simply the fact that Mapplethorpe paid his models: but then, what painter or photographer does not, when his models are studio models? Similarly, Longley's title makes Mark Stevens anonymous as 'Mr 10½', whereas Mapplethorpe's title very prominently and punctiliously gives him his proper name: Danto has argued that this lack of anonymity evidences a trust between photographer and model of a kind which very precisely differentiates between pornography and eroticism. I would also say that such moralising tends to miss something else about many of Mapplethorpe's images, including this one: the fact that, when the initial shock of, or erotic reaction to, the image has worn away, as it does quite quickly, the residue is often a kind of comedy, and often also, as in this photograph, a comedy of discrepancy. Mapplethorpe, that is to say, is serious enough, but not *that* serious: although, indeed, the casual, even whimsical humour of the Longley poem may itself include precisely such a recognition.

However, if Longley overinterprets, he does so in the interests of reducing male presumption and arrogance and of reminding us of the instabilities of gender differentiation. This huge displayed phallus is relocated at its point of origin in the womb where, prior to sexual differentiation, it was not yet phallus at all, but a non-specialised shape. The poem is, it is probably worth saying, physiologically knowledgeable here in a way that people are, sometimes, surprisingly, not. The point has been made with brilliant wit and aplomb by Stephen Jay Gould in his essay 'Male Nipples and Clitoral Ripples', where he says that if you ask the majority of people why men have nipples they can't tell you, being ignorant of what he calls 'the most elementary fact of sexual anatomy – the homology of penis and clitoris', an ignorance prompted by the pervasiveness of the functionalist model in evolutionary theory. Gould writes:

The external differences between male and female develop gradually from an early embryo so generalized that its sex cannot be easily determined. The clitoris and the penis are one and the same organ, identical in early form, but later enlarged in male fetuses through the action of testosterone. Similarly, the labia majora of women and the scrotal sacs of men are the same structure, indistinguishable in young embryos, but later enlarged, folded over, and fused along the midline in male fetuses.[4]

Gould's insistence on the point is of course continuous with his sense that such physiological knowledge may have consequences in psychology and sociology. If the penis is a clitoris too, that is to say, its arrogant place on the pedestal may not be so securely held or, possibly, even desired: competition won't count. I think this is Longley's point too, and he is finely discriminating to have made it in a poem, and particularly in this exquisitely brief and witty poem.

My theme is botany in Longley, however, not physiology, and I am probably taking an inordinately long time to broach it. But, on the other hand, perhaps I am not, since by broaching botany through physiology – human physiology – I am holding in the same thought things that are almost always held together in Michael Longley's poems too. As they are, of course, in 'Mr. 10½', where the unreconstructed penis and scrotum are two plums and a cucumber; the penis and scrotum reconstructed as clitoris and vagina are plum-blossom and a yellowy flower. In these figures Longley has appropriated the Mapplethorpe photographic image to the most consistent imagery of his own poetry, an imagery of botany – of plant, wildflower and herb – through which some of his most central preoccupations are insinuated, an appropriation enforced by the languid revision of Mapplethorpe's New York *chic* into the Northern Irish demotic of that 'wee girl'. On the other hand,

Longley's biomorphism here is continuous with Mapplethorpe's own, where his flower pictures – of calla lily, poppy, baby's breath, chrysanthemums and orchid – rhyme their flowers with the human genitalia. In Longley's poem 'Mr. 10½' it is almost, therefore, as though the male floral rhyming of Mapplethorpe is being revised into the female biomorphism of a Georgia O'Keeffe, those flowers which enfold, invite and caress rather than assert, rise up and strut.

II

If physiology is read under the figure of botany in 'Mr. 10½', then, it is an instruction in the way botany in Longley is instinct with human significance. It is a botany frequently eroticised, and in ways sometimes subversive of masculine norms; it offers a series of figures for the processes of psychological identity and differentiation; it attempts to act as palliation for the afflictions of history and mortality. Before all of these metaphorical and figurative functions, however, botany in Longley is what it is. As in the other botanical poets named in his work – John Clare and Edward Thomas, but also those momentary botanists of the battlefields, Isaac Rosenberg and Keith Douglas – the naming of species is itself a rich poetic resource. There is in Longley a sweet lyricism of the onomastic, ambivalently caught between wildflower delight and something more melancholy and resigned. Edward Thomas is, as Seamus Heaney has said, the 'sponsoring presence from the literary tradition' for this strain in Longley – 'a sponsorship with just as much political significance as we want to assign it'[5] – and certainly such poems as Thomas's 'Old Man', 'Lob' and 'Household Poems' seem generative of the whole Longley procedure. At a very early stage in his writing career he clearly deeply internalised and newly synthesised the way such poems 'like the names', as 'Old Man' has it – 'And yet I like the names'. Longley's poetry likes the names too, nowhere more than in 'The Ice-cream Man' in *Gorse Fires*, where the liking of the names builds into a perfectly cadenced catalogue:

> Rum and raisin, vanilla, butter-scotch, walnut, peach:
> You would rhyme off the flavours. That was before
> They murdered the ice-cream man on the Lisburn Road
> And you bought carnations to lay outside his shop.
> I named for you all the wild flowers of the Burren
> I had seen in one day: thyme, valerian, loosestrife,

My Botanical Studies: The Poetry of Natural History in Michael Longley 105

> Meadowsweet, tway blade, crowfoot, ling, angelica,
> Herb robert, marjoram, cow parsley, sundew, vetch,
> Mountain avens, wood sage, ragged robin, stitchwort,
> Yarrow, lady's bedstraw, bindweed, bog pimpernel.
>
> (*GF* 49)

This is a little triumph of its kind, a *tour-de-force* which paradoxically calls no attention to itself, but only to its object. If Edward Thomas's sponsorship is somewhere behind this, the poem reminds us too that the naming of wildflowers goes a long way further back than Thomas in English poetry, since it is not Thomas but Milton and Shakespeare with whom these lines connect more immediately, the Milton of the elegiac strewing of flowers in 'Lycidas' and the Shakespeare of Ophelia's last appearance in *Hamlet*, 'Larded all with sweet flowers', and of Perdita's catalogue of flowers in *The Winter's Tale*. The persistence suggests Longley's resourcefulness as the discoverer of potential in a long English tradition of the melancholy collocation of human death and botanical life.

This does not, however, detract from the originality of this poem, which is a poem almost purely catalogue, but very artfully managed catalogue. The list of ice-cream flavours in the first line culminates in a flavour – peach – which is also a plant: so the poet's recitation of the names of the wild flowers of the Burren seems doubly continuous with the daily recitation made in the ice-cream man's shop by the poem's addressee. This continuity between the activity of the shop and the activity of the poem is enforced by the way the recitation in the shop is defined as a 'rhyming', where the colloquialism is at once conventional and inflected with regard. It is probably heavy-handed to point this out, but the word makes of the activity of the ice-cream shop a kind of poetry too and, in doing so, indicates something entirely characteristic of Longley: an aesthetic unpresumptuousness in which other – it may seem more mundane – activities are accorded a properly generous appreciation. This implies, too, something else generally true of his work: its tactful hesitation about any consolation poems might offer for human suffering and its deep unease about the legitimacy of making poems from violent deaths.

These elements of this poem's behaviour – its good behaviour – are forwarded also by the way the poem is an address to another who has been distressed by the murder. That person's testimonial – the wreath of carnations laid outside the shop – is a gesture of affection and helplessness, as all such gestures are; but behind the poem's catalogue there is presumably a conversation in which distress and helplessness have been articulated. To offer consolation for, or palliation of, these feelings is manifestly impossible, since there is none, and behind this poem too there may therefore be the accurate cliché that 'there are no words'. The poem offers, therefore, no words at all of the conventionally consolatory or analytical kind; but it does nevertheless offer words, the words for wild flowers offered as if they are themselves a wreath, to join the wreath of carnations, but a wreath now offered not to the ice-cream man himself but to this other, the poem's addressee, in his or her grief. The list asserts, I suppose, the fact of botanical persistence, the wonderful rich profusion of the natural world, even in the face of the grotesque damage done by human atrocity; but it also, beyond that, offers to helplessness the resistance that is the act of naming itself, the patient onomastics of recital in which rhyming and naming, however tentatively and pitifully, bravely encounter and resist that other verb prominent in 'The Ice-cream Man', 'murdering'. There is a Rilkean vigour and defiance in this, that luminous defiance of the Duino Elegies, in which Rilke discovers that what we are here for is naming – 'such saying as never the things themselves / hoped so intensely to be'.[6] In this context, 'I named for you' is the most that can be done for anyone in distress, and the verb accrues a new strength from the patient punctiliousness of the list of names which succeeds it.

III

So botany is what it is in Longley, the thing and the name of the thing; but 'The Ice-cream Man' also suggests something of the way it is intricated with themes of identity, death and political history. The self in Longley's poetry is recorded but also rendered oblique or, as it were, hesitated before; and the way this hesitation is often profoundly intertwined with the botanical is clear from the poem 'Alibis' in *An Exploded View*. In a mode continuous with such metamorphic fantasias of Derek Mahon's as 'Lives', this poem's lyric first person wanders in and out of a set of variant selves: he is saxophonist on the Souza Band's Grand Tour of the World, diarist, music teacher, the drafter of appendices to lost musical manuscripts, the saviour of damaged birds, the author of an *Apologia Pro Vita Mea*, and so on. But the poem, before briefly glancing over these various alternative selves, actually opens with its first person identifying himself as a botanist:

My Botanical Studies: The Poetry of Natural History in Michael Longley

> My botanical studies took me among
> Those whom I now consider my ancestors.
> I used to appear to them at odd moments –
> With buckets of water in the distance, or
> At the campfire, my arms full of snowy sticks.
> Beech mast, hedgehogs, cresses were my diet,
> My medicaments badger grease and dock leaves.
> A hard life. Nevertheless, they named after me
> A clover that flourished on the distant slopes.
>
> (P 104)

The humoresque of this poem, its lighthearted buoyancy and flourish, keep the matter of identity in play as itself a form of play, a feinting at and wavering among possibilities; the poem is the place where you do not keep yourself to yourself, but where you do indeed find an answer to the far from simple question 'Of being in two places at the one time'.

The ways in which the botanical alibi may articulate historical attitude or veiled biography under the forms of natural history are suggested by many other poems in the Longley *oeuvre*. The elegantly fluent little poem 'Flora' in *Man Lying on a Wall* virtually defines this kind of simultaneity when it imagines the bookmark of a flower staining pictures of the poet. The whole poem may be read as a kind of unravelling of the pun on the word 'leaves' which closes its first line, the leaves of both plant and book, the pun which Joyce actually employs at the close, or recommencement, of *Finnegans Wake*; and indeed the entire botanical element in Longley is coincident with the fact that the Greek word 'anthology' means a collection of flowers: 'flora' in Longley are flowers and poems too. Frequently, therefore, Longley poses himself in his poems, as Nicholas Hilliard's miniatures pose their subjects, intertwined with flora, or at nest or at ease in a vegetable world. When he offers, in 'Watercolour', for instance, a poetic version of his portrait by Jeffrey Morgan, he notes that his shirt is 'a running / Together of earth-colours, wintry grasses, bracken'; but it is the third part of 'Spring Tide' in *The Echo Gate* that seems almost paradigmatic in this respect:

> The spring tide has ferried jelly fish
> To the end of the lane, pinks, purples,
> Wet flowers beside the floating cow-pats.
> The zig-zags I make take me among
> White cresses and brookweed, lousewort,
> Water plantain and grass of parnassus

> With engraved capillaries, ivory sheen:
> By a dry-stone wall in the dune slack
> The greenish sepals, the hidden blush
> And a lip's red veins and yellow spots –
> Marsh helleborine waiting for me
> To come and go with the spring tide.
>
> (P 157)

This is as minutely particular as can be, and suggests an affinity between Longley and the botanical psychodrama to be found in the work of Theodore Roethke, very influential during the 1960s, but not much read now, as far as I can tell. Utterly unlike Roethke, however, it has a poised, lucid calm; and if we are to read psychic distress out of these lines, it is only the generalised distress which realises that the psyche, that consciousness itself, is intrusive in the botanical realm, when the line-break and the cumulative syntactical sway of the penultimate line dramatise both longing and disappointment: not 'Marsh helleborine waiting for me', alas, but 'March helleborine waiting for me / To come and go with the spring tide'. The helleborine will persist, as this personification or psychologising of the plant proposes, whereas the poet's intrusive subjectivity will not: so botany becomes *memento mori*, as it does more than once elsewhere in Longley too. There is a range of poems in his work in which, with great delicacy, botany and psychology interpenetrate in a way that seems almost to constitute identity as evanescence; a lyric subjectivity discovers itself only in the act of witnessing or recording its own vanishing. This occasionally runs the risk of the over-exquisite or the exiguous, and its reticences and hesitations, its decorums of diction and rhythm, sometimes come close to what Hopkins called the 'Parnassian', a term used to distinguish 'the language of inspiration' from a language which 'can only be spoken by poets, but is not in the highest sense poetry'.[7] These may, however, be regarded as necessary risks for a poetry so devoid of the will to self-aggrandisement, so little preoccupied with making a show or cutting a figure. And all this, I hope it's not nugatory to remark, in the context of modern and contemporary poetry written by Irish men, where the firm inscription of characteristically identifiable signature is virtually taken as normative.

There is one poem, however, 'Eurycleia' from *Gorse Fires*, in which some more immediate psychic distress does seem to be addressed, and in a way which to some extent refocuses all those poems in which the lyric self is present at the centre of a botanical realm. As in a significant number of Longley's later poems in which personal experience or feeling is refracted through parallels in other writing, notably the texts of Homer and Ovid, 'Eurycleia' revisits the moment in the *Odyssey* when Odysseus's old nursemaid recognises him, while washing his feet, when she sees the scar of a wound inflicted by a boar during his youth. Longley's version of the recognition scene composes the first part of the poem. This is the second, which accompanies it:

> I began like Odysseus by loving the wrong woman
> Who has disappeared among the skyscrapers of New York
> After wandering for thousands of years from Ithaca.
> She alone remembers the coppice, dense and overgrown,
> Where in a compost of dead leaves the boar conceals
> Its bristling spine and fire-red eyes and white tusks.
>
> (GF 31)

The story of Longley's relationship with his own nursemaid, and of his difficult relationship with his mother, is one he has told in his prose piece, *Tuppenny Stung*.[8] In this mythologising parallel, the psychic pain is read as an Odyssean scar: a mark of secret recognition, certainly, but also of permanent damage done. The poem 'remembers' the coppice, dense and overgrown too, where the damage is inflicted; but that compost of dead leaves may well be the germinant source of a great deal of the botany in Longley's compositions.

If these have their Marvellian elegance, wit and grace, making Longley too, sometimes, as Marvell describes himself in 'Upon Appleton House', an 'easie philosopher, / Among the birds and trees confer[ing]', they also have their darker side, where botany names distress and is sought for succour. Frequently, the lyric self is situated in womb-like, protective covering: in 'In Aillwee Cave' in *Gorse Fires* he is wombed below the botanical, 'Darkness above the darkness of the seepage of souls'; in 'The White Garden' in *The Ghost Orchid* he disappears into the garden's white 'lace and veils', at the still centre of a kind of white nowhere which is the origin of writing, the place where words begin, mysteriously, to emerge; and in the same book's lighthearted pastiche sequence, 'Chinese Occasions', 'I fall into the flowerbed (drink taken), / Soil and sky my eiderdown and pillow'. This longing for the security of a botanical space as a psychic shelter is finely figured too, and most memorably, in another Odyssean parallel-poem, 'A Bed of Leaves' in *The Ghost Orchid*, where Odysseus beds himself down into a 'mattress of leaves, / An eiderdown of leaves' – 'So was his body in the bed of leaves its own kindling / And sleep settled on him like ashes and closed his eyelids'. In the context of these linkages between botany and psychology it is unsurprising – although this is the only unsurprising thing about this strangely dislocating poem – to discover a botanical relation too when Longley contemplates, in 'X-Ray' in *Gorse Fires*, the womb in which he was actually gestated. He has written in prose, in *Tuppenny Stung*, about this experience too, that of scrutinising an x-ray photograph of his mother's womb while she was pregnant with himself and his twin brother.[9] The poem appears to contain distress or even rage, when its first person wants the mother to 'eat the world, giblets, marrow, / Tripes and offal, fish, birds, fields of grain'; but this language of rapacity and engorgement dissolves into the language of forgiveness and retrospective assuagement, a medicinal healing in which the lyric self prescribes 'in the dark a salad of landcress, / Fennel like hair, the sky-blue of borage flowers'. That curative capacity, the capacity to make whole again what has been wounded or broken, is the profoundest element of the botanical in Longley.

IV

It is not only personal history, however, which Longley's botanical poems plot into their figures and forms; it is also public, political history, as we have seen already in 'The Ice-cream Man'. The poem 'Finding a Remedy' from the sequence 'Lore' in *The Echo Gate* has the same quality of desired reparation as the conclusion of 'X-Ray', but, in this volume published in 1979, the desire is manifestly turned out towards the public life of its time more than it is turned inwards to personal distress. This poem too is an herbal prescription, containing an instruction in its use:

> Sprinkle the dust from a mushroom or chew
> The white end of a rush, apply the juice
> From fern roots, stems of burdock, dandelions,
>
> Then cover the wound with cuckoo-sorrel
> Or sphagnum moss, bringing together verse
> And herb, plant and prayer to stop the bleeding.
>
> (P 159)

This is reticent about the actual source of the bleeding, but, in a poem from Northern Ireland in the 1970s, there is a political subtext. The concept of the poem as a spell, as a careful and patient instruction in a healing ritual, as a measured contemplation of desperation: all of these are implicit in the botany of 'Finding a Remedy'. The scrupulous hesitation of this way of addressing the Troubles – where 'addressing' is altogether too emphatic a word – is continuous with Longley's stated unease in *Tuppenny Stung*: 'I find offensive the notion that what we inadequately call "the Troubles" might provide inspiration for artists; and that in some weird *quid pro quo* the arts might provide solace for grief and anguish'; and again, 'In the context of political violence the deployment of words at their most precise and most suggestive remains one of the few antidotes to death-dealing dishonesty'.[10] This is a view consistent with all of the poems in which the Troubles figure at some level in Longley; and I have myself written elsewhere about the pains he takes to 'establish credentials' in these poems, the way he manages 'an authenticating relationship between public and private'.[11]

A further mode of authentication is the way, occasionally and obliquely, the Troubles are caught up into Longley's permanent botanical poetic. His poem 'Peace', after Tibullus, in *The Echo Gate*, is one such case, when its version of the Latin elegist concludes in a dream of alterity, where Peace is figured as feminised, maternal, erotic and botanical all at once, in a kind of sudden Arcimboldo effect in language – 'As for me, I want a woman / To come and fondle my ears of wheat and let apples / Overflow between her breasts'. John Kerrigan has written well about the way this poem secretes, in its reference to a statue carved out of bog-oak, a reclamation of a harmless household god from the always ominous bogland territory of Seamus Heaney's poems; and it would be possible to write at some length about the variant uses of the bog in early Longley and Heaney, where it is very much common ground trodden with a difference.[12] Such a comparison might also have 'as much political significance as we want to assign it', or possibly even more. What I want to do in this context, however, is to offer a reading of the poem in which Longley does very much bring together herb, plant and prayer, and bogland too, 'Bog Cotton' from *The Echo Gate*:

> Let me make room for bog cotton, a desert flower –
> Keith Douglas, I nearly repeat what you were saying
> When you apostrophised the poppies of Flanders
> And the death of poetry there: that was in Egypt
> Among the sandy soldiers of another war.
>
> (It hangs on by a thread, denser than thistledown,
> Reluctant to fly, a weather vane that traces

> The flow of cloud shadow over monotonous bog –
> And useless too, though it might well bring to mind
> The plumpness of pillows, the staunching of wounds,
>
> Rags torn from a petticoat and soaked in water
> And tied to the bushes around some holy well
> As though to make a hospital of the landscape –
> Cures and medicines as far as the horizon
> Which nobody harvests except with the eye.)
>
> You saw that beyond the thirstier desert flowers
> There fell hundreds of thousands of poppy petals
> Magnified to blood stains by the middle distance
> Or through the still unfocused sights of a rifle –
> And Isaac Rosenberg wore one behind his ear.
>
> (P 167)

This poem does indeed 'make room' for bog cotton in that it finds a poetic space for this local flower among other flowers already made over into significant poems: Keith Douglas's 'Desert Flowers', a poem of the Middle East in the Second World War, a subtle, fluid poem of turning-points, dissolvings, dreams and transitions, and Isaac Rosenberg's 'Break of Day in the Trenches', that bravely ironic and insouciant poem of the First World War with its 'Poppies whose roots are in men's veins', which ends with an almost dandyish flourish of defiance – 'But mine in my ear is safe – / Just a little white with the dust'.[13]

Longley's poem is, as it were, doubly intertextual in that it refers not only to these two poems, but in that it also mimics Douglas's own reference to Rosenberg, since the second line of 'Desert Flowers' reads, 'Rosenberg I only repeat what you were saying'. Longley makes space for his flower, then, by bracketing it between other men's flowers; and this makes 'Bog Cotton' implicitly a kind of war poem too. 'Bog Cotton' reads these experiences and previous poems with deference, by opening literal brackets to celebrate its flower, the lunulae of the parenthesis acting as an index of humility before an acknowledged and respected tradition. The brackets, as it were, visibly make room for the flower; they make a room which is within a tradition but to one side of it too. This is a fine tact, I think, and a necessary one, since unlike Douglas and Rosenberg, Longley is not of course a combatant soldier, although he may well be a victim of the general depredations of a province at war for a very long time: naming bog cotton a 'desert flower' may imply precisely that. The parenthesis itself repeats the parenthesis Douglas makes for his acknowledgement of Rosenberg in 'Desert Flowers', an acknowledgement of his own anxiety as a latecomer which is sharpened by those prose statements in which he has no illusions about the fact that the great war poems have all, long since, been written. This is, I assume, one of the implications of the concluding stanza of Longley's poem too, where the address to Douglas has him seeing beyond the desert flowers of the Second World War to the 'hundreds of thousands of poppy petals' of the First.

The bog cotton may make room for itself in this tradition, however, because it shares qualities with the already-written desert flowers and poppies. Manifestly, Longley admires in Douglas and Rosenberg strengths which are both poetic and moral, attitudes of irony and self-deflation which enable the bravery of endurance: 'Desert Flowers' and 'Break of Day in the Trenches' manage their ironies in the face of almost certain death – Douglas knows that 'the body can fill / the hungry flowers', and the roots of Rosenberg's poppies are in men's veins. The bog cotton is perhaps less ambivalently ominous a flower than these, but it is certainly an emblem of endurance, in place and in function, even if this is endurance at the very edge of capacity, 'hanging on by a thread'. The cotton is therefore like people compelled to remain in their places or at their posts, whatever the circumstances; but is is also like poetry, 'useless' in that it can offer nothing directly, although it may well bring a great deal to mind – 'Cures and medicines as far as the horizon / Which nobody harvests except with the eye'.

Poetry as the curative harvest of the eye is a richly beneficent figure, and one informed by the range of Longley's botanical tropes elsewhere; but the lines probably also pick up the conclusion of 'Desert Flowers', where Douglas writes 'I see men as trees suffering / or confound the detail and the horizon'. Men as trees suffering is a half-allusion to Mark's gospel, 8: 23–6, where Christ cures the blind man – 'And he looked up and said, I see men as trees walking'; and that is the harvest of the eye too. So that, if John Kerrigan is right to read an intertextual debate with Heaney into the bog-oak statue of the poem 'Peace', we could claim the same of this poem: that the bog cotton is a reclamation of beneficence from the bogland territory of so many early poems of Heaney's, that territory which so authoritatively provokes images and emblems of terror, punishment, shame and suffering. When, in the sequence 'Kinship' in *North*, 'catkin and bog-cotton tremble', they 'raise up / the cloven oak-limb' of the sacrificial goddess Nerthus; in Longley it is the unsubduable bog cotton itself which is raised up.

V

When Heaney discusses Longley in his essay 'Place and Displacement', it is not as a botanist of history or generalised psychology, but as an erotic botanist whose very eroticism may at times, in poems such as 'The Linen Industry' and 'Self-heal', be read as analogous with a politics and history of Northern Ireland. I want to think a little more about the link between botany and eroticism in Longley and, in doing so, to return this paper to its origin and, I hope, bring something back. Longley's is a poetry, Heaney says, 'of direct amorous address, its dramatic voice the voice of indolent and occasionally deliquescent reverie, its subject the whole matter of sexual daydream . . . even when the poem is ostensibly about landscape or seascape, about flora and fauna ... the intonation of the verse is seductive, its melody allaying and cajoling, its typical mood one of tender insinuation and possibility'.[14] It may be that Heaney gives his own tendency towards a critical erotics its head here, and the temper of this is itself more seduced and enraptured than the poems themselves seem to me to warrant. Even where an intimacy of erotic address or evocation is being expressed in these poems, they often maintain a classical poise and lucidity which stills the cajolement and insinuation into something different from itself – not at all unlike, indeed, the combination of erotic subject matter and classical form in the photographs of Robert Mapplethorpe. Heaney is of course right, however, to have noticed the way botany is, as it were, both the tenor and the vehicle of an erotics in Longley. In some of his poems the process of metaphorisation of the botanical is so complete as to maintain a kind of equivalence.

It is possible to identify several different kinds of erotic botany in Longley. There are those poems such as the sequence actually called 'Botany', in which botanical species are themselves sexualised: duckweed draws in its skirts; the dock may 'blossom into blush or birthmark', and so on. These seem to me in some ways the most conventional of the kind, in which the traditional poetic figuring of women as flowers is given a new configuring and a different perspective or inflection, certainly, but in which the basis of the conceit is an obvious and easily overworked one and one not entirely free, it may be, of an element of masculinist condescension. The second kind is the obverse of this when, in poems like 'Sulpicia', 'Martinmas', 'Patchwork', 'Light Behind the Rain' and 'Couplet', the body itself is botanised, so that nipples are read as flowers, lovers are seen as a harvest to be gathered in, the female body is a 'little country'. This is a more complex kind because more alert to the ways in which it takes its place in what is almost a sub-genre of erotically inflected landscape – in photographers and painters such as Mapplethorpe and O'Keeffe, as we have already seen, but also in the sculpture of Henry Moore, for instance, and in the earlier poems of Seamus Heaney. Then there is the trope – if it is that, precisely – of lovemaking in the open air, in poems like 'Mountain Swim', 'On Mweelrea' and 'Autumn Lady's Tresses'; the patron saint of this kind is possibly the 'Sheela-na-gig' in the eponymous poem from *The Ghost Orchid*; at Kilnaboy, 'Where the orchids have borrowed her cunty petals. / A proper libation would be sperm and rainwater'. The same may be said for the poems which reverse this figure, those in which the landscape enters the bedroom: 'The Linen Industry' is one such, and I shall return to it in a moment, and 'An Amish Rug' is another, where the rug in the lovers' bedroom, to be stepped over as they undress, becomes a 'flowerbed'.

I am unsure whether these categories exhaust the Linnaean taxonomy of Longley's botanical erotics, but it would be exhausting, certainly, to pursue them much further. I offer the catalogue to indicate how deeply the figuration goes in the work, how intimately coterminous it is with an essential kind of poetic energy and address in this poet. There is a classical, primarily – although not exclusively – Ovidian sanction for all of this, which has been picked up on by John Kerrigan in his essay 'Ulster Ovids',[15] and which Longley makes explicit in the beautiful poem 'A Flowering' in *The Ghost Orchid*, where a theme of ageing, sexual desire and timidity is run through glancingly collocated versions of the metamorphoses of Hyacinthus and the anemone – 'Ovid's lovely casualties – all that blood / Colouring the grass and changing into flowers'. This reminds us that in the *Metamorphoses* sexual desire is the agent of transformation, but also the agent of violence. The flowerings of Longley's poems are ambivalently inflected with both of these qualities; and they make him one of the finest contemporary poets of sexual longing and its possible fulfilment. But they are also, we will remember, a way of being in two places at the one time. They are, that is to say, the opposite of confessional declaration: the poems are turned out towards resolution and clarification, not in upon themselves in any of the customary erotically self-advertising modes of vaunt, challenge or depreciation. Which is why Heaney's terms seem over-heated to me: Longley's finest work has a genuine impersonality and objectivity, of a Gravesian rather than an Eliotic kind – of, in other words, an authentically, rather than a self-deludingly classicising kind.

But now that I have completed what I can offer in the way of taxonomy, let me return to 'The Linen Industry', which is one of the finest distillations of the botanical-erotic essence in Longley.

> The Linen Industry
> Pulling up flax after the blue flowers have fallen
> And laying our handfuls in the peaty water
> To rot those grasses to the bone, or building stooks
> That recall the skirts of an invisible dancer,
>
> We become a part of the linen industry
> And follow its processes to the grubby town
> Where fields are compacted into window-boxes
> And there is little room among the big machines.
>
> But even in our attic under the skylight
> We make love on a bleach green, the whole meadow
> Draped with material turning white in the sun
> As though snow reluctant to melt were our attire.
>
> What's passion but a battering of stubborn stalks,
> Then a gentle combing out of fibres like hair
> And a weaving of these into christening robes,
> Into garments for a marriage or funeral?
>
> Since it's like a bereavement once the labour's done
> To find ourselves last workers in a dying trade,
> Let flax be our matchmaker, our undertaker,
> The provider of sheets for whatever the bed —
>
> And be shy of your breasts in the presence of death,
> Say that you look more beautiful in linen
> Wearing white petticoats, the bow on your bodice
> A butterfly attending the embroidered flowers.
>
> (P 179)

Heaney reads this emphatically but tactfully too as a political allegory, 'the internalisation and affirmation of those feminine powers repressed by man's, and in particular the Ulsterman's, adaptation to conditions in the technological factory world'.[16] This sophisticatedly pulls out one strand of this poem's complex interweavings, and suggests how subtle and implicative a poet Longley is at his best. But there are other strands which can be pulled too in this poetic text which has surely taken into itself the etymology of the word 'text', from the Latin 'textum', 'that which is woven, web, texture'; and I want, naturally, to pull the one that most fittingly suits my own purpose here.

'The Linen Industry' may well, as Heaney says, anchor itself in its Northern Irish location, since it is an historical fact that the industry developed from the availability of flax in the province was the source of Belfast's industrial strength; but the poem also allies itself very strangely and originally with traditions of love poetry in which the woman's dress and accoutrements are eroticised or even fetishised. The concluding reference to the linen petticoats is a kind of transformation of all those poems of clothing, and the slippage of clothing from the body, in Herrick, poems such as 'Upon Julia's Clothes':

> When as in silks my Julia goes,
> Then, then (me thinks) how sweetly flowes
> That liquefaction of her clothes.
>
> Next, when I cast mine eyes and see
> That brave Vibration each way free;
> O how that glittering taketh me!

'The Linen Industry', we might say, takes the clothes back to their original liquefaction, when they were flax in the peaty water. In doing so, it offers for account, as Herrick's leisured poems of course do not, the industrial basis of pleasure. It uncovers the labours necessary to delight and thereby extends the realm of the love poem: a community as well as a privacy is involved in this act of attic love. Despite which, it manages to make privacy contingent like this without in any way courting intrusion. This poem, like all of those Longley poems in which the act of love is central, is quite without the disfiguring element of display; 'The Linen Industry' is no encouragement to the voyeur.

If Herrick, or a tradition of erotic lyric which the name Herrick may represent, is somewhere at the back of 'The Linen Industry', so is Yeats, in a way uncharacteristic of Longley. The grand rhetorical question, 'What's passion but a battering of stubborn stalks. . . ?', is a Yeatsian rhetoric ('What's water but the generated soul?', asks 'Coole Park and Ballylee, 1931'), and the word 'passion' is, of course, an emphatically Yeatsian word. 'The Linen

Industry' therefore accommodates Yeats, and the Yeatsian love lyric which must shadow any subsequent poet writing love poems in Ireland, but accommodates him also to the most typical figures and images of Longley's own poems. I think this is managed very deftly here, when the sudden flowering of the Yeatsian tone, with its almost bravado assurance and command, is only the briefest interruption in a poem otherwise so tonally unlike Yeats: not so much a 'battering' as a 'gentle combing out'. And in that combing out, what comes clear in the final stanzas of 'The Linen Industry' is the presence of death, the reminder that the linen which makes the white petticoats of love also makes both swaddling and shroud. The use of the word 'bereavement' and the presentation of the lovers as 'last workers in a dying trade' runs a submerged pun on sexual consummation as 'le petit mort', and it reminds us of that mortuary voluptuousness which is also one of the most peculiar features of Longley's eroticism, in poems such as 'Obsequies', 'Oliver Plunkett' and 'According to Pythagoras'. In these he establishes sudden connection with another kind of seventeenth-century lyric, even if his more immediate source is the conclusion of Louis MacNeice's poem, 'Mayfly' – 'But when this summer is over let us die together, / I want always to be near your breasts', a poem which Peter McDonald has shown to be deeply influential on Longley.[17] The unflinching recognition that the awareness of death is profoundly involved in the act of love is what steadies 'The Linen Industry' into authority; it places a serious concentrated premium on pleasure because it knows what pleasure must contest. Thinking of the seventeenth-century lyric too, one might say of 'The Linen Industry', finally, that it is a remarkable contemporary instance of how a little room may be made an everywhere.

VI

I want to end with 'The Ghost Orchid' itself, which brings flower and poem self-consciously together once more, in one of Longley's most delicate lyrical figurings:

> Added to its few remaining sites will be the stanza
> I compose about leaves like flakes of skin, a colour
> Dithering between pink and yellow, and then the root
> That grows like coral among shadows and leaf-litter.
> Just touching the petals bruises them into darkness.

(*GO* 52)

The opening of that may remember the opening of 'Bog Cotton', where, as we have seen, the poetic act of making room is evoked, since a stanza is, etymologically, a 'room' too; and the poem reminds us of the ecology implicit in Longley's whole output and endeavour. But this little hymn to fragility, ephemerality and evanescence is a reminder to the critic that poems as delicate as this can be bruised too by the heavy critical touch; and one would do better to retire and leave poem and flower to their mutually supportive and nurturing creative darkness.

LONGLEY'S LONG LINE: LOOKING BACK FROM *THE GHOST ORCHID*

MICHAEL ALLEN

Like earlier creative silences, the one[1] that followed the publication of Michael Longley's *Poems 1963–1983* (1985) can be seen as a time of rhythmical retrenchment. *Gorse Fires* (1991) and *The Ghost Orchid* (1995) show a much greater use of the long line (a loose iambic pentameter often verging on hexameter whose more precise definition I will return to later).[2] This formal development (Table I) corresponds to a widening of range, a movement towards

Table I

	NUMBER OF 'LONG LINE' POEMS
MAN LYING ON A WALL, 1976	0/34
THE ECHO GATE, 1979	3/36
POEMS 1963–1983, 1985	
'MAN LYING ON A WALL' SECTION	1/28
'THE ECHO GATE' SECTION	3/35
'NEW POEMS' SECTION	0/15
GORSE FIRES, 1991	15/57
THE GHOST ORCHID, 1995	40/74

Table II

```
POEMS 1963-1983 ◄──────► GORSE FIRES ◄──────► THE GHOST ORCHID
      (1985)                 (1991)                 (1995)
    PRIVATE ◄───────────────────────────────────► PUBLIC
    INTIMATE ◄──────────────────────────────────► SOCIO-POLITICAL
    ESOTERIC IDIOM ◄────────────────────────────► DEMOTIC IDIOM
    ATTRACTS WORD-HOARD ◄──► EXCLUDES WORD-HOARD*
    SHORTER LINES ◄─────────────────────────────► LONGER LINES
```

*See Donald Davie, *Purity of Diction in English Verse*: 'words thrusting at the poem and being fended off'.

the 'public' as opposed to the 'private' extreme of the continuum represented in Table II. The penultimate binary in that Table comes from Donald Davie's *Purity of Diction in English Verse* and the opposition Davie sets up between the richly associative language which accrues to a poem from deeply varied sources (in, say, Hopkins) and a word-hoard 'thrusting at the poem and being fended off from it'[3] (in, say, Gray or Johnson) does illustrate one of the directions in which the classics can push Anglophone poetry. But while his long line and its concomitant stylistic qualities bear some relationship (particularly when a hexametric tendency is visible) to Longley's increased practice of translation in his later career, I will argue that the effect of his classical training only complements that opening of himself up to society which is my major concern.

Peter McDonald was, in fact, perfectly right to say when reviewing *Poems 1963–1983* that in comparison with Heaney the Longley of that book had a tendency 'to move away from a public voice'.[4] And even when we come to *Gorse Fires* and *The Ghost Orchid* we are never talking about 'a vatic rhetoric that can quarrel with itself'[5] in the manner of 'Whatever You Say Say Nothing'. Nevertheless, there is now undoubtedly a wider range of voices: witness in *The Ghost Orchid* the powerfully sardonic note of 'According to Pythagoras' or the Ulster Scots dialect of 'Phemios & Medon'. The long line is important to both; the first certainly demonstrates Davie's classicised 'purity of diction'. The second is demotic whether it represents 'an aesthetic brand of revolutionary action, perhaps more linguistic reclamation than decolonisation'[6] (Edna Longley's description of Heaney's 'A New Song') or a satiric response to the possible 'dialectical counter-hegemony' (Clair Wills) which Tom Paulin associates with 'the elevation and organization of two aspects of the language – accent, or regional pronunciation, and lexicon, or regional vocabulary'.[7] In either event, Longley's lexically and idiomatically North-East Irish insurgent (Odysseus by name), while he bears a distant relationship to the paramilitary speaker of Derek Mahon's 'A Rage for Order', has an identity precipitated by the socio-political resonances of 'The Butchers', the last poem of *Gorse Fires*, and the long line is a key component in the whole enterprise. (The demotic impulse is more moderately at play in the latter poem too, whether in the borrowing of the title from city folklore[8] or the carefully ambiguous disposition of localised words like 'disloyal' and 'haggard' at key points in the story.) (*GF* 51)

Of course, it is in poems like 'Ceasefire' and 'Poppies' that *The*

Longley's Long Line: Looking Back From The Ghost Orchid

Table III

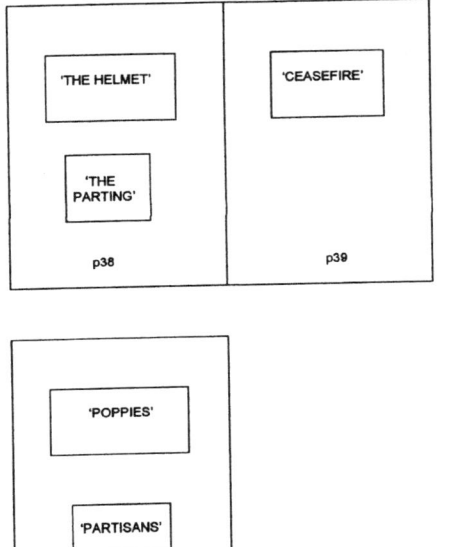

Ghost Orchid's public and political meanings come to the fore, in 'Ceasefire' again because of the contemporary relevance that 'The Butchers' had made possible for Longley's Homeric pieces as well as because of its own timely appearance in *The Irish Times* in the week of the IRA ceasefire in 1994. A third factor here is the way Longley's interest in the transcendence of gender stereotypes (pursued in an intimate and textually esoteric poem like 'A Flowering') (*GO* 14) is extended into the public arena. And it is characteristic that he uses the minutiae of the page-arrangement of poems to relate political violence to the gender values of society (see Table III). The reader's positive response to the redemptive implications of 'Ceasefire' (where the reconciled male characters 'stare at each other's beauty as lovers might') is reinforced by the build-up to it on p. 38: Hector praying in 'The Helmet' that his own martial machismo will be passed on and his son 'grow up bloodier than him'; Andromache (who in Homer tried to persuade Hector to forswear the heroism of single combat in favour of a defensive strategy)[9] capitulating in 'The Parting' to his patronising instruction, 'Leave it to the big boys', with the consequence we know (the kind that 'Ceasefire' aims to mitigate).

But the life-affirming 'stare' of bereaved king and victor on p. 39 (carrying contrasting gender implications in Greek and modern contexts and implying in 1994 the roots in repression of Irish violence) is ironically subverted the minute we turn over. Page 40 repeats the pattern of p. 38, insinuating the power of the cycle of violence. 'Poppies' (identically placed to 'The Helmet') shows Irish (male) Republican savagery in the aftermath of the 'ceasefire' of 1918 ('Some people tried to stop other people wearing poppies / And ripped them from lapels . . . ') and retaliatory Loyalist savagery when 'the others hid inside their poppies / Razor blades and added to their poppies more red poppies'. 'Partisans', located on p. 40 just where 'The Parting' appears on p. 38, recapitulates the irony of the latter poem in terms of the gendered division of labour as the male partisan 'hacks at a snowdrift' and his domesticated partner skims from the soup 'Ideograms of "peace" / And "love", suchlike ideals'. The short line (trimetric) of 'Partisans' (crudely represented in Table III) provides a mocking diminuendo, picking up on the satiric force of the strict iambic of 'The Parting' –

> He: 'Lēave it tŏ the bīg bŏys, Andrōmăche.'
> 'Hēctor, my dārling husband, ōch,och,' shē. –

while contrasting sharply with the hexametric propensity of 'Poppies':

> Sōme pĕople triēd tŏ stōp ŏther peōple wēaring pōppies
> And rīppĕd them frŏm lapēls ăs though upr̄ooting pōppies
> From Flanders fiēlds, but the ōthers hid insīde their pōppies
> R̄azor blades and ādded to their pōppies mōre rēd pōppies.

When the long line is at full stretch as it is here and in 'The Butchers'[10] the hexameter, with its gathering of a potential caesura in the middle of the line, sometimes seems not just an irregularity in the loose iambic pentameter, but an ominously brutal alternative rhythmic possibility. In these lines it reinforces the plangency with which, in Donald Davie's terms, the word-hoard of private lyric is being fended off by a limited and cruelly effective vocabulary. In comparison the loose pentameter of 'Ceasefire' implies restraint:

> When they had eaten together, it pleased them both
> To stare at each other's beauty as lovers might,
> Achilles built like a god, Priam good-looking still
> And full of conversation, who earlier had sighed:
>
> 'I get down on my knees and do what must be done
> And kiss Achilles' hand, the killer of my son.'

The overspill six stresses and attendant caesura in the third line quoted above confer unexpected equality on the two negotiators in the aftermath of concession: the metre however can contract into strict iambic in the last line to render the necessity and pain of that concession.

Clair Wills has written well on the public dimension of Northern Irish poetry (including its gender concerns) but when she speaks of 'a precarious balance between the formal pleasures of the lyric . . . and the broader sweep of public statement'[11] her last phrase seems closer to what we find in Heaney and Paulin than to Longley. By the latter we are almost reminded of the Frost who told Louis Untermeyer that while 'you get more credit for thinking if you restate formulae or cite cases that fall in easily under formulae . . . all the fun is outside saying things that . . . won't formulate – that almost but don't quite formulate'[12] (for 'fun' here perhaps we would want to read 'play'). We have already seen the effect of this at various local levels (and the snow imagery of 'Partisans' becomes both more mischievous and more self-aware when the poem is seen alongside 'Snow Hole' or 'Form' which I will discuss shortly). This refusal to be formulaic is clear when one examines the counterpointed structures of *Gorse Fires* and *The Ghost Orchid*. In the former, Odysseus's return and the reconstruction of his familial and marital relationships are paralleled (often on facing pages) with the speaker's ('Longley''s) shifting but redemptive intimate re-engagements with his mother, with his nurse, with his wife.[13] The whole artefact seems to be engineered towards a closure predicated upon an italicised epigraph (which meditates on the grave in which the poet's parents are united) yet it finally jibs at closure, 'The Butchers' giving to the theme of repossessing the 'home' territory[14] a raw and public dimension which will resonate through the succeeding collection.

The Ghost Orchid yokes private and public dimensions like an extended conceit. The text proper begins with a love poem:

> Trying to tell it all to you and cover everything
> Is like awakening from its grassy form the hare:

> In that make-shift shelter your hand, then my hand
> Mislays the hare and the warmth it leaves behind.
>
> 'Form' (*GO* 1)

Hand finally meets hand (as in a later poem in the book, 'Snow Hole') in erotic foreplay. The poem is close to the private, intimate and esoteric pole of Table II, delving into a word-hoard that assumes some of the power and irrationality of 'dream work'. In this respect the way the long line can tense up into a hexameter is crucial:

> Trȳing to tēll it āll to yōu and cōver ēverythīng
> Is līke awākening from its grāssy fōrm the hāre . . .

The initial laborious hexameter acts out the speaker's reluctance to meet the demand of the beloved for serious and comprehensive discourse or reportage. The four unstressed syllables in the middle of the five-beat second line accommodate both the start of the hare and the shock to the lyric poet's language habit (or dream-work in the half-awake state simulated by the poem), as can be seen if one reads it alongside the prose version, 'awakening the hare from its grassy form'. Because of the second line's rhythmic hiatus there is a moment before one captures the 'prose meaning' during which 'awakening from' functions intransitively to intensify our sense of lyric resistance to 'public' discourse. Under the surreptitious pressure of this alternative reading not only does the word 'form' become self-referential but the metonymic life of the animal in question evokes both the precarious accessibility of the 'dream-work' which leads to lyric poetry ('first catch your hare') and the knowledge-oriented demands of the beloved ('can a poet run with the hare and hunt with the hounds?'). The language possibilities which corresponded to the left and right hand extremes of Table II are balanced against each other, only provisionally resolved by the erotic closure, and one is reminded that the beloved in an earlier poem was also an intermediary between the poet and the public world:

> Love has diminished to one high room
> Below which the vigilantes patrol
> While I attempt to make myself heard
> Above the cacophonous plumbing, and you
> Who are my solitary interpreter
> Can bear my company for long enough
> To lipread such fictions as I believe
> Will placate remote customs officials,

> The border guards, or even reassure
> Anxious butchers, greengrocers, tradesmen
> On whom we depend for our daily bread,
> The dissemination of manuscripts,
> News from the outside world, . . .
>
> 'Company' (1975, P 140)

Notice though that the beloved of the later poem has a more active role, is urging a transformation of the speaker's utterance rather than functioning as the 'solitary interpreter' of his 'attempt to make himself heard' from his 'high room'.[15]

Working by way of its structure towards the meaning of *The Ghost Orchid* is like stripping an onion and in every layer the private ⇌ public dialectic of Table II is imprinted. If 'Form' (the text proper's first poem) suggests one of the pressures which are producing a wider range of voices than ever before in his work (consider three more long-line poems, 'Spiderwoman', 'Mr 10 1/2' and 'The Rules of Baseball', in addition to those I have already mentioned) its final (trimetric) poem carries a curiously world-weary note:

> Do they ever meet out there,
> The dolphins I counted,
> The otter I wait for?
> I should have spent my life
> Listening to the waves.
>
> 'Out There' (*GO* 60)

Referring back to the second poem of *The Ghost Orchid*, 'Autumn Lady's Tresses' (and behind that to the third poem of *Gorse Fires*, 'Insomnia') this poem seems surprised and bemused by the flurry of articulation into which these last two books have developed, ready to discount their multiplicity of active voices as all beside the point. (Its title, perhaps, could have different implications.) Again one is reminded (while crediting that something programmatic has now been substantiated) of a Longley tactic which first emerged in *An Exploded View* (1973, note the title) where different personae (John Clare, a decadent mid-European musician poet, a macho football supporter hurtling to join 'among the police files / My obstreperous bigfisted brothers') are all undercut:

> I could always have kept myself to myself
> And, falling asleep with the light still on,
> Reached the quiet conclusion that this

> (And this is where I came in) was no more than
> The accommodation of different weathers,
> Whirlwind tours around the scattered islands,
> Telephone calls from the guilty suburbs,
> From the back of the mind, a simple question
> Of being in two places at the one time.
>
> 'Alibis' (1972, P 105)

Both *loci* here, the recent and the retrospective, remind us how intensively textual Longley's writing is, how his creative space is an emptiness to be filled with words rather than a transcendentally validated space like that in Heaney's 'Clearances'. Apparently mimetic details ('leveret', 'snipe', 'clump of nettles') in a poem like 'Remembering Carrigskeewaun' for instance are confirmed in their textuality by the self-referential last line:

> The leveret come of age, snipe
> At an angle, then the porpoises'
> Demonstration of meaningless smiles.
> Home is a hollow between the waves,
> A clump of nettles, feathery winds,
> And memory no longer than a day
> When the animals come back to me
> From the townland of Carrigskeewaun,
> From a page lit by the Milky Way.
>
> (*GF* 12)

Or Longley's innate textual binarism[16] ('bigfisted brothers ... two places at the one time') ensures that the Lacanian nostalgia of a poem like 'Brothers' ('Or I paraded naked in front of him / As though I was looking in a mirror') is insinuated into the readerly collaboration we are engaged in:

> It's his peculiar way of putting things
> That fills in the spaces of Tullabaun.
>
> (*P* 161)

There is nevertheless no way of ignoring the paradoxical structuring of *The Ghost Orchid* whereby Longley's increasing openness to public utterance plays against this insistent textuality. *After* 'Out There' (the last poem of the text proper) and the 'Notes and Acknowledgements' there is an 'Afterword' in italics apparently repudiating one of the most public of poetic genres, the elegy (which is quite a prominent form in the book itself), in favour of lyric intimacy:

Longley's Long Line: Looking Back From The Ghost Orchid 129

> *Love poems, elegies: I am losing my place.*
> *Elegies come between me and your face.*

At the same time, however, *in front* of the table of contents and what I have called the first poem, 'Form' (in italics also and presuming that a dedication might be written last of all), Longley has placed a lyric which reactivates the whole public/private issue:

> For John & Janet
>
> *You walked with me among water mint*
> *And bog myrtle when I was tongue-tied:*
> *When I shouted at the ferny cliff*
> *You adopted my echo like a child.*

We cannot ignore the fact that 'John' here is John Banville who, as literary editor of *The Irish Times*, held 'Ceasefire' poised while Longley was away from Ireland in order to publish it on the right day in 1994 and cement into culture Longley's most politically public moment as an Irish poet. And this fact is by no means unrelated to the 'private' content of this epigraph in which a shy poet's utterance, delivered into the void, is fostered by his companions. The Longley who had written the epigraph for the Opsahl[17] report on Northern Ireland in 1993 is already an Irish public figure who can appropriately find himself, according to the title of another poem in *The Ghost Orchid*, 'Sitting for Eddie' ('Eddie' being Edward McGuire the expected portrait-painter for such people). How is Longley the textual strategist to deal with the dangers of the stereotypical and the formulaic which, according to Ciaran Carson, inevitably ensue when a poet plays a public role?

Badly reproduced on the literary pages, beside the reviews, Edward McGuire's portrait of Seamus Heaney is blurred and ambivalent; it appears both as an advertisement and as a record of literary achievement. Idealized almost to the point of caricature (the foreshortened legs, the hen-toed boots, the squat fingers resting on the table, the open book) – it seems to forestall criticism; the poet seems to have acquired the status of myth, of institution.[18]

'Sitting for Eddie' may be off the hook because it turns out to be an elegy for this well-known painter (whatever Longley will end up saying about elegy) as well as because of its strangely surrealist quality. But the question reasserts itself if we compare Jeffrey Morgan's picture[19] of Longley (reproduced between pp. 136 and 137) with the poem he is there depicted writing, 'Watercolour'. The figure in Morgan's very affectionate portrait, placed symmetrically between sculpted egg and dolphin's skull, is undoubtedly a public figure: the titles of the books which surround him, the whooper swans and lazy-beds seen through the window organize much of the paraphernalia of Longley's poetry into a recognisable conspectus at once 'Irish', ecologically aware and international. As soon as one turns to the poem however it becomes clear how important the management of the long line is in evading any such stereotypical version of identity:

> Between a chicken's wishbone on the mantlepiece
> And, on the window sill, a dolphin's skull, I sit,
> My pullover a continuation of the lazy-beds ...
>
> (GO 3)

Longley has spoken of what poetry can achieve 'through syntax, the arrangement of a sentence'[20] and if one compares these lines (as we did in 'Form') with their prose equivalent it becomes clear that the poet's rearrangement of prepositional phrases has heightened the absurdity of that 'I' and of the activity of 'sitting' in both senses: 'I sit between a chicken's wishbone on the mantlepiece and a dolphin's skull on the window sill'. But the absurdity is primarily established metrically by the ghost of a strict iambic pentameter ('And on the window sill a dolphin's skull') which plays against the overspill effect of the hexametric line and marginalises and deflates the sitting 'I'.

How then (and this is the opposite question) can a poet who so diminishes himself take a public ecological stance on behalf of the vegetation of the Burren or of the planet as he does on p. 52 of *The Ghost Orchid*, coupling the title poem with 'The White Garden'?

> So white are the white flowers in the white garden that I
> Disappear in no time at all among lace and veils.
> For whom do I scribble the few words that come to me
> From beyond the arch of white roses as from nowhere,
> My memorandum to posterity? Listen. 'The saw
> Is under the garden bench and the gate is unlatched.'

We have to decide how ephemeral (in comparison with 'Watercolour') in fact is the 'I' here[21] whose disappearance 'among lace and veils' introduces a gendered but not necessarily disempowering suggestion of nuns and weddings. The pronoun may be pushed to the end of the first line but the strong sense of a word-hoard suppressed for the sake of a powerful but limited vocabulary carries a counter-suggestive weight and authority:

three of the first line's six stresses fall on the word 'white', the sixth on the internally rhyming 'I'. As the poem relaxes into loose pentameter the lack of stress on 'me' at the end of line 3 necessitates the authoritative ring (enforced again by internal rhyme) of the 'My' in the penultimate line. (The poem's poise between personal and public voice is reinforced too by the knowledge that the words on an Athenian shard which are translated to convey the speaker's anger on behalf of the trees – and not just those at Sissinghurst,[22] his contempt for the depredator, were probably a matter-of-fact memo from master to gardener.)[23]

It must be apparent by now that the long line we are talking about is different from either Ciaran Carson's seven-beat simulation of the mode of the Irish storyteller[24] or the deliberately counterpointed metric which Derek Mahon uses to purge his 'Yaddo' and 'Hudson' letters[25] of wanton lyricism. Longley's own working definition, 'loose iambic',[26] would imply that the six-beat line emerges as an 'irregularity' out of the interplay between the pentameter and a speech rhythm governed partly by syntax. I can go along with that with the reservation that in some circumstances the hexametric possibility can momentarily threaten to take over, can become the ghost of an alternative metre (perhaps because of Longley's classicism and often when violence is the subject).[27] At its full stretch the metre I have just been defining appeared in two[28] poems in *The Echo Gate* (1979) which nicely disentangle two aspects of my more general theme: one anticipates Longley's increased impact as a literary personality after 1985, the other shows him universalising out of his Irish concerns as he does in 'The Ghost Orchid' or one of his finest long-line poems, 'Ghetto'. What is interesting about the first of the two poems in question, 'Dead Men's Fingers', is that its distinctive rhythms impart an intensity of feeling to something that in 1979 must have seemed private or esoteric:

> Indeed, I soon find myself, wherever a fire is lit,
> Crossing my legs, putting my feet up on the mantelpiece
> And talking to my shoes, with glances in her direction.
> The first time we meet is really the last time in reverse.
> We kiss for ever and I feel like the ghost of a child
> Visiting the mother who long ago aborted him.
>
> (*P* 181)

The coiled hexameters here intensify the sense that the callow nonchalance of the male speaker is retaliatory but to assimilate the precise implications of that last line the original readers would have to wait for the publication in 1985 of Longley's revealing autobiographical essay, 'Tuppenny Stung', to which I shall turn shortly.

The other long-line poem from *The Echo Gate* which I want to discuss puts the link between gender and violence in a public context and uses Longley's classical inheritance as a conscious resource. 'Peace' (subtitled 'after Tibullus') was commissioned in the mid-seventies by the Northern Irish Peace People. It was Longley's first considerable poem to emanate from translation since a version of Propertius completed in the early sixties and one could speculate that the classical metre is rubbing off on his loose iambic at the beginning of both the first and the third stanzas:

> Who was responsible for the very first arms deal –
> The man of iron who thought of marketing the sword? . . .
>
> A man could worship there with bunches of early grapes,
> A wreath of whiskery wheat-ears, and then say Thank You . .
>
> (P 169)

Admittedly the pentameter takes over to render the actively pacifying female presence:

> As for me, I want a woman
> To come and fondle my ears of wheat and let apples
> Overflow between her breasts. I shall call her Peace.
>
> (P 171)

But the hexameter is always available to simulate the ominous and omnipresent possibility of male violence:

> Compost for the vines, grape-juice turning into wine,
> Vintage years handed down from father to son;
> Hoe and ploughshare gleaming, while in some dark corner
> Rust keeps the soldier's grisly weapons in their place . . .
>
> (P 170)

Both the unexpected central caesura in that third line and the way the line itself lingers 'in some dark corner' are extremely effective.

Longley's next foray into the long line came when he was preparing *Poems 1963–1983*. Male brutality on the part of 'Grandpa George' who had disowned and thrown out 'his only son – / My sad retarded uncle' was the subject of a short-lined poem in *Man Lying on a Wall* (1976). Preparing to republish the poem ('Master of Ceremonies') (*MLW* 37) in 1984 Longley must have seen it in a prosodic context that now included the experiments in the long line I have just discussed and he ran the pairs of two- or three- beat lines together:

> In old age my grandfather demoted his flesh and blood
> And over the cribbage board ('Fifteen two, fifteen four,
> One for his nob') would call me Lionel. 'Sorry. My mistake.
> That was my nephew. His head got blown off in No Man's Land.'
>
> (P 133)

There is little subtlety about the hexametric tendency here and Longley himself has spoken of the poem as a little clumsy, but the slow build-up, the even distribution of six stresses in the last line and the consequent pressure to pause after 'head' seem to me to dramatise very well the domineering insensitivity of the poem's central figure.

It was probably important that this revision (picking up on an innovation which would later be developed to articulate both the energies of male violence and the public – or civilised – note which can accommodate and transcend them) coincided with the mood of contemplative reminiscence which was shortly to surface in 'Tuppenny Stung'.[29] Longley was there presenting a public version of his personal identity in a London poetry magazine (later book-publication in Belfast would confirm his Irish public status), yet it is obviously the result of quite painful introspection. Significant changes in a poet's rhythm stem not only from changes in his pattern of communication with the world, but also from revised internal contacts with the physical and psychological self. The new poems in *Poems 1963–1983*, while they were accompanied by the kind of rhythmical diminuendo which had alarmed Longley before,[30] also encompass the poet's imaginative negotiations with the death of his mother. *Tuppenny Stung*, in taking stock of a new emotional situation, finds itself interrogating (for admittedly a fairly narrowly literary public in the first instance) the gender implications of violence.

The myth-making possibilities of this theme (needing, as it turned out, Homer for their realisation) are apparent from the characteristically binary iconography of Longley's illustrations for the *Poetry Review* publication of the piece (which are reproduced here between pp. 136 and 137).[31] The photographs show us (and a whole familial dimension of the poetry is increasingly organised around these figures): two twins; two 'mothers', Lena and 'Mother' ('my mother concentrated on Peter, the slightly more difficult child. Lena looked after me and turned into my mother.')

(*TS* 15); and two patriarchal figures 'Captain Longley' and 'Grandpa George'. At the heart of Longley's binary obsession are the figures of himself and his twin, their identities first established in a conflict later transcended:

> We fought a lot, our differences so freely expressed that it is only recently that Peter and I have recognised how much we have in common as personalities. Beneath the tussles, tangles, power struggles an affection developed, natural, quotidian, inexpressible, so deep and lasting that to comprehend it would be a madness . . . When he was ten Wendy and I visited Peter in hospital where he was recovering from an eye-operation . . . His eyes were still in bandages when he returned home. I remember reading to him at night from *The Water Babies* and *The Snow Queen* and feeling completely fulfilled – fraternal, paternal, maternal. Being a lover, a husband, a father has since enabled me to draw parallel lines only.
>
> <div align="right">(<i>TS</i> 24)</div>

Longley is constructing what classicists would call an ascending scale of affection,[32] placing a relationship which transcends gender at its pinnacle. An early treatment of the same experience had subverted conventional gender-roles in its speaker ('me reading to you like a mother') and in the indirect fantasy identification of one or both twins through Tom, the 'chimney sweep' from *The Water Babies*, with a 'beautiful girl' whose face is 'a reflection in clean water':

> I remember your eyes in bandages
> And me reading to you like a mother;
> Our grubby redeemer, the chimney-sweep
> Whose baptism among the seaweed
> Began when he stopped astounded beside
> The expensive bed, the white coverlet,
> The most beautiful girl he had ever seen –
> Her hair on the eiderdown like algae,
> Her face a reflection in clean water;
>
> <div align="right">'Readings' (<i>P</i> 75)</div>

In the mordant world of another story 'The Snow Queen', however, gender- and incest-taboos seem to accompany existential isolation and the making of a sacrificial victim:

> Kay and Gerda in their separate attics;
> The icicle driven into Kay's heart –
> Then a glance at the pillow where you

Longley's Long Line: Looking Back From The Ghost Orchid

Twisted your head again and tried to squeeze
Light like a tear through the bandages.

The pressurised fantasy world of the twins (or, again, of one of them, the speaker) generates the further binary, 'two mothers' in its contrast between a Kleinian bad mother (the Snow Queen responsible for the 'icicle driven into Kay's heart') and a 'good mother':

The Irishwoman haunting Tom's shoulder –
The shawl's canopy, the red petticoats
Arriving beside him again and again,
The white feet accompanying his feet,
All of the leafy roads down to the sea.

The poem, of course, secure in its ambience of rich textuality, did not need such disclaimers as 'an affection developed, natural, quotidian, inexpressible, so deep and lasting that to comprehend it would be a madness'. But in 'Tuppenny Stung' Longley is vitalising channels of communication with a wider public upon which he will rely for the less private resonance of his next book of verse, *Gorse Fires*. In autobiographical prose two twins can now be explicitly seen, according to the involuntary logic of the emotional life, as necessitating two mothers:

I began by loving the wrong woman.
In 1936, when she was seventeen, Lena came from County Fermanagh to work for my parents as a maid. At approximately 4 pm on July 27 1939 I was born, followed half an hour later by my twin, Peter. My sister Wendy was nine when we arrived. According to her we were cranky babies, victims of the now discredited Truby King method of feeding by strict regime rather than demand. We did not get enough milk and because we yelled day and night were kept in separate rooms and prams – one at the back of the house, the other in the porch at the front. My mother concentrated on Peter, the slightly more difficult child. Lena looked after me and turned into my mother. She exchanged the uniform of a maid for that of a nurse, but this was for her much more than a promotion. She was a natural and devoted surrogate mother: the two of us became inseparable.
(*TS* 15)

The potential of 'Mother' as she is titled in Longley's choice of photographs, to be the 'bad mother' (already implicit in her use of the Truby King feeding method and perhaps in her concentration 'on Peter') is reinforced by her active hostility to the two children when first conceived:

My father died in 1960 when I was twenty and too young to appreciate his strengths or understand his weaknesses. My mother died in April 1979. For about a year beforehand we both knew that she was going to die. I wanted to feel free to embrace her as I had embraced Lena, and agreed to call with her every day for five minutes or five hours – for as long as both of us could stand it. Over several tumultuous months we lived out her childhood and mine. She gave me X-ray pictures in which the shadowy shapes of Peter and me curl up and tangle about five months after conception. ('Tuppenny Stung for a penny bung,' my father had said.) She confessed that in the early days of the pregnancy she had attempted in an amateurish way to abort us – or 'it' as we then were. I registered neither shock nor pain. Somehow this knowledge made it easier for me to hug her dying lopsided body. It was like a courtship, and I accompanied her on my arm to death's door.

(TS 28–29)

In retrospect it is interesting that the threat of violence to the then unborn 'I' of the poems, first attributed to (male against male) warfare

> (. . . your proper funeral urn
> Had mercifully smashed to smithereens,
> To shrapnel shards that sliced your testicle.
> That instant I, your most unlikely son,
> In No Man's Land was surely left for dead,
> Blotted out from your far horizon.
> As your voice now is locked inside my head,
> I yet was held secure, waiting my turn.)[33]

shifts, subsequent to the confession detailed above, to the speaker's companion in the womb

> (I came into being alongside a twin brother
> Who threatened me at first like an abortionist
> Recommending suicide jumps and gin with cloves.
> Then he blossomed into my guardian angel.)[34]

and to the Belle Dame Sans Merci figure of the erotic adventure poem 'Dead Men's Fingers' mentioned above

> (We kiss for ever and I feel like the ghost of a child
> Visiting the mother who long ago aborted him.)[35]

before emerging into autobiographical light. What is crucial about that last passage from 'Tuppenny Stung' is that maternal violence and filial forgiveness are seen in such close proximity to the 'strengths or ... weaknesses' of 'Captain Longley' and his cynically humorous insinuation that the very engendering of twins is somehow unnatural, a penalty, Nature's revenge ('Tuppenny Stung for a penny bung'). In his formally retaliatory creative initiative ('waiting my turn' as he says in the stanza I quote above from 'In Memoriam') Longley detaches these words from their original context, using them to provide a title to categorise his own disorientatingly binary maternal predicament ('I began by loving the wrong woman') which he will elsewhere connect (with, as we shall see, certain sacrificial overtones) to his poetic vocation. ('Captain Longley' himself, in contrast to 'Grandpa George',[36] is given an honourable place in Longley's redemptive scale of gender values as one can see by comparing the account (*TS* 19) of him behaving 'most vitally in women's company, and most peacefully as well' with the sly concluding lines from 'Peace' quoted above.)

To see the mythic potential of Longley's binarily obsessional personal universe one has only to set it against the extraordinary extended meditation on the worlds of Sophoclean drama, folklore and primitive religion contained in René Girard's *Violence and the Sacred*:[37]

At the core of the Oedipus myth, as Sophocles presents it, is the proposition that all masculine relationships are based on reciprocal acts of violence.

(p. 48)

And if the lost sexual difference [when women in Greek tragedy are violent] makes it easier to shunt the responsibility for violence onto the women, it still cannot explain away the necessity for violence. Like the animal and the infant, but to a lesser degree, the woman qualifies for sacrificial status by reason of her weakness and relatively marginal social status.

(pp. 141–2)

Twins invariably share a cultural identity, and they often have a striking physical resemblance to each other. Wherever differences are lacking, violence threatens.

(p. 57)

The antagonists . . . invariably believe themselves separated by insurmountable differences. In reality, however, these differences gradually wear away. Everywhere we now encounter the same desire, the same antagonism, the same strategies – the same illusion of rigid differentiation within a pattern of ever-expanding uniformity. As the crisis grows more acute, the community members are transformed into 'twins', matching images of violence. I would be tempted to say that they are each *doubles* of the other.

(pp. 78–9)

Girard makes it quite clear that the worlds he describes are different from our world but they are not totally different. With Longley's penchant for the phantasmagorical in mind one could say that they are not different from the world of our dreams. What is more, as Frank Wright has revealingly shown in *Northern Ireland: a Comparative Analysis*,[38] they resemble in a number of ways the behavioural patterns that obtain at particular periods in particular geographical areas (the American South early this century, 'The Balkans' at irregular intervals, Northern Ireland on and off since its inception) which Wright calls 'ethnic frontiers'. Girard's version of mythic space offers a ready commentary on a poem like 'Poppies' with its antagonists who 'believe themselves separated by insurmountable differences', while they 'are transformed into "twins", matching images of violence'. But Longley's overall vision is different from Girard's in its redemptive scale of gender values and its recourse to the earlier classical terrain of Homer where negotiation is usually (cf. 'Ceasefire') but not always (cf. 'The Butchers') at a premium.[39]

Of course, Longley's outreach to the public domain by way of Homer begins in dialogue with the autobiographical materials, so confirming Clair Wills's recognition that the Northern Irish poet must 'root public statement in personal experience, from which it derives its authenticity and hence the authority to speak of more communal concerns.'[40] Longley was already doing this in 'Wounds' when he enlarged on his father's war experience (told him in childhood) as a mode of access to the varieties of Northern Irish violence. In retrospect, though, one can see the force of the mythic dimension now provided by Homer: the over-anxious twin, taking first a vatic and later an almost maternal responsibility for the wounded parent in, respectively, 'In Memoriam' ('Let yours / And other heartbreaks play into my hands') (*P* 48) and 'Wounds' ('I touched his hand, his thin head I touched') (*P* 86) gives way to the well-adjusted filial presence of 'Northern Lights' (*GF* 32) precisely because on the facing page (33) of *Gorse Fires*

> ... Laertes recognised his son and, weak at the knees,
> Dizzy, flung his arms around the neck of great Odysseus
> Who drew the old man fainting to his breast and held him there
> And cradled like driftwood the bones of his dwindling father.

Portrait of Michael Longley, 'Light from Two Windows' by Jeffrey Morgan, now hanging in the Waterfront Hall, Belfast. Reproduced by courtesy of the artist.

Above left: ML as a sixth former at the Royal Belfast Academical Institution, 1957. Above right: ML as an undergraduate at Trinity College, Dublin. This photo accompanied a profile in the undergraduate weekly, *Trinity News*. Below: ML with Derek Mahon, John Hewitt and Seamus Heaney at Cushendall, Co. Antrim, 1969.

Above: a literary evening at the Lyric Theatre, Belfast. Back row, left to right, Paul Muldoon, John Hewitt, Patrick Galvin, Frank Ormsby and Ciaran Carson; front row, Seamus Deane, John Boyd and ML, *c.* 1975. Photo: George Craig. Below: ML with Francis Stuart, and the painter Neil Shawcross at Stuart's reading for The Queen's University English Society, *c.* 1985. Photo: Geraldine Sweeney.

Above: ML with co-tutor Paul Muldoon at the Arvon Foundation, Lumb Bank, Yorkshire, 1985. Below: ML with John Montague, the American poet Donald Hall, and Frank Ormsby, in the Crown Bar, Belfast, November 1998.

Above: ML with his daughter Rebecca, photographed by Solly Lipsitz in 1969. Below: ML photographed at the Arts Council of Northern Ireland in 1985, when he was Combined Arts Director.

ML with his wife Edna, and children Dan and Sarah, photographed by the composer George Newson at his home in Stone-in-Oxney, Kent, Summer, 1986.

Longley's Long Line: Looking Back From The Ghost Orchid

My stress-markings are intended to show how the long line in the Homeric context has amplified what Douglas Dunn called Longley's characteristic 'release into gentleness and into an affection which seems bewildered but always benevolent, always strange, always at an imagined angle to reality'[41] to bring authenticity to something like the opening of 'Ceasefire':

> Pūt in mīnd of his ōwn fāther and mōved to teārs
> Achilles tōok him by the hānd and pūshed the ōld kīng
> Gēntly awāy. . .
>
> (*GO* 39)

Longley's selective use of the Homeric materials (often incorporated in a kind of collage along with original lines and stanzas) engineers a kind of gapped discourse, across which the reader can make tenuous associative links between the lyric, autobiographical, epic and socio-political dimensions of what he/she is reading. We come closest to identifying the origins of the recent work's ever-increasing range of voices in 'Eurycleia' where Odysseus, the 'great Odysseus' of 'Laertes' as well as the brutal aggressor of 'The Butchers' is identified[42] with the poet by way of the late-Romantic/Modernist[43] trope of the creative wound:

> Odysseus shifted out of the firelight, afraid
> She might notice his scar, the key to his identity,
> A wound a boar inflicted years back, a flesh wound.
>
> (*GF* 31)

If the key to the speaker's (creative) identity is his wound, then the source of the wound becomes significant:

> I began like Odysseus by loving the wrong woman
> Who has disappeared among the skyscrapers of New York
> After wandering for thousands of years from Ithaca.
> She alone remembers the coppice, dense and overgrown,
> Where in a compost of dead leaves the boar conceals
> Its bristling spine and fire-red eyes and white tusks.

It is no accident that the first prose sentence of 'Tuppenny Stung' has been extended into a pentameter in the first line quoted here, equating for the reader the mythic with the autobiographic, suggesting that the 'flesh-wound' has a cross-gendered source. The final line would at first seem to be a hexameter tensed up to embody the threat of male violence on the part of the 'boar' which

> concēals
> Its brīstling spīne and fīre-red ēyes and whīte tūsks.

Table IV

```
                    ┌─────────────┐
                    │ 'EURYCLEIA' │
                    │     p31     │
                    └─────────────┘

    ┌─────────────┐  ┌─────────────┐
    │  'NORTHERN  │  │  'LAERTES'  │
    │   LIGHTS'   │  │             │
    │     p32     │  │     p33     │
    └─────────────┘  └─────────────┘

    ┌─────────────┐  ┌─────────────┐        ⇌
    │'THE BALLOON'│  │ 'ANTICLEIA' │
    │     p34     │  │     p35     │
    └─────────────┘  └─────────────┘
```

But rereading the stanza as a whole there seems no doubt that the 'right woman', tactically absent from the poem, is illogically, explosively and inextricably implicated in those final three lines. Or, to put the point another way: in this poem an ambiguous textuality is again to be seen (cf. 'Readings') at the heart of Longley's concern with gender. One final diagram (Table IV) is needed to show the way this esoteric core resonates outwards through pp. 31–35 of *Gorse Fires*, the individual poems confirming each other in their oblique enactment of the dilemma made public property in 'Tuppenny Stung':

> I begān like Odȳsseus by lōving the wrōng wōman ...
> 'Eurycleia'(p. 31)

> Your hānd on my shōulder, your tobācco-y brēath
> And the sōlar wīnd that rŭffled your thĭnning hāir,
> 'Northern Lights' (p. 32)

> Odȳsseus
> Who drēw the ōld mān faīnting to his brēast and hēld him there
> And crādled ...
> 'Laertes' (p. 33)

> Yōu are a chīld in the drēam and nōt my mōther ...
> 'The Balloon' (p. 34)

> And you āsk her whȳ she kēeps avoīding your tŏuch and wēep
> Because hēre is your mōther and ēven hēre in Hādes
> You could cŏmfort eāch ōther in a shŭddering embrāce, ...
> 'Anticleia' (p. 35)

Each of the Homeric treatments of the familial (examples 3 and 5) engages the full extent of the long line to at once complement and undercut, intensify and distance the gender-implications of the facing autobiographical poem. Once more while documenting Longley's move from left to right in the private ⇌ public continuum depicted in Table II above it is important to stress (and this would be true of any good poet) the interdependence of these poles.

'HOW DO YOU SEW THE NIGHT?':
THE WEATHER IN JAPAN

ALAN J. PEACOCK

The Ghost Orchid closes with a haunting couplet which asserts once again Longley's central preoccupation with the antinomies of love and death:

> Love poems, elegies: I am losing my place.
> Elegies come between me and your face.

There is a sense here of the ascendancy of elegy, as if the speaker is confusing the genres of elegy and love lyric and 'losing my place' like a faltering reader. There is also a hint of philological play in that Tibullus' and Propertius' love poems are technically 'elegies' (i.e., poems in the elegiac metre: a hexameter followed by a pentameter), and in the fact that both are famously death-haunted poets – whose importance for Longley is reasserted in 'Remembering the Poets' in *The Weather in Japan* and in their citation as exempla of the true poetic spirit in 'Damiana'. This latest collection of poems subsumes the material in the 1998 booklet *Broken Dishes* (which consists largely of elegies),[1] but incorporates it within a more broadly articulated thematic and allusive overall context.

What this elegiac core in *The Weather in Japan* luminously reminds us of, however, is the fact that an elegy is both a poem of loss and one of celebration (just as the tone of the programmatic couplet quoted above is poised between sadness and wit), and this ambiguous chemistry pervades the volume. In 'The Altar Cloth: in memory of Marie Ewart', for instance, a sense of vital human presence is movingly set in counterweight to mortal loss. The 'addressee' is vividly evoked in her Italian domicile –

> Your laughter a wild duck's navigational call,
> Your argumentativeness Alexandrian, obstreperous
> Your liking for big obstreperous dogs with big tails . . . –

but this summoning of presence is 'in retrospect', and qualified by a *memento mori* which turns on a Latin pun but draws its imagery from the intimately observed natural world:

> Shouldn't we be sheltering beneath the altar cloth's
> Pattern of grapes and vine-leaves, for this is our last
> Conversation and the crab is nipping your synapses,
> Sifting your memory through its claws and frilly lips?[2]

This unsettling, equivocal memorial gesture, humane but unillusioned, disturbing but strangely beautiful, represents the ethos of the volume in concentrate. In the movement within the poem from past to present tense and then again to past, and in the following of the elegiac convention of direct address together with the use of imagery suggesting the materiality of consciousness, Longley realizes the potential for consolation in the formal elegiac mode, while simultaneously acknowledging the assuaging fictions endemic in the received conventions.

The elegy for Sean Dunne, 'A Sprig of Bay', formally memorializes and celebrates in a similarly affective mix. Within the relaxed, familiar overall tone of the poem ('I wish I could introduce you to this friend of mine'), the neoclassical dedication of bay leaves is both a formal tribute and a warm human gesture as the sprig is wittily offered to 'Sean, cook and poet' – something to go with 'the dried beans in your Cork bed-sit'. The suggestion of practical usefulness subtly and affectionately humanizes dedicatory convention to balance a sense of presence against absence, sentiment against rationality – the same kind of human impulse which led MacNeice, in 'Memoranda to Horace', to voice his intimate sense of fellow-feeling with the Roman poet across the millenia 'on the offchance'.[3]

The Weather in Japan contains many formal elegies, or poems of an elegiac cast, to friends, family, fellow-artists, animals and, notably, war casualties in a variety of stylistic and emotional registers – but with a developing impression of inter-relatedness. Once again, Longley's father's status as a 'belated' war casualty provides intimate familial linkage, as in 'January 12, 1996' (quoted in the Introduction); but see also 'The Moustache':

> The moustache Edward Thomas grew to cover up
> His aesthete's features, the short-back-and-sides hair-do
> That moved him to the centre of modern times, recall
> My father, aged twenty, in command of a company ...

Thomas is a talismanic presence in this volume (cf. also, in this

'How do you sew the night?': The Weather in Japan

connection, 'Poetry' and 'The War Graves'), and the conflation of his image with that of Captain Longley is as significant in context as the twinning of Laertes and Longley senior in *Gorse Fires* where, in a way that recalls Longley's comforting of his 'slowly' dying father in 'Wounds' ('I touched his hand, his thin head I touched'):

> ... Laertes recognised his son and, weak at the knees,
> Dizzy, flung his arms around the neck of great Odysseus
> Who drew the old man fainting to his breast and held him there
> And cradled like driftwood the bones of his dwindling father.
>
> (*GF* 33)

Consistently in *The Weather in Japan* the personal meshes with the general, the past with the present, in webs of association which often ingeniously or idiosyncratically reinforce an inclusively compassionate, but stark and unblinking apprehension of mortality and existential exigency which, typically, extends beyond the merely human predicament. 'Death of a Horse', for instance, with controlled pathos describes the individual animal's unquestioning submission to its fate:

> Its expression resigned, humble even, as if it knows
> And doesn't mind when the man draws the first diagonal
> In white across its forehead, from ear to eyeball, then
> The second, death's chalky intersection, the cross-roads
>
> Where, moments before the legs stiffen and relax and
> The knees give way and like water from a burst drain
> The blood comes jetting out, black almost, warm and thick,
> The horse goes on standing still, just staring ahead.

Longley does not provide a specific narrative situation for what however reads like a kind of 'execution'; and the sub-title 'after Keith Douglas' inevitably suggests a war ethos, so that the animal's mute acceptance of its fate takes on something of a parabolic dimension.

In fact, a comparison with the prose vignette by Douglas from which Longley gleans his poem by a process of excerption shows how decisively he has made the animal's meek stoicism the emotive focus of the poem – and the poem itself more decisively a 'war' poem. (In Douglas, the chalked cross is not, as it might seem in Longley, a target but a marker for the application of a device for putting down a broken-legged horse, prior to an instructional dissection by a vet and his orderly; and the locale is probably that of a training camp in England.) The whole emphasis of Douglas' piece – on the various responses of his characters to the slaughter and then messy dissection, right up to the fainting of the narrator – is jettisoned in a deft process of phrasal collage where, for instance, the first stanza is an almost verbatim conflation of phrases culled from four separate paragraphs of Douglas' prose piece:

Its expression was resigned and humble . . . 'It does know, but it doesn't seem to mind.' . . . And he [the vet] drew a line with the chalk, diagonally across the horse's forehead: from the base of the left ear, more or less towards the right eye. Then he drew another line, diagonally the other way . . . The orderly moved forward holding something, a sort of tube, which he put against the intersection of lines on the horse's forehead.[4]

In Longley's poem, the intensifying 'eyeball' replaces 'eye', and the added image of 'the cross-roads' graphically and dramatically pivots into the second stanza, but the remainder is essentially pared-down Douglas; and creative editing is even more in evidence in the second stanza, where 'like water from a burst drain / The blood comes jetting out . . . ' simultaneously with the killing, whereas in Douglas this is part of an extensive post-mortem procedure. By this technique of excerption and subtle shifting of emphasis, Longley creates a stark, elemental poem, restricted to no particular time or place (if anything, without the Douglas sub-title, the *mise en scène* might appear to be First World War), which functions as a moving companion-piece to 'The Horses'. This poem, which begins with a similarly generalised (but this time with a strong First World War coloration) tribute to 'all of the horses butchered on the battlefield, / Shell-shocked, tripping up over their own intestines', finds their 'best war memorial'

> . . . in Homer: two horses that refuse to budge
> Despite threats and sweet-talk and the whistling whip . . .
> Because they are still in mourning for Patroclus
> Their charioteer, their shiny manes bedraggled
> Under the yoke-pads on either side of the yoke.

As so often in Longley, whether in the context of the Northern Irish Troubles, Homer, or twentieth century World War experience and the Holocaust, the focus is upon the innocent victim – the human (or animal) consequences of inhuman processes. 'The poetry is in the pity' and when, in 'All of these People' in *The Weather in Japan*, he shifts to a more rhetorical note of protest, the impact of his outrage draws strength from his previous intimate memorial celebrations of the inestimable value of the same 'ordinary' lives (cf. 'The Greengrocer' (*P* 148) – 'He ran a good shop, and he died . . . ' – and 'The Ice-cream Man' (*GF* 49)) whose consequence in the larger scheme of things this poem continues to insist upon: 'All of these people, alive or dead, are civilised'. This final, unifying use of the present tense keys in with similar acts of reclamation, assertion and celebration elsewhere in the volume.

In the long, meditative poem, 'The War Graves', there is a literally tactile attempt to make contact, across many decades, with casualties who are otherwise just names:

> I don't know how Rifleman Parfitt, Corporal Vance,
> Private Costello of the Duke of Wellingtons,
> Driver Chapman, Topping, Atkinson, Duckworth,
> Dorrell, Wood come to be written in my diary,
>
> For as high as we can reach we touch-read the names
> Of the disappeared . . .

That last term vibrates ominously in the modern political context, and it also has a familial resonance for Longley, whose mentally retarded uncle 'disappeared' in the trenches of the First World War; but the attempt, in 'The War Graves', to conjure a presence out of names also recalls George Seferis' inch-by-inch searching over an archaeological site in the Peloponnese for some kind of reality attaching to a name mentioned fleetingly in Homer in his poem, 'The King of Asine'.[5] In the context of Longley's own poetry, it is also yet another variant on 'Longley's lists'[6] (cf., especially, 'The Ice-cream Man'), and a compressed meditation on the metaphysics of naming. As Neil Corcoran notes in the present volume in connection with Longley's botany, in his work 'the onomastic' is 'ambivalently caught between wildflower delight and something more melancholy and resigned'; and within such poles of implication a poem like 'The War Graves' can pulse between a sense of absence and presence, between closed and open perspectives:

> At the Canadian front line permanent sandbags
> And duckboards admit us to the underworld, and then
> With the beavers we surface for long enough to hear
> The huge lamentations of the wounded caribou.

At base, in the ambivalent, poignant vacillations between 'wildflower delight' and 'something more melancholy and resigned', there is an application of the familiar Horatian trope where death and love are located within a natural 'decorum' of seasonal change and renewal, and where the one presupposes the other in a continuing cycle; but in Longley the usage is less formulaic, less dramatically managed than in Horace's *Odes*. There is an edgier awareness of the limits of the artist's power or prerogative in the face of existential realities.

Thus, in a number of elegies in the volume, as in 'The War Graves' ('we pick from a nettle bed / One celandine each, the flower that outwits winter'), reference to plant, creature or natural landscape allows an ending at a rising point along the broader life-death continuum. 'The Snow Leopard', dedicated to the memory of Fiona Jackson (1970–1995), gently chafes, in section I, against conventional consolatory formulae:

> I couldn't recommend to you the Elysian Fields
> At the world's end with fair-haired Rhadamanthus,
> Though there, Fiona, you would still be you, your body
> Temperature controlled by westerlies off the waves,
>
> No snowfall, according to the old man of the sea,
> No cold spells or cloudbursts to help you feel at home,
> No wreaths of frost-flowers on your bedroom window,
> No snowman in the garden as your memorial.

In section II, conventional bouquets are offered, but in III a mythicised detail from the natural world provides the final, salving image:

> The snow leopard that vanishes in a whirlwind of snow
> Can be seen stalking on soft paws among the clouds.

Similarly, on a broader, more public scale, in 'A Poppy' the commonality of human experience in war is inclusively suggested by reference to a literary motif which loops back from the First World War (cf. Charles Sorley: 'When you see millions of the mouthless dead . . . '[7] and Longley's reference to his 'monumental sonnet' in 'The War Graves') to Homer and then forward again, via Virgil, to the present moment:

> When millions march into the mincing machine
> An image in Homer picks out the individual
> Tommy and the doughboy in his doughboy helmet:
> 'Lolling to one side like a poppy in a garden
> Weighed down by its seed capsule and rainwater,
> His head drooped under the heavy, crestfallen

> Helmet' (an image Virgil steals – *lasso papavera*
> *Collo* – and so do I) . . .

This sense of a tradition of humane literary response to war and its casualties then allows the possibility of an assuaging conceit whereby the historical experience of millenia is related to processes of recurrence in the natural world and human rituals of sacrifice and renewal:

> And the poppy that sheds its flower-heads in a day
> Grows in one summer four hundred more, which means
> Two thousand petals overlapping as though to make
> A cape for the corn-goddess or a soldier's soul.

In 'The Mustard Tin' however, a poem of more immediate familial loss, adequate consolatory formulae are unavailable:

> You are dying and not sleeping soundly because
> Your eyes stay open and it doesn't seem to hurt.
> We want you to blink and find three of us standing
> For a few seconds between you and the darkness.
>
> Your mouth has opened so wide you appear to scream.
> We will need something to close your terrible yawn.
> I hoke around in my childhood for objects without
> Sharp edges and recover the oval mustard tin.
>
> A daughter strokes your forehead and says: 'There. There.'
> A daughter holds your hand and says: 'I'm sorry.'
> I focus on the mustard tin propping your jaw,
> On the total absence of the oval mustard tin.

The poet has no more to offer in consolatory terms than others at the bedside. The importance of poetry and the poet's prerogative are relative to other human values, utterances and observances.

Of course, this humble sense of aporia is expressed in a poem of masterful technical resource (the unsparingly apt conceit of the 'terrible yawn'; the use of anaphora in the final stanza; the haunting, strategic repetition of 'the oval mustard tin'; the insistent use of the present tense which leaves that terminal repetition suspended and unresolvable, like an image in a recurring nightmare); but the governing ethic, the sense of candour and humility in the face of 'ordinary' human experience is only the more powerfully registered by virtue of the paradox. The only formula which seems adequate to the situation is in fact the form which the poem actually finds: the stark, unsentimental bearing of witness in strict stanzaic form, where unflinchingly honest observation is given a disturbing oneiric edge by the fantasy of 'the oval mustard tin'.

'Pascoli's Portrait' in a less extreme situation similarly puts into equivocal or diminishing perspective the poet's status:

> Dining under your portrait at Ponte di Campia
> I need hardly apologise for not knowing
> Your poetry, although I hear wingbeats and see
> An eye that sees the skylark and the skylark's eye.
>
> Since a poem's little more than a wing and a prayer,
> I turn back to my dinner and pretend our souls
> Are roosting on the broken lamp beneath the eaves.
> Splashes of birdlime on the pavement give us away.

Fanciful ghostly communings between poets in the eaves are a side-show to the actual meal in hand. A poem is 'little more than a wing and a prayer', and fame is (geographically and culturally) relative. The civic memorial, like the 'hero-courageous tomb' in Kavanagh, is of questionable status, and in this provincial Italian hamlet the Northern Irish 'blow-in' is logically more of a culturally invisible presence than his defunct, locally celebrated, addressee. Marginality and invisibility are however equably embraced as the two poetic souls are wittily seen as making their impression on the scene in the form of 'birdlime on the pavement'. The idea of souls as birds[8] is thus, with mellow humour, 'grounded' in the observable phenomena of the natural world. Metaphysics cedes to quotidian reality in a wry comparison where term, in the avian comparison, is mischievously allowed to become anarchically over-graphic (an ironic, philosophically rueful variant on such an earlier, lyrical subversion of the expected relationship between term and referent as 'snipe the weight of the human soul' (P 119)).[9] The cautiously sceptical approach to metaphysics and the appeal to nature are Horatian, but the intimate witness, in this connection, to the processes of the biological and zoological world is distinctively Longley's own.

The naturalist's aim is to be invisible, to be an unobtrusive part of a landscape, to merge with it; and imagery of evanescence and disappearance within and into a landscape, has been a notable feature of, in particular, Longley's Mayo poems. The means of ultimate merging with a 'place of dispersals' where 'I ... disintegrate / Like a hillside neighbour / Erased by sea mist' ('Landscape', P 126) and a landscape where 'separating vertebrae

/ And scapulae litter a sandy wind' ('In Mayo', P 118) is of course to become, in the inevitable cycle, a part of this detritus. Any identification prior to that runs the risk of presumption; and in 'Detour' (GF 7), in the social sphere, only in imagined death does the protagonist see himself as 'part of the action', an unnoticed part of the quotidian scene. Longley's winning, seasoned irony in this poem on the issue of death and belonging or not belonging (see Introduction) turns precisely on the ambiguous import of 'invisibility': i.e. denoting on the one hand what is unseen or marginal; or, simultaneously, what is so much a natural, integrated part of things as to be beyond noticing. Hence in 'Between Hovers':

> I watched a dying otter gaze right through me
> At the islands in Clew Bay, as though it were only
> Between hovers and not too far from the holt.
>
> (GF 5)

The 'holt', the permanent domicile, is associated with death; and the dying animal's diminished sensory awareness does not distinguish the protagonist from the landscape, as the common social application of the term 'looked right through me' is revised – and its effect deepened by the echo of MacNeice's ambivalent use of it in the final stanza of 'The Taxis':

> As for the fourth taxi, he was alone
> Tra-la when he hailed it but the cabby looked
> Through him and said: 'I can't tra-la well take
> So many people, not to speak of the dog.'[10]

MacNeice's, however, is a surreal poem of absurdist alienation: Longley's by contrast is a muted paean to place and fellow-creature.

In *The Weather in Japan*, then, Longley's profound scruple concerning belonging or authentic presence in landscape or locale continues to be voiced with an intense, plangent sense of identification, but with a lack of presumption which amounts to a territorial ethic:

> A moment before the comber turns into
> A breaker – sea-spray, raggedy rainbows –
> Water and sunlight contain all the colours
> And suspend between Inishbofin and me
> The otter, and thus we meet, without my scent
> In her nostrils, the uproar of my presence,

> My unforgivable shadow on the sand –
> Even if this is the only sound I make.
>
> ('The Comber')

The stand-off, the sense of intrusion and trespass in Carrigskeewaun territory which, as the term goes, Longley has otherwise 'made his own', the intimate tuning into the magnified register of the animal's sensory systems in 'the uproar of my presence' – all these qualify any easy sense of communion; and respect for the 'otherness' of animals, as represented by the otter, is characteristically articulated by the speaker's reference to his problematic status in *their* world. In this sense the poem continues the self-effacing ethic of 'Autumn Lady's Tresses' or 'The Eel-trap', in *The Ghost Orchid*; but now ethical scruple exerts a firmer control upon symbiotic lyricism. In 'The Eel-trap', the naturalist's non-interventionist discipline adds pathos to the sense of affinity and concern –

> I lie awake and my mind goes out to the otter
> That might be drowning in the eel-trap . . . –

but the otter is nevertheless part of a lyrically apprehended nexus of relationships:

> your breathing
> Falters as I follow you to the other lake
> Below sleep, the brown trout sipping at the stars.
>
> (*GO* 34)

In this connection, then, 'The Comber' and the other nature poems which open *The Weather in Japan* signal a subtly modified angle of vision in the volume. 'Water-burn' for instance looks back to 'Phosphorescence' – a lyrical high-spot of *Gorse Fires* ('water-burn' is Scots for 'phosphorescence'); and Carrigskeewaun remains magical territory:

> We should have been galloping on horses, their hoofprints
> Splashes of light, divots kicked out of the darkness,
> Or hauling up lobster pots in a wake of sparks. Where
> Were the otters and seals? Were the dolphins on fire?
> Yes, we should have been doing more with our lives.

But the idyll is shadowed now by a sense of something vaguely amiss, in a way that becomes clear in 'The Lapwing':

> Carrigskeewaun in May light has unsettled me.
> Each butterwort flourishes an undertaker's lamp

> For the poisoned swan unfolding on David's pond
> Like a paper flower in a saucer . . .

As that equivocal, bitter-sweet image indicates, the lyric response to place and creature is complicated by a hint of pollution, of ecological threat – even in this sequestered (as yet not seriously 'developed') corner of western Ireland. The sense of disturbance, however, is not over-stated, and may even intensify a poignant feeling of mutuality; but it pushes lyric communion into an embattled, exposed, elegiac register:

> . . . 'Milkwort',
> I mumble to the piss-scattering wind. 'Why me?'
> The lapwing replies and falters like a bi-plane
> Above her nest. 'Why me?' The lapwing and I
> Watch over each other and we speak in tongues.

The ambiguous collocation of beautiful and disturbing images in this poem is characteristic of the volume (cf. the comments on 'The Altar Cloth' above) and perhaps the key to its strange intensities; and this is not any sort of single-issue matter, such as that of pollution. 'Pale Butterwort' for instance utilizes imagery derived from *undisordered* nature for an effect not dissimilar to that in 'The Lapwing':

> . . . a buzzard distracted me
> As it quartered the tree-tops and added its skraik
> Or screel to the papery purr of the dragonflies'
> Love-flight, and with so much happening overhead
> I forgot the pale butterwort there on the ground
> Spreading its leaves like a starfish and digesting
> Insects that squirm on each adhesive tongue and
> Feed the terror in your eyes, your smoky blue eyes.

It is not so much the recognition of both the apparently benign and the more savage aspects of nature which is at issue (this has been a regular trade-mark of Longley's poetry over the years), but the delicately poised contiguity of seductive and unsettling detail.

Translated into the sphere of human mortal destiny, this equivocal vision produces 'the crab . . . nipping your synapses, / Sifting your memory through its claws and frilly lips . . . ' ('The Altar Cloth') or, in 'Sweetie Papers', a radical mixture of childhood recollection and mature response to the visual arts which, through imagery of papery delicacy, disconcertingly opens up vistas of the most extreme and brutal experience of our era:

> When sweeties came back to Mrs Parker's shop we
> Drooled over the look of them and smoothed out at home
> Tinfoil and cellophane, a little bit like Pierre
> Bonnard's collection of sweetie papers, his 'sparkles'
> Pinned to the wall, light-conductors for the late
> Self-portraits as Japanese soldier or collaborator
> Punched and kicked in the face until his eyes close
> Or death-camp survivor, the skin across his chest
> Transparent as cigarette paper . . .

The revisionist 'take' upon Bonnard's famous Second World War quietism, whereby 'escapism' is re-imagined as an intense domestic filter through which highly coloured impressions of war and atrocity are registered, provides that remarkable, sickly-sweet image of the 'death-camp survivor, the skin across his chest / Transparent as cigarette paper . . . ' which with disturbing visual finesse meshes with the 'tinfoil and cellophane' of the poem's naive, child's eye overall frame. It is the same kind of subtly unnerving conflation as produced 'the poisoned swan unfolding . . . Like a paper flower in a saucer . . . ' in 'The Lapwing'.

This kind of tensioning, this *recto* and *verso* response to a given thematic element, is a consistent reflex through the volume. There is, for instance, a continuation of Longley's characteristically measured, free translations of selected material from Homer in poems such as 'The Garden' and 'The Vision of Theoclymenus'; but there is also a vein of wilder Homeric spin-offs in poems like 'Heartsease', 'The Parody' and 'In the Iliad'. Here witty and idiosyncratic angles of approach to the *Iliad* disrupt easy categories. In 'Heartsease', a seemingly genially colloquial gloss on a detail from Homer suddenly (like the disconcerting Holocaust images in 'Sweetie Papers') moves into a second frame of reference –

> When Helen, destroyer of cities, destroyer of men,
> Slipped the lads a Mickey Finn of wine and heartsease,
> Unhappiness's cure, a painkiller strong enough
> To keep you dry-eyed for a day even if mummy
> Or daddy pegs out, or your brother or son's been bumped off
> On the doorstep in front of you . . . –

but as suddenly tempers the shock of this with a playful, witty development of the Irish parallel:

> . . . (an Egyptian drug?),
> She hadn't a clue that where I hail from - beyond

> The north wind, Hyperborean, or nearly - heartsease
> Is kiss-me-quick, kiss-me-behind-the-garden-gate,
> That in Donegal this pansy gets mixed up with selfheal.

The salving ending however does not dissipate the unnerving, slipped-in impact of the reference to sectarian murder in Ireland; and the whole tenor of the poem undermines facile optimism. The optative force of the final 'selfheal' is disruptively 'mixed up' with the equivocal connotations of 'pansy', and the overall sense of intimacy and familiarity with Homeric material which, since *Gorse Fires*, has replaced the mock-heroic disparity and distance of the ebullient Odyssean impersonations of *No Continuing City* is in turn qualified by the recognition that Helen 'hadn't a clue' about Longley's world – a mere mythic possibility 'beyond / The north wind, Hyperborean'.

Throughout the volume, this restless, disturbed, obverse and reverse sense of related poles of experience in tension (then and now; grief and celebration; good and bad; nature and pollution) provides a constant elaboration and expansion of the central, elegiac preoccupation with the life-death opposition/symbiosis. Hence, exempla of authentic artists in 'Remembering the Poets' are balanced by their opposite in 'Damiana'; and the conventional allusion (at least by Poundian standards) to Ovid's *Tristia* in the former[11] is in tension with the more mischievously radical method, in this connection, of the latter. Similarly, in a more intimate fusion, in 'The Shaker Barn' New World wooden architecture metamorphoses into Gothic European stone, and life and love are twinned with death as a shared bed becomes an effigy tomb:

> I would lie down with you here, side by side,
> Our own memorials in what amounts to
> The Shakers' cathedral, this circular hay barn,
> The two of us fieldmice under storeys of hay . . .

Domestic life as a counter to thoughts of mortality and transience is a recurrent theme in the volume – asserted in challenging terms in 'Sweetie Papers', but more often tenderly asserted, as here in the ironic reductiveness of the final line quoted, or in the short poem which closes the volume where death only glancingly disturbs an image of marital union which once again takes its coloration from nature:

> There's a dip in the mattress where I sleep.
> Rise out of your hollow hours before me

Every morning, and on the last morning
Tuck me in behind our windbreak of books.

This poem, with its reflexive irony, its canvassing of the option of quietistic retreat from ultimately intractable questions *(permitte divis cetera*: 'leave the rest to the gods')[12] and its appeal to nature and the inevitable processes of nature (as sleep is lightly equated with death) is Horatian in spirit – particularly in its ironic self-effacement, its lack of presumption. Contextualised however with the overall, sometimes harrowing, elegiac content of the volume it is an affective and valid assertion of concern with what Longley has consistently identified as his two basic themes: love and death, Eros and Thanatos.

* * *

The most remarkable poem in the volume in this connection, and perhaps its masterpiece, is 'Etruria'. It is set, as the title suggests, in Tuscany where, for some years now, the Longleys have had access to a small house owned by a friend in the remote village of Cardoso, a short distance from the hamlet of Ponte di Campia, the setting of 'Pascoli's Portrait'; and Italy now seems to have an accelerating importance in Longley's work. 'Couchette', 'Cathedral' and 'Il Volto Santo', grouped together in *Gorse Fires*, were an instance of this development; but perhaps a more powerful indication of the way in which Cardoso in particular has steadily infiltrated Longley's consciousness is 'Laertes' (*GF* 33). It was suggested earlier how, in this poem, the returned Odysseus' confrontation with his aged 'dwindling' father meshes with Longley's memory of his own father's final days, as evoked in 'Wounds'. In a recent interview, however, Longley has revealed how there is in fact a third term to be added to the comparison: 'And then I was in Italy in about 1989 and I had a view from the bathroom window of this little villa of our friends, where we were staying, and I looked down to the bottom of the village and there was this octogenarian tending his flowers. I had a volume of Homer with me, and I wrote the Laertes poem which is also a lament for my father.'[13]

In *The Weather in Japan*, this Cardoso-affiliation is explicitly to the fore. Other geographical locations figure, such as America (which Longley has visited frequently on reading tours), Poland, France, the Orkneys, Scandinavia and, of course, Japan (see below). Italy, however, and Tuscany in particular, seem to have assumed an importance in Longley's life and work in a way which begins to be comparable with that of Mayo and Carrigskeewaun. In the last five years or so an annual sojourn there has tended to parallel the longer personal and familial tradition of visits to Mayo; and commitment to place is reinforced by close friendships – in both locales tragically shadowed, in recent years, by deaths. The resulting elegies, 'Between Hovers' and 'The Altar Cloth', are central achievements in *Gorse Fires* and *The Weather in Japan* respectively; and both are indissolubly linked to the ethos of place.

It is considerations such as these which perhaps most cogently imprint a locale and a community in Longley's scheme of belonging – a symbiosis of human and environmental attachment, registering simultaneously in elegiac and vitalistic terms; and 'Etruria' exemplifies both of these polarities. It is voluptuously responsive to the sensory and, especially, visual particularities of place, but it is also hauntingly infused with an oblique sense of the inexorable drift towards dissolution of these, of the individual consciousness and even, by implication, of whole civilizations.

In this latter connection, the title itself 'Etruria' (rather than 'Tuscany') significantly picks up on the pre-Roman civilization of the region – defunct for over two millenia, and affording cultural access now notably through its funerary remains, its cemeteries and tombs, with their representations of death and the afterlife. These are the kind of associations which play around 'Etruria' – not in any direct, pointed or systematic way, but in terms of the persistent life-death preoccupations of *The Weather in Japan*. The famous practice, for instance, of the Etruscan *haruspices* of divination by observation of the entrails of sacrificed animals provides the imagery for a superbly concentrated stanza of mysterious, vaguely apprehended threat or anxiety –

> A liver concocted out of darkness and wine
> Dregs, the vinegar mother sulking in her crock
> Haruspicates fever, shrivelled grapes, vipers
> On the footpath to a non-existent waterfall –

and the poem closes on the disturbed, nocturnal, ancient and 'underground' note of

> ... my space in this cellar
> Beneath old rafters and old stones, Etruria,
> Nightmare's cesspit, the mosquito-buzz of sleep.

The broad, first order frame of reference of the poem however is local, domestic – keyed to fragments of Longley's quotidian existence in Cardoso. (The 'non-existent waterfall' with its footpath and vipers, for instance, is not a phantom, but the same as the one mentioned in 'The Altar Cloth' with its dozing adder and path, which also figures in 'The Waterfall'.)

As Longley has stressed: 'Many of my poems have their beginnings in ordinary domestic experience. (Though nothing remains ordinary if you look at it for long enough. Anyone's back garden can become a gold mine . . .)';[14] and what is strangely, mesmerically distinctive to this poem is the way in which a series of imagistic stanza-length vignettes of everyday pottering about a familiar locale can exfoliate into a constellated sequence of condensed reveries of inclusive and even cosmic reach. Stanza one, for instance, establishing a mood of disturbed, restless passivity, and incongruously juggling English and Italian cultural referents, jags suddenly into surreal, mortuary associations:

> Pavese's English poems, an English setter barking –
> Too hot and clammy to read, sleep, dander, so
> Snap my walking stick in two and lay it out beside
> My long bones in an ossuary that tells a story . . .

These, however, lead syntactically (but, thematically, utterly unpredictably) into the self-contained cosmos of the second stanza (and from now on, each stanza will be a free-standing sentence, until the final two stanzas repeat the run-on of the first two):

> . . . The apprentice ivory carver's yarn, for instance,
> Who etched those elderly twinkling Chinese pilgrims
> On a walnut, shell-crinkles their only obstacle,
> Globe-trotters in my palm, the kernel still rattling.

The casually instanced apprentice-piece can work these shifts of perspective between microcosm and macrocosm; but it is the ironically self-effacing protagonist ('You can find me under the sellotaped map-fold / Stuck with dog-hairs . . . ') who can transform them into imaginative life through the vivacity of metaphor – just as in stanza four, while democratically, and with genial irony at his own expense, acknowledging that other creatures may work their perceptual transformations on *him* ('Was it a humming bird or a humming bird moth / Mistook my navel for some chubby convolvulus?') he can observe with a 'Martian' eye how: 'Paolo steps from his *casa* like an astronaut / And stoops with smoky bellows among his bees.'

The rich, seamless transfer from image to image however

reaches a peak in the interplay between domestic and stellar frames of reference in:

> Gin, acacia honey, last year's sloes, crimson
> Slipping its gravity like the satellite that swims
> In and out of the hanging hornet-traps, then
> Jukes between midnight planes and shooting stars.

Possibly behind the central lines here is Edward Thomas' 'The Wasp Trap' –

> Nothing on earth,
> And in the heavens no star,
> For pure brightness is worth
> More than that jar,
>
> For wasps meant . . . [15] –

though the shift in Longley from sloe-gin to the satellite, first framed in the heavens like an artificial star, and then 'juking' through a kinetic twentieth century sky-scape, shows a generative density of metaphoric play which is Longley's own – particularly in his ability to introduce the playful, Ulster-demotic 'juking' (dodging about) without disruption into the magical transformative process. Stanza after stanza there is this same rapt, open passivity of response whereby the ordinary swiftly metamorphoses into the extra-ordinary:

> The melon Adua leaves me on the windowsill
> Gift-wrapped in a paper bag and moonlight,
> Ripens in moon-breezes, the pipistrelles' whooshes,
> My own breathing and the insomniac aspen's.

'Gift-wrapped in a paper bag and moonlight' achieves the transformation in one deft metaphoric touch, and the transferred epithet of the fourth line quoted allows a concise echo of the final lines of Thomas' 'Aspens', while avoiding direct use of the device of anthropomorphism which runs rhetorically through that poem:

> We cannot other than an aspen be
> That ceaselessly, unreasonably, grieves . . . [16]

A sense of unease is retained, but in muted terms – and qualified by the relaxed linguistic and sensuous exuberance of 'the pipistrelles' whooshes'.

Through the poem, this poised, equivocal susceptibility to the tug of contradictory moods, impressions or emotions registers not in polarised, antithetical or oppositional terms, but as a simultaneous, integrative experience; and here perhaps is its special distinction. In the ultimate descent towards the 'underground' situation of the final stanza, there is a Cerberus to be negotiated, but a playfully benign one (or is it, as D.H. Lawrence puts it in *Etruscan Places*, 'the dog who is man's guardian even on the death journey . . . '?)[17] – and the descent, and the dog, are (as ever in the poem) identifiable aspects of Longley's domestic life in the Cardoso villa:

> I escape the amorous mongrel with dew-claws
> And vanish where once the privy stood, my kaftan
> Snagging on the spiral staircase down to the small
> Hours when house and I get into bed together . . .

The more disturbed and even sombre atmosphere of the final stanza, with its 'scorpion-shapes', 'old stones' and sense of 'Etruria, / Nightmare's cesspit, the mosquito-buzz of sleep', is thus not so much in antithetical relation to the openness and sensuality of response to quotidian experience and sensation elsewhere in the poem as in fusion: Eros and Thanatos are mutually implicated. In a way, Longley's position is reminiscent of Lawrence's response to Etruscan tombs and their artefacts: 'and death, to the Etruscan, was a pleasant continuance of life, with jewels and wine and flutes playing for the dance. It was neither an ecstasy of bliss, a heaven, nor a purgatory of torment. It was just a natural continuance of the fullness of life.'[18] Longley's poem is however rather more unsettlingly and inclusively poised between blitheness and plangency than this: Janus-like, it looks in both directions, and in its avoidance of rhetorical finality or closure it is in contrast with the insistent rhetoric of Lawrence's championing of the life-affirming nature of Etruscan culture as he perceives it. Moreover, its achievement of this poised vision (and hence its importance at the heart of *The Weather in Japan*) is indissolubly linked to formal developments in Longley's work which, as will be seen, are of complex provenance – and which open up new possibilities.

* * *

In a recent radio interview, Longley has stated that structure in a poem should, for him, ideally be 'cellular'.[19] He was referring to 'The Linen Industry', but the term might serve very usefully to suggest how the stanzas in 'Etruria' are in suspension with each other: they have their individual integrity, but they are also permeable to mutual influence. The eschewing of linear relationship in this is in fact, as has been suggested, a key part of the import of the poem. The pattern is emergent rather than directed, and a matter of cluster rather than line: indices of meaning may run in more than one direction; and in fact Longley has in recent years been indicating the emergence of a praxis exactly along these lines. In 1994 he observed how: 'I'm interested in forms that are, if you like, more organic. I wouldn't want to think that the forms in my earlier books are inorganic but I have now to let the poems happen. There's very little deliberation in what I do. It's the difference between trimming a hedge and building a wall.'[20] The emphasis away from linear coercion and towards form as amalgam is clear; and the 1999 formulation of 'cellular' structure succinctly characterizes this mode of development. Meanwhile, Longley had, in 1998 (i.e., in the later stages of the preparation of *The Weather in Japan*), given a revealing account of how the relationship of stanza to poem may also, in this respect, be echoed in the relationship of poem to volume:

In my first four books I had indulged a tendency to write short intense lyrics and then arrange them in sequences. Something different began to happen in *Gorse Fires* – some kind of involuntary denial of that urge to string poems together in rosaries. The book emerged like a big patchwork. I wanted any given poem to draw resonances from other poems ten or twenty pages in front or behind. I was aiming for a deeper cohesiveness. In more confident moments the book looks to me like one big poem, although each piece has its own title and independence.[21]

The patchwork metaphor here stresses once again the idea of a non-linear accumulation of constituent elements, and in this connection it is notable that Longley's interest in Amish quilting (cf. 'An Amish Rug' in *Gorse Fires*) is continued in *The Weather in Japan* in 'The Quilt', 'The Sunburst', 'The Design' and 'The Sewing Machine'; moreover, these 'quilting' poems also exemplify Longley's point about individual poems picking up 'resonances' diffused through a volume.

'The Quilt' picks up a recurrent preoccupation in *The Weather in Japan* with art and creativity – in this case broached by dual reference to patchworking and Emily Dickinson. Illness and bereavement also figure (the friend who is the addressee has an 'ill father' and the protagonist styles himself an 'antique orphan') and, as elsewhere within this elegiac volume, the affiliation of human experience to the processes of the natural world offers assuaging perspectives: 'instead of snow the bushes / Wear quilts left out all night to dry, like one enormous / Patchwork spring-cleaned, well-aired, mended by morning'. 'The Sewing Machine', in a similar but even more intricately resonating way, features the work of George Fleming, a retired sailor and quilter whose work incorporates the 'cap tallies' of submariners, elegiacally evoking the vessels they served on (and perhaps, for Longley, also recalling the meticulous patchworks made by First World War convalescent soldiers).[22] Beyond this, it is also yet another of 'Longley's lists', and, in a volume containing a number of poems deriving from Homer's *Iliad*, it inevitably recalls the epic formula of the 'Catalogue of the Ships'. Playing simultaneously against this affiliation however is the way in which the submarines' highly suggestive names (e.g.: 'Spearfish', 'Salmon', 'Tempest', 'Thunderbolt', 'Porpoise') temper both martial and elegiac elements by their insistent reference to a vital natural world, mirroring the life-death interrelations of the volume as a whole. Meanwhile, within Longley's extended oeuvre, 'The Sewing Machine' also echoes the evocative naming of Northern Irish navigation locks, apples, pipes and fishing boats in 'Trade Winds' (*GF* 50) (a technique of listing which Longley associates with the work of Ian Hamilton Finlay, the dedicatee of 'Paper Boats' in *The Weather in Japan*).[23] Throughout the volume such elements 'resonate' together in a mutually implicative way, just as the individual stanzas of 'Etruria' amalgamate in subtle interaction; and in this sense 'Etruria' may therefore be seen as a concentrated instance of a compositional method which pervades *The Weather in Japan*, and which has broader implications.

The premium put, for instance, on the contracted two-, three- or four-line unit within the individual poem or the volume is, in a sense, a formal variant on the thematic symbiosis of 'great' and 'small' which has been such a notable feature of Longley's poetry since *Gorse Fires*; and hence 'The Design' in *The Weather in Japan* can offer a drastically condensed perspective on the central theme of life and death:

> Sometimes the quilts were white for weddings, the design
> Made up of stitches and the shadows cast by stitches.
> And the quilts for funerals? How do you sew the night?

The latter is the question this volume centrally poses – sometimes, as in this poem, with the same paradoxically masterful kind of helplessness in the face of mortality as was seen in 'The Mustard Tin', but sometimes, as was seen earlier in respect of the formal elegies, with an openness to assuaging or countervailing perspectives. Hence, within the context of the volume as a whole, the importance of, for instance, the gnomic sense of continuity between the domestic and the natural world in the haiku-like title poem:

> *The Weather in Japan*
> Makes bead curtains of the rain,
> Of the mist a paper screen.

Within Longley's concept of a book of poems as a 'patchwork' of inter-related but independent items, this delicately beautiful poem has a specific role. It represents one possible position along the elegiac-celebratory or 'life and death' continuum and its status as title-poem indicates the ultimately life-affirming weighting of the volume in this respect. It is also a pointer as to how the Japanese material generally in *The Weather in Japan*, and in particular Longley's obvious susceptibility to the exquisite formalities associated with Japanese art and culture, may be regarded.

Longley himself is very much aware of the fact that the Japanese cultural elements which feed into his work might, by popular conception or prejudice, seem to be self-indulgent in the work of a contemporary Northern Irish writer:

> I went to Japan in – I think it was 1991. But I had been interested in things Japanese before that, Japanese poetry, and especially Japanese wood-engraving and porcelain. And it was – part of it was a bit like going home. Here I get my leg pulled, and they think it's a bit effete to write about birds and petals and feathers. There I was reading my poems to people whose culture circulates around things like that.[24]

It is not, as becomes clear, a case of 'effeteness', preciosity or self-indulgent exoticism. Rather, as Longley observes: 'part of it was a bit like going home'. Moreover, as Chris Agee has remarked in connection with the Japanese elements in Longley's poetry:

> The reverential sensibility running through all his books; his feeling for things and events as symbols, for the *lares* and the social rite (a funeral, a baptism, a laying of flowers) – make him a creative natural for the tea ceremony, the Zen garden, the aesthetic and spiritual ceremoniousness of Japanese gestures.[25]

Agee is reviewing *The Ghost Orchid*, but a poem such as 'Invocation' in *The Weather in Japan* exemplifies Longley's continuing affinity with 'the aesthetic and spiritual ceremoniousness of Japanese gestures' –

> Begin the invocation: rice cakes, say, buckwheat
> Flowers or temple bells, bamboo, a caged cricket
> Cheeping for the girl who plants the last rice seed . . . –

just as 'Birds and Flowers', written for Fuyuji Tanigawa, warmly celebrates family and *lares*. But such poems are not simply products of what Longley has, with ironic self-deprecation, referred to as 'the slightly Japanese, Chinese, feathery, leafy, butterfly-wingy side of my imagination'.[26] They are contextualised with other elements in a way that is exemplified in the graphic juxtapositions of 'Sweetie Papers'. Longley's admiration for the delicate formalities of Japanese poetry, then, is not insulated from other realities which might pressure an aesthetic of 'birds and petals and feathers'. This was exactly the point of his irony when deploying that formulation – an irony anticipated in fact as early as 'Options' in *An Exploded View* with the observation how 'at a pinch, I could have / Implied in reduced haiku / A world of suffering . . . ' (P 106). Hence, in connection with *The Weather in Japan*:

> My next collection will take its title from a two-line poem, a new form I've invented and am trying to impose on the world in the belief that the haiku is garrulous and overweight. Should I call it the low-ku? The title runs into the first line, and the couplet has to be as short as possible, and it has to rhyme . . . And in naming the book after such a brevity I might be making a point about scale and importance.[27]

Behind the wit and irony is a principled diffidence about dilating on certain thematic areas: 'Sometimes the brevity is a kind of tact, the only way I have of dealing with momentous subject matter without being offensive or impertinent . . . '.[28] 'Terezín' (*GF* 39) is cited as an instance of this; and it might be observed that the same principle is at work in the three four-line poems ('Eva Braun', 'Geisha' and 'Blitz') which precede 'Terezín' in *Gorse Fires* (and which, together with it, comprise a remarkable 'exploded' unrhymed sonnet, its three quatrains and a couplet spaced over two pages). They combine historical and tragic resonance with reduced format in a way that anticipates a run of four-line poems in *The Weather in Japan* on 'momentous' themes. 'The Exhibit', for instance, poignantly returns to the Holocaust theme, and finds a characteristically unusual and humane approach which hauntingly envisions the persistence of the ordinarily, instinctively human in an inhuman situation –

> I see them absentmindedly pat their naked bodies
> Where waistcoat and apron pockets would have been.

> The grandparents turn back and take an eternity
> Rummaging in the tangled pile for their spectacles –

and 'January 12, 1996' once again memorializes Longley's father's First World War trench experience. Similarly, 'A Prayer' focuses on Northern Ireland – as, more obliquely, does 'At Poll Salach':

> While I was looking for Easter snow on the hills
> You showed me, like a concentration of violets
> Or a fragment from some future unimagined sky,
> A single spring gentian shivering at our feet.

Only the subtitle, 'Easter Sunday, 1998', relates the fragile imagery here to the 1998 'Good Friday' agreement in Northern Ireland,

As Longley observes, sometimes in connection with such subject-matter only 'a touch and no more'[29] is appropriate. The 'single . . . shivering' flower is, like the short-lived Homeric truce of 'Ceasefire', both a celebration and a caution, and is contextualised within the themes of disturbed and undisturbed nature, bellicosity and quietism, love and death, celebration and elegy which populate the volume. Moreover, the concentrated imagistic-epigrammatic suggestiveness of a poem such as this, however much it may owe to Longley's interest in Japanese poetry (and in particular the suggestive brevity of the haiku), also, for a poet with his educational background and cultural purview, inevitably draws on the Graeco-Roman epigrammatic tradition including, in particular, the succinct and emotionally charged short personal epigrams of Catullus – as well as (given his strong presence in the volume) four-line poems in Edward Thomas such as 'The Cherry Trees' and 'In Memoriam (Easter, 1915)' which make an oblique approach to themes of conflict and mortality by reference to natural, and, in the latter case, specifically floral imagery.

* * *

Such ranging literary and cultural syncretism is typical of *The Weather in Japan* and subtly underpins the characteristic shifts and reversals in the volume between elegy and celebration, love and death, plangency and lyricism; and certain geographical, cultural and historical sources of reference weigh specifically in this respect. Japan, as has been noted, tends to figure in terms of the more life-asserting, ceremonial and celebratory end of the spectrum, whereas Italy (from 'Couchette' in *Gorse Fires* onwards, where on an Italian train journey, family and protagonist are stored in couchettes like coffins disposed 'in layers up the walls' of 'the family vault') carries with it accentuated Horatian implications of mortality, qualifying a sensuous response to quotidian stimulus and gratification – as suggested by the Etruscan substratum in 'Etruria'. The categories are not, however, within the shifting perspectives of the volume, hard and fast – and, in fact, in 'She-wolf' in *The Ghost Orchid,* Longley had already anticipated the subtle ambiguities of 'Etruria' by softening, in the poem's allusive play, the archaic Etruscan stiffness of the famous Capitoline Wolf and making it maternally responsive to Rome's infant founders (as represented in the sixteenth century additions to the original bronze sculpture): 'She licks Romulus and Remus / The moment they piddle, / Her cold nose tickling the heads / That nod off and nuddle' (*GO* 10) – an 'art or nature?' or art-into-life trope taken up again in 'Scrap Metal' in *The Weather in Japan* where, in a poem written in appreciation of sculptress Helen Denerley's assemblages from scrap metal:

> A wolf
> At the forest's edge where scrap metal multiplies
> Waits on claw-hammer feet for the rest of the pack.

The shift from celebration of the transformative creative imagination into an equivocal, poignant image of a threatened natural world is typical of the volume's swerves away from, and then back into, an elegiac mode where terrain and its flora and fauna are the constant, unifying referential matrix.

From the initial, programmatic Carrigskeewaun poems of disturbed and undisturbed nature onwards, this hesitation between, and sometimes simultaneous visionary apprehension of, a *recto* and *verso* vision of ecology in the widest possible sense (and with particular reference to the Greek root of the term in *oikos* – 'house' or 'home') remains the source of the book's moving and varied descants upon a central elegiac preoccupation. Ideas of loss and celebration, transience and persistence, life and death, grief and joy, are not so much in dialectical tension but rather, in a synoptic view which outflanks contrariety and antithesis, presuppose and complete one another. Panoptic historical, cultural and geographical allusive vistas may be involved, or the microcosm of village (Cardoso) or townland (Carrigskeewaun) may provide the human and territorial focus: but, crucially, belonging and authentic *presence*, remembered or current, are the salient criteria. In this way, death and transience can be seen

'How do you sew the night?': The Weather in Japan

within a nexus of concepts which allows the artist to achieve a counterbalancing vision of continuity and reclamation intimately bound up with place and environment – all of which is superbly concentrated in 'The Fox':

> Where the burn separating Carrigskeewaun
> From Thallabaun crosses the path to the cottage
> And fencing crosses the water, flood water
> Has hung among grass clumps and black plastic
> A fox who tries to sidestep death, decay
> And barbed wire by foxtrotting upside down
> Against the camber of the Milky Way.

This poem (which, I understand, post-dates by some months the rest of the content of *The Weather in Japan*) reasserts Carrigskeewaun territory at the centre of Longley's preoccupations. Transience, decay and ecological threat are given due acknowledgement, but in the precise, observant celebration and evocation of the dead creature's distinctive *living* presence there persists, as ever in the volume, the lyrical, unsentimental impulse to elegize and celebrate simultaneously – to turn death on its head.

ETRURIA

MICHAEL LONGLEY

Pavese's English poems, an English setter barking –
Too hot and clammy to read, sleep, dander, so
Snap my walking stick in two and lay it out beside
My long bones in an ossuary that tells a story,

The apprentice ivory carver's yarn, for instance,
Who etched those elderly twinkling Chinese pilgrims
On a walnut, shell-crinkles their only obstacle,
Globe-trotters in my palm, the kernel still rattling.

You can find me under the sellotaped map-fold
Stuck with dog-hairs, and close to a mulberry bush
The women tended, coddling between their breasts
The silkworms' filaments, vulnerable bobbins.

Was it a humming bird or a humming bird moth
Mistook my navel for some chubby convolvulus?
Paolo steps from his *casa* like an astronaut
And stoops with smoky bellows among his bees.

Gin, acacia honey, last year's sloes, crimson
Slipping its gravity like the satellite that swims
In and out of the hanging hornet-traps, then
Jukes between midnight planes and shooting stars.

The trout that dozed in a perfect circle wear
Prison grey in the fridge, bellies sky-coloured
Next to the butter dish's pattern, traveller's-joy,
Old man's beard when it seeds, feathery plumes.

The melon Adua leaves me on the windowsill
Gift-wrapped in a paper bag and moonlight,
Ripens in moon-breezes, the pipistrelles' whooshes,
My own breathing and the insomniac aspen's.

A liver concocted out of darkness and wine
Dregs, the vinegar mother sulking in her crock
Haruspicates fever, shrivelled grapes, vipers
On the footpath to a non-existent waterfall.

I escape the amorous mongrel with dew-claws
And vanish where once the privy stood, my kaftan
Snagging on the spiral staircase down to the small
Hours when house and I get into bed together,

My mattress on the floor, crickets, scorpion-shapes
In their moonlit square, my space in this cellar
Beneath old rafters and old stones, Etruria,
Nightmare's cesspit, the mosquito-buzz of sleep.

NOTES

INTRODUCTION

Alan J. Peacock

1. Published by Abbey Press, Newry and Belfast. *The Weather in Japan* was published by Jonathan Cape while the present volume was in press. A pre-publication typescript was kindly made available to the editors by the author.
2. Michael Allen, 'Louis MacNeice and Michael Longley: Some Examples of Affinity and Influence', in *Louis MacNeice and his Influence*, ed. K. Devine and A.J. Peacock (Gerrards Cross, Colin Smythe, 1998), p. 99.
3. Cf. 'The Longley Tapes', *The Honest Ulsterman*, No. 78, Summer 1985, p. 27.
4. Brian John, 'The Achievement of Michael Longley's *The Ghost Orchid*', *Irish University Review*, Vol. 27, No. 1, Spring/Summer 1997, p. 139.
5. Peter McDonald, 'Michael Longley's Homes', in *Mistaken Identities: Poetry and Northern Ireland* (Oxford, Clarendon Press, 1997), p. 121.
6. Michael Longley, *Tuppenny Stung: Autobiographical Chapters* (Belfast, Lagan Press, 1994), pp. 25–6.
7. Cf., e.g., 'The Longley Tapes', pp. 23–4: 'then when I went to Trinity there was the ban. It was a mortal sin, according to the dreadful Archbishop McQuade, for Irish Catholics to go to this Protestant bastion. So apart from Brendan Kennelly . . . I only had two Catholic friends . . . and it wasn't until I'd come back to Belfast at the age of 23 and had met Seamus and Marie Heaney that . . . I realised that they were the first Northern Irish Catholics who were close friends.'
8. *Ibid.*, p. 20.
9. Fran Brearton, '"Walking Forwards into the Past": an Interview with Michael Longley', *Irish Studies*, No. 18, Spring 1997, p. 37.
10. 'The Longley Tapes', p. 21.
11. *Round Midnight*, B.B.C. Radio 2, February 4, 1985.
12. 'An Interview with Michael Longley' by Dermot Healy, *The Southern Review*, Vol. 31, July 1995, pp. 558–9.
13. March 19, 1991.

14 *Tuppenny Stung*, p. 70.
15 Louis MacNeice, *Selected Poems*, ed. Michael Longley, (London, Faber and Faber, 1988).
16 Reading, March 19, 1991.
17 David Wheatley, 'Unsuspected Shapes', *The Irish Review*, No. 19, Spring/Summer 1996, p. 126.
18 Ezra Pound, *ABC of Reading* (London, Faber and Faber, 1951), p. 46.
19 Reading, March 19, 1991.

MICHAEL LONGLEY AND THE IRISH POETIC TRADITION

Terence Brown

1 Michael Longley, *Tuppenny Stung: Autobiographical Chapters* (Belfast, Lagan Press, 1994) pp. 36–37.
2 'Michael Longley' in 'The State of Poetry: A Symposium', *the Review*, No. 29–30, Spring/Summer, 1972, p. 47.
3 Longley published his selection of MacNeice's verse in 1988. It is a much more generous, celebratory volume than W.H. Auden's somewhat grudging selection of 1964.
4 Michael Longley, 'A Misrepresented Poet', *The Dublin Magazine*, Vol. 6, No. 1, Spring, 1967, p. 69. All quotations from MacNeice's poetry in what follows are from Louis MacNeice, *Collected Poems*, ed. E.R. Dodds (London, Faber and Faber, 1966).
5 *Ibid.*
6 See 'The Longley Tapes', *The Honest Ulsterman*, No. 78, Summer 1985, p. 20 and p. 15.
7 See my 'Louis MacNeice and the Second World War' in *Modern Irish Writers and the Wars*, ed. Kathleen Devine (Gerrards Cross, Colin Smythe Ltd., 1999), pp. 165–77.
8 'A Misrepresented Poet', pp. 72–3.
9 *Ibid.*, p. 74.
10 *Ibid.*, pp. 69–70.
11 Michael Longley, 'Poetry', in *Causeway: the Arts in Ulster*, ed. Michael Longley (Belfast, the Arts Council; Dublin, in association with Gill and Macmillan, 1971), p. 97.
12 Michael Longley, 'Introduction', *Louis MacNeice: Selected Poems* (London, Faber and Faber, 1988), p. xxii.
13 *Ibid.*, pp. xvii–xviii.
14 Longley, 'A Misrepresented Poet', p. 68.
15 Longley, 'Poetry', p. 97.
16 'The State of Poetry', p. 47.
17 *Ibid.*, p. 48.
18 See W.B. Stanford, *Ireland and the Classical Tradition* (Dublin, Allen Figgis and Co. Ltd, 1976; Totowa, N.J., Rowman and Littlefield,

1977). Stanford was one of Longley's teachers in Trinity College, Dublin, where he read Classics.
19 'The Longley Tapes', p. 16.

LONGLEY'S METRIC

Douglas Dunn

1 W.B. Yeats, *Collected Poems* (London, Macmillan, 2nd ed., 1950), p. 400.
2 T.S. Eliot, *Ezra Pound, His Metric and Poetry* (1917) in *To Criticize the Critic* (London, Faber and Faber, 1965), pp. 162–82.
3 Yvor Winters, *Primitivism and Decadence* (1937) in *In Defense of Reason* (Chicago, Swallow Press, n.d.), p. 23.
4 *The Honest Ulsterman*, No. 78 (Summer 1985), pp. 13–31.
5 P, 17–19, 24–25, 27–29, 40–43.
6 I quote from memory, and can no longer trace the source of Levi's remark.
7 Louis MacNeice, *Collected Poems* (London, Faber and Faber, 1966 (1979)), pp. 327–439.
8 Toni Morrison, *Playing in the Dark: Whiteness and the Literary Imagination* (London, Picador, 1993).
9 A favourite phrase of Derek Mahon's, it seems, and quoted by Longley, via Mahon, in his interview in *The Honest Ulsterman*.
10 W.H. Auden, 'In Memory of W.B. Yeats', *Collected Shorter Poems 1927–1957* (London, Faber and Faber, 1966), pp. 141–3.
11 Newcastle upon Tyne, Bloodaxe Books, 1987.
12 T.S. Eliot, *Selected Prose of T.S. Eliot*, ed. Frank Kermode (London, Faber and Faber, 1975), p. 110.

LAPSED CLASSICS: HOMER, OVID, AND MICHAEL LONGLEY'S POETRY

Peter McDonald

1 Interview with Robert Johnstone, 'The Longley Tapes', *The Honest Ulsterman* 78 (Summer 1985), p. 17.
2 *Ibid.*, p. 24.
3 *The Honest Ulsterman* 95 [1994], p. 36.
4 Bernard O'Donoghue, *Seamus Heaney and the Language of Poetry* (Hemel Hempstead, Harvester Wheatsheaf, 1994), p. 118.
5 Robert Welch (ed.), *The Oxford Companion to Irish Literature* (Oxford, Oxford University Press, 1996), p. 351.
6 See Peter McDonald, 'The Greeks in Ireland: Irish Poets and Greek

Tragedy', *Translation and Literature*, Vol. 4 Part 2 (1995), pp. 183–203.
7   *Tuppenny Stung: Autobiographical Chapters* (Belfast, Lagan Press, 1994), p. 15.
8   *The Odyssey*, trans. E.V. Rieu (Harmondsworth, Penguin, 1946), p. 310.
9   'Memory and Acknowledgement', *The Irish Review* 17–18 (Winter 1995), p. 158.
10 Michael Hofmann and James Lasdun (eds.), *After Ovid: New Metamorphoses* (London, Faber and Faber, 1994), p. xi.
11 John Lyon, 'Michael Longley's Lists', *English*, Vol. 45 No. 183 (Autumn 1996), p. 232.
12 *Odyssey* XI, 134.

MICHAEL LONGLEY AND THE WEST

Robert Welch

1   A phrase from Jonathan Swift, according to Austin Clarke, but I cannot find it in Swift.
2   'A Letter of the Authors to Sir Walter Raleigh' in A.C. Hamilton (ed.), *Spenser: The Faerie Queene* (London, Longman, 1977), p. 737.
3   C.S. Lewis, *The Allegory of Love* (London, Oxford University Press, 1958), p. 297 *et seq*.
4   'Bogland', *Selected Poems* (London, Faber & Faber, 1980), p. 54.
5   H.M. Margoliouth (ed.), *The Poems and Letters of Andrew Marvell* (Oxford, The Clarendon Press, 1927), p. 49.
6   *Ibid.*, p. 75.

CONFLICT, VIOLENCE AND 'THE FUNDAMENTAL INTERRELATEDNESS OF ALL THINGS' IN THE POETRY OF MICHAEL LONGLEY

Elmer Kennedy-Andrews

1   Stan Smith, 'At One Remove', in *The Literary Review*, 22, Aug. 8, 1980, pp. 11–12.
2   Michael Longley, *Tuppenny Stung: Autobiographical Chapters* (Belfast, Lagan Press, 1994), pp. 75–6.
3   'Interview with Michael Longley' (Neil Johnston), *Belfast Telegraph*, 30 Jan. 1996.
4   Michael Longley, 'The Neolithic Night: A Note on the Irishness of Louis MacNeice', in Douglas Dunn (ed.), *Two Decades of Irish Writing* (Cheadle Hulme, Carcanet Press, 1975), pp. 101–2.
5   Michael Longley, quoted in Terence Brown, *Northern Voices: Poets from Ulster* (Dublin, Gill and Macmillan, 1975), p. 211.

6   Tom Adair, 'Of Flock and Fold: A Consideration of the Poetry of Michael Longley', in *The Linen Hall Review*, Vol. 4, No. 1 (Spring 1987), pp. 16–19.
7   Frank Ormsby, Introduction to *Poets from the North of Ireland* (Belfast, Blackstaff, rev. ed. 1990), p. 11.
8   *The Collected Poems of Edward Thomas*, ed. R.G. Thomas (Oxford, The Clarendon Press, 1978), p. 477.
9   Seamus Heaney, *Preoccupations: Selected Prose 1968–1978* (London, Faber and Faber, 1980), pp. 54–5.
10 Chris Agee, 'Chinese Whispers, Epic Recensions', in *Poetry Ireland Review*, 49 (Spring 1996), p. 76.

MY BOTANICAL STUDIES:
THE POETRY OF NATURAL HISTORY IN MICHAEL LONGLEY

Neil Corcoran

1   See Arthur C. Danto, 'Playing with the Edge: The Photographic Achievement of Robert Mapplethorpe', in Mark Holborn and Dimitri Levas (eds.), *Mapplethorpe* (London, Jonathan Cape, 1992), pp. 311–39.
2   Hugo Williams, 'Siren', *London Review of Books*, 15 August 1991, p. 22.
3   Roland Barthes, *Camera Lucida: Reflections on Photography*, trs. Richard Howard (London, Jonathan Cape, 1982), pp. 55–9.
4   Stephen Jay Gould, 'Male Nipples and Clitoral Ripples', in *Bully for Brontosaurus* (1991; Harmondsworth, Penguin Books, 1992), p. 127.
5   Seamus Heaney, 'Place and Displacement: Reflections on Some Recent Poetry from Northern Ireland', in Elmer Andrews (ed.), *Contemporary Irish Poetry: A Collection of Critical Essays* (London, Macmillan, 1992), p. 142.
6   Rainer Maria Rilke, 'The Ninth Elegy', in *Duino Elegies*, trs. J.B. Leishman and Stephen Spender (London, Chatto and Windus, 1939; 1981), p. 85.
7   Hopkins, Letter to A.W.M. Baillie, Sept. 10, 1864, in *Further Letters of G.M. Hopkins*, ed. C.C. Abbott (London, Oxford University Press, 1938; 1956), pp. 215–7.
8   Michael Longley, *Tuppenny Stung: Autobiographical Chapters* (Belfast, Lagan Press, 1994).
9   *Ibid.*, p. 29.
10 *Ibid.*, pp. 73, 74.
11 Neil Corcoran, *English Poetry since 1940* (London, Longman, 1993), p. 187.
12 John Kerrigan, 'Ulster Ovids', in Neil Corcoran (ed.), *The Chosen Ground: Essays on the Contemporary Poetry of Northern Ireland* (Bridgend, Seren Books, 1992), p. 246.

13 Hugh MacDiarmid had, it should be said, already found such room in his beautiful poem 'Milk-Wort and Bog-Cotton', published in *Scots Unbound and Other Poems* (1932). I am grateful to Patrick Crotty for bringing this poem to my attention.
14 Heaney, 'Place and Displacement', p. 140.
15 See above, n. 12.
16 Heaney, 'Place and Displacement', p. 141.
17 Peter McDonald, 'Michael Longley's Homes', in *The Chosen Ground*, p. 75.

LONGLEY'S LONG LINE: LOOKING BACK FROM *THE GHOST ORCHID*

Michael Allen

1 Compare Longley's discussion of this particular 'period of silence' in Clive Wilmer's *Poets Talking: Poet of the Month Interviews from BBC Radio 3* (Manchester, Carcanet, 1994, p. 117) and 'The Longley Tapes', an interview by Robert Johnstone in *The Honest Ulsterman* 78 (1985), p. 27 with his anticipatory account of an earlier one in the Introduction to *Secret Marriages* (Manchester, Phoenix Pamphlet Poets Press, 1968, p. 2). See also Michael Allen, 'Rhythm and Development in Michael Longley's Earlier Poetry', *Contemporary Irish Poetry: a Collection of Critical Essays*, ed. Elmer Andrews (Basingstoke, Macmillan, 1992), pp. 220–26.
2 See p. 131 below.
3 Donald Davie, *Purity of Diction in English Verse* (New York, Schocken, 1967), p. 12.
4 Peter McDonald, 'From Ulster with Love': review of Michael Longley, *Poems 1963–1983, Poetry Review* 74/4 (1985), p. 16.
5 *Ibid.*
6 Edna Longley, *Poetry in the Wars* (Newcastle upon Tyne, Bloodaxe, 1986), p. 146.
7 Clair Wills, *Improprieties: Politics and Sexuality in Northern Irish Poetry* (Oxford, Clarendon Press, 1993), p. 91.
8 See *Poets Talking*, p. 117 and Martin Dillon, *The Shankill Butchers* (London, Arrow Books, 1990).
9 *Iliad* VI 429–39 (I am grateful to Maureen Alden for this point and for the reference).
10 Cf.

> ... hanged the women
> So none touched the ground with her toes, like long-winged thrushes
> Or doves trapped in a mist-net across the thicket where they roost,
> Their heads bobbing in a row, their feet twitching but not for long ...
> (*GF* 51)

11 *Improprieties*, p. 37.

12 *The Letters of Robert Frost to Louis Untermeyer* (London, Cape, 1964), p. 47.
13 See *GF* 13, 25, 31–35.
14 See Peter McDonald, 'Michael Longley's Homes', *The Chosen Ground*, ed. Neil Corcoran (Bridgend, Seren Books, 1992), p. 81.
15 Cf.
>   Somewhere beyond the scorched gable end and the burnt-out buses
>
>   there is a poet indulging
>   his wretched rage for order –
>   or not as the case may be, for his
>   is a dying art,
>   an eddy of semantic scruples
>   in an unstructurable sea.
>
>   He is far from his people,
>   and the fitful glare of his high window is as
>   nothing to our scattered glass.
>
>   Derek Mahon, 'Rage for Order', *Poems 1962–1978* (Oxford, Oxford University Press, 1979), p. 44.

16 See Allen, 'Rhythm and Development in Michael Longley's Earlier Poetry', *Contemporary Irish Poetry*, pp. 228–232 and below.
17 *A Citizens' Inquiry: the Opsahl Report on Northern Ireland*, ed. Andy Pollak (Dublin, Lilliput Press, 1993).
18 Ciaran Carson, Review of *North*, *The Honest Ulsterman* 50 (1975), p. 183.
19 Reproduced here by permission and with the co-operation of the artist.
20 Robert Johnstone, 'The Longley Tapes', p. 15.
21 He is certainly much less ephemeral than the superficially similar speaker of an earlier poem and the expansiveness of the long line is part of the reason:
>   I am clothed, unclothed
>   By racing cloud shadows,
>   Or else disintegrate
>   Like a hillside neighbour
>   Erased by sea mist.
>   'Landscape' (1975, *P* 126)

22 Vita Sackville-West's garden at Sissinghurst, Kent, the original inspiration of the poem.
23 I am grateful to the poet for both the identification of his source and his explanation of the original meaning.
24 For instance in 'Judgement', *The Irish for No* (Dublin, Gallery Press, 1987), pp. 17–20.
25 See *The Hudson Letter* (Oldcastle, Gallery Press, 1995).
26 'The best thing that was ever said about English prosody was by

Robert Frost, who said, "There's strict iambic and loose iambic".' – 'The Longley Tapes', p. 16. (Longley makes it clear on the same page of that interview that he interprets 'iambic' to mean 'iambic pentameter'.)

27 With prosody there is always a choice between a narrow but idiosyncratic methodological precision and widely accepted but inexact notation. To talk about the 'iambic' in Anglophone poetry without considering the unstressed syllables and their organization into feet (a procedure of which both Longley and I are guilty) is to choose the second of these alternatives. I should add here that scansion of English verse has always a subjective component and while I think my own stress-markings correspond to those heard when Longley reads his own poetry, this does not mean that other readers will not sometimes legitimately accentuate different syllables.

28 The third poem in that book (see Table I) to show Longley experimenting with the long line is 'Martinmas' (*P* 177). There are also some unexperimental but appropriately jog-trotting long lines in sections of 'Lore' (*P* 158–9).

29 *Poetry Review* 74/4 (1985), pp. 5–11. Reprinted with other autobiographical pieces in *Tuppenny Stung: Autobiographical Chapters* (Belfast, Lagan Press, 1994). My subsequent references will be to this edition, abbreviated to *TS*.

30 See note 1 above.

31 By permission of the poet.

32 See J. Th. Kakrides, *Homeric Researches* (Lund, C.W.K. Gleemp, 1949), pp. 20–64. I am grateful to Maureen Alden for this reference.

33 'In Memoriam' (1968, *P* 48).

34 'Self Portrait' (1979, *P* 183).

35 'Dead Men's Fingers' (1979, *P* 181).

36 Though 'Grandpa George' is treated more sympathetically in 'Tuppenny Stung' than in 'Master of Ceremonies'.

37 René Girard, *Violence and the Sacred*, tr. Patrick Gregory (Baltimore and London, Johns Hopkins U.P., 1977).

38 See Frank Wright, *Northern Ireland: a Comparative Analysis* (Dublin, Gill and Macmillan, 1987).

39 The whole disaster of the *Iliad* is due to the failure of Agamemnon and Achilles to submit to Nestor's arbitration of their quarrel and at the end of the poem Menelaus and Antilochus negotiate a speedy resolution to a similar quarrel by mutual concession. I am grateful for this point to Maureen Alden who discusses it further in a forthcoming work.

40 *Improprieties*, p. 37.

41 Douglas Dunn, review of Michael Longley, *Selected Poems 1963–1980*, *TLS* 31 July 1981, p. 886.

42 Another of Longley's binaries emerges here and overlaps with his preoccupation with twins. At least since the writing of 'Birthmarks'

(P 58) he has been interested in something very like the Jungian 'shadow', a dark alter-ego which according to Anthony Stevens develops in the individual because of 'a fear of being *abandoned* by the mother for being unacceptable' (*Jung*, Oxford University Press, 1994, p. 49).

43 '... a further implication [of Sophocles's *Philoctetes*] ... which must occur to the modern reader: the idea that genius and disease, like strength and mutilation, may be inextricably bound up together', Edmund Wilson, *The Wound and the Bow* (London, Methuen, 1961), p. 259.

'HOW DO YOU SEW THE NIGHT?': *THE WEATHER IN JAPAN*

Alan J. Peacock

1 *Broken Dishes* (Newry and Belfast, Abbey Press, 1998).
2 All quotations from *The Weather in Japan* are from a typescript kindly provided by the author. It is now published by Jonathan Cape (London, 2000).
3 Louis MacNeice, *Collected Poems* (London, Faber and Faber, 1966), p. 541.
4 Keith Douglas, *A Prose Miscellany*, ed. Desmond Graham (Manchester, Carcanet Press, 1985), p. 137.
5 George Seferis, *Collected Poems 1924–1955*, ed. and trans. E. Keeley and P. Sherrard (London, Jonathan Cape, 1969), pp. 258–65.
6 Cf. John Lyon, 'Michael Longley's Lists', *English*, Vol. 45, No. 183 (Autumn 1996).
7 Charles Sorley, *Marlborough and Other Poems* (Cambridge, Cambridge University Press, 1916), p. 69.
8 Cf. Longley's comment that birds are 'a symbol for me of the human soul' in Clive Wilmer, *Poets Talking* (Manchester, Carcanet Press, 1994), p. 119.
9 Derek Mahon observes (not in direct connection with this poem) how 'The late T.R. Henn estimated the weight of the human soul as that of a mature snipe ...': see 'Careful Footprints: *Poems 1963–1983* by Michael Longley' in Derek Mahon, *Journalism*, ed. Terence Brown (Loughcrew, The Gallery Press, 1996), p. 100.
10 *Collected Poems*, p. 523.
11 Cf. Ovid, *Tristia* 4,10,41 *seq*. Longley's free version of Ovid's lines coalesces, at the mention of Tibullus, with Horace's friendly evocation of Albius (Tibullus) strolling or 'creeping' (*reptare*) among the 'health-giving woods' (*silvas ... salubres*) in *Epistles* 1,4,4. Hence Longley's protagonist speaks of 'Albius / Tibullus strolling in the woods a little while / With me before he died ...'; whereas Ovid records (51–2) how fate 'gave no time' for friendship between himself and Tibullus, who died in 19 B.C.

12 Horace, *Odes*, 1,9,9.
13 Sarah Broom, 'Interview with Michael Longley', *Metre*, No. 4, Spring/Summer 1998, p. 18.
14 Michael Longley, 'A Tongue at Play' in *How Poets Work*, ed. Tony Curtis (Bridgend, Seren Books, 1996), pp. 113–4.
15 *The Collected Poems of Edward Thomas*, ed. R.G. Thomas (Oxford, The Clarendon Press, 1978), p. 147.
16 *Ibid.*, p. 233.
17 D.H. Lawrence, *Etruscan Places* in *Mornings in Mexico* and *Etruscan Places* (London, Heinemann, 1956), pp. 11–12.
18 *Ibid.*
19 'Fine Lines', Radio 4, February 14, 1999.
20 *Poets Talking*, p. 115.
21 Peter McDonald, 'An Interview with Michael Longley', *Thumbscrew*, No. 12, Winter 1998/9, p. 7.
22 It may also be noted that Fleming is the author of the military biography *Magennis VC*, and hence 'The Sewing Machine' 'resonates' with what is thus a companion-poem within the volume – namely, 'Ocean: Homage to James "Mick" Magennis VC', which was published in *The Irish Times* on August 22, 1998, side by side with Longley's review of Fleming's book (which he begins by recalling his father's unassuming account of the act of bravery which won him the Military Cross).
23 Cf. Michael Longley, 'Paper Boats' in *Green Waters*, ed, Alec Finlay (Edinburgh, Morning Star and Polygon, 1998), p. 81.
24 Broom, p. 25.
25 Chris Agee, 'Chinese Whispers, Epic Recensions', *Poetry Ireland Review*, Vol. 49, Spring 1996, p. 76.
26 McDonald, p. 12.
27 *Ibid.*, p. 9.
28 *Ibid.*
29 *Ibid.*

NOTES ON CONTRIBUTORS

MICHAEL ALLEN teaches American and Irish writing at Queen's University, Belfast. He has written on American, English and Irish fiction and on American poetry but of late has given his main attention as reviewer and critic to contemporary Irish poetry. He recently edited a collection of critical essays on Heaney and is preparing a book on Longley's poetry.

TERENCE BROWN is Professor of Anglo-Irish literature in Trinity College, Dublin where he is a Fellow of the College. He is a member of the Royal Irish Academy and also a member of the Academia Europaea. He has lectured on Irish literature and on Irish cultural history in many parts of the world. Among his publications are *Louis MacNeice: Sceptical Vision* (1974), *Northern Voices: Poets from Ulster* (1975), *Ireland: A Social and Cultural History* (1985), *Ireland's Literature: Selected Essays* (1988) and *The Life of W. B. Yeats: A Critical Biography* (1999).

NEIL CORCORAN is Professor and Head of the School of English in the University of St Andrews. He taught previously at the Universities of Sheffield and Swansea. His publications include *English Poetry Since 1940*, *The Chosen Ground: Essays on the Contemporary Poetry of Northern Ireland*, *The Poetry of Seamus Heaney: A Critical Study*, *After Yeats and Joyce: Reading Modern Irish Literature* and *Poets of Modern Ireland: Text, Context, Intertext*. He is currently writing a book about Elizabeth Bowen.

DOUGLAS DUNN teaches at the University of St Andrews. His most recent books of poems are *The Donkey's Ears* (Faber & Faber, 2000) and *The Year's Afternoon* (Faber & Faber, 2000).

ELMER KENNEDY-ANDREWS is Senior Lecturer in English at the University of Ulster at Coleraine. His books include *The Poetry of Seamus Heaney: All the Realms of Whisper* (1988), *Seamus Heaney: A Collection of Critical Essays* (1992), *Contemporary Irish Poetry: A Collection of Critical Essays* (1992), *The Art of Brian Friel* (1995), *The Poetry of Seamus Heaney: Icon Critical Guides* (1998) and *Nathanial*

Hawthorne: The Scarlet Letter: Icon Critical Guides (1999). He has also published essays on American and Irish writers in various books and journals.

PETER McDONALD has published two volumes of poetry, *Biting the Wax* (1989) and *Adam's Dream* (1996); a third collection, *Pastorals*, is forthcoming. He is the author of two critical books, *Louis MacNeice: The Poet in His Contexts* (1991) and *Mistaken Identities: Poetry and Northern Ireland* (1997), and has written widely on modern and contemporary poetry. He is Christopher Tower Student in Poetry in English and Tutor at Christ Church, Oxford.

ALAN J. PEACOCK has lectured at Magee University College and the University of Ulster. He has written articles on English poetry from the seventeenth to the twentieth century and on a number of modern Irish writers. He has edited *The Achievement of Brian Friel* (1993) and co-edited *Louis MacNeice and His Influence* (1998).

ROBERT WELCH is Professor of English at the University of Ulster. He is the author of several books on Irish literature, including *Changing States* (1993) and *A History of the Abbey, 1899–1999: Form and Pressure* (1999), poetry collections, and fiction in Irish and English, including *Groundwork* (1997).

INDEX

Aeschylus, xii
Agee, Chris, 98, 99, 163
Allen, Michael, ix–x
Amis, Kingsley, 31
Andersen, Hans Christian, *The Snow Queen*, 134–35
anthropomorphism, xiii
Armstrong, Louis, 20
Arnold, Matthew, 35, 51, 52; 'Thyrsis', 94
Arts Council of Northern Ireland, xiv, xviii, 75
Auden, W.H., xii, 17, 31; 'squares and oblongs', 3, 27; 'In Memory of W.B. Yeats', 21; 'New Year Letter', 21

B Specials, xi
Banville, John, 129
Barthes, Roland, *Camera Lucida*, 102
Baudelaire, Charles, 2
Beatles, Magical Mystery Tour, 82
Belfast, xiv–xv, 59, 86
biomorphism, 104
Blake, William, 51, 52, 54
Bloom, Harold, 5; *The Anxiety of Influence*, 4
bogs and bogland, 74, 88, 90, 111–14
Bonnard, Pierre, 154
Brecht, Bertolt, 2
Brown, George Mackay, 52
Browning, Robert, 15, 16
Burns, Robert, 21

Callanan, J.J., 58
Camus, Albert, 21
Cardinal, Marie, *The Words to Say It*, 20
Cardoso, 156, 158, 160, 166
Carrigskeewaun, xiv, xviii, 57, 82, 152, 157, 166–67
Carson, Ciaran, 29, 129, 131
Cary, Joyce, 53
Catholicism and poetry, 59, 61, 79
Catullus, xii, 36, 165
Clapham Common, xv
Clare, John, xii, 104
Clarke, Austin, 2, 11
classicism, 11, 39–40, 41, 50
Collins, William, 57
Conor Mor, 79
Conquest, Robert, *New Lines*, 31
Corcoran, Neil, 147
countermythology, 82
Crane, (Harold) Hart, 1
Criterion, The, 39
Cultural Traditions Group, xviii, 75
Cummings, E.E., 1
Custer, General George, 81

Danto, Arthur C., 101, 102
Davie, Donald, 2, 124; *Purity of Diction in English Verse*, 121–22
Denerley, Helen, 166
Dickinson, Emily, 161
Didsbury, Peter, *The Classical Farm*, 30
Discourses of Master Po Shan, 51

183

Dolmen Press, 2
Donne, John, xii, 6, 62; *Satyres*, 29
Donnelly, Charles, 94
Douglas, Keith, war poet, xviii, 10, 85, 88, 104, 145–46; 'Desert Flowers', 112–13
Dryden, John, 51, 52
Dublin Magazine, The, 2, 3
Dunn, Douglas, x, 139
Dunne, Sean, 144

Eagleton, Terry, 76
Eliot, George, 54
Eliot, T.S., 2, 14, 27, 30, 39
Emerson, Ralph Waldo, 16
Empson, William, 52
Encounter, 2
Enright, D.J., 31
eroticism, 5–6, 36, 62, 101–04, 114–18, 125–26, 136
experimentalism, 2

Fenton, James, 13, 15
Ferguson, Samuel, 58
Finlay, Ian Hamilton, 162
Fleming, George, 162
Ford, John, *The Quiet Man*, 58
Friel, Brian, *Translations*, 39–40
Frost, Robert, 15, 16, 125
Fuller, John, 13

Gardner, Helen, 55
Ghost Orchid, The, xvii, 11, 60, 96, 143, 152; botany and psychology in, 109–10; conflict and violence in, 74, 89, 95–99; erotic poems, 115–16, 125–26; Homeric poems, 40, 42, 44, 45–46, 97–98; long line in, 29, 121, 122–31, 139; and *Metamorphoses*, xii; natural history poetry, 109; paradoxical structuring, 136, 129–31; protean energy, ix; reviewed, xx, 163; short poems, 48–49, 98–99; stylistic mode, ix–x; visionary intensity, 98
Girard, René, *Violence and the Sacred*, 137–38
Glor-na-nGael language group, 75
Good Friday Agreement, 165
Gorse Fires, 11, 57, 62–63, 145; a book of names, 93–95; botany and psychology in, 108–110; conflict and violence in, 89–95; and 'Etruria', 161; first public reading, xv; home and 'belonging', xviii–xix, 152; Homeric poems, 36, 40–46, 48–49, 89–92, 123, 138–41; listing and naming in, 7–8, 28, 91, 93–95, 104–06, 147, 162; long line in, 29–30, 121, 122, 138–41; lyric intensity, ix; poems of imaginative transformation, 92; public and private dimensions, 135; stylistic mode, ix–x
Gould, Stephen Jay, 'Male Nipples and Clitoral Ripples', 103
Graves, Robert, 1
Gray, Thomas, 'The Bard', 57

Hardy, Lena (ML's nurse), 109, 125, 133, 135–36
Hardy, Thomas, xii, 15
Harrison, Tony, 13, 29, 31, 33
haruspices, 157
Heaney, Seamus, 11, 29, 54, 84; artistry of poetry, 13; attitude to violence, 74; bogland in, 74, 88, 111, 113; ceremony and customary rhythms, 99; eroticism in, 114, 115, 116, 117; freestyle poetic, 39; sense of irrelevance and ineffectualness, 91; long poem sequences, 98; 'moral project', 33; portrait by Edward McGuire, 129; public and private voice, 125; 'Clearances', 128; 'Feeling into Words', 88; 'Glanmore Sonnets', 98; 'Kinship', 113–14; 'Letters' addressed to, 21, 23; 'A

Index

New Song', 122; North, 113; 'A Personal Statement' dedicated to, 16, 56; 'Place and Displacement', 114; *Seeing Things*, 98; 'Squarings', 98; 'Station Island', 98
hedonism, 14–15
Herbert, George, 2, 6, 15, 16, 17, 56
Herrick, Robert, 117
Hewitt, John, xviii
Hill, Geoffrey, xii; *Mercian Hymns*, 2
Hilliard, Nicholas, 107
Hobsbaum, Philip, 3
Hofmann, Michael, *After Ovid: New Metamorphoses*, 47, 48
Holocaust, xx, 90, 154, 164–65
Homer, 11, 146, 148; in Longley's classicism, xxi, 36, 40–49, 89–90, 97–98, 123, 138–41; *Iliad*, xvii, 40, 44, 45, 97, 154, 162; *Odyssey*, 40–44, 109
Hopkins, Gerard Manley, 59, 108
Horace, x; *Odes*, 148
horses, 81, 82, 145–46
Hughes, Ted, xii, 1, 52; *Lupercal*, 2; *Tales from Ovid*, 47

i ching ('doubt sensation'), 51, 56–57, 59, 61, 63, 64
Imlah, Mick, 14, 15
interconnectedness, xii–xiv, xvi, xix, **73–99**; see also intertextuality
intertextuality, 84, 87–88, 112, 113
IRA (Irish Republican Army), 46, 123
Irish Times, The, 46, 80, 123, 129

Jackson, Fiona, 148
John, Brian, x–xi
Johnson, Dr Samuel, 62
Johnstone, Robert, 15, 25
Jonson, Ben, 21
Joyce, James, 11; *Finnegans Wake*, 107; *A Portrait of the Artist as a Young Man*, 58, 80

Kavanagh, Patrick, xix, 150; *Collected Poems*, 2; 'Lines Written on a Seat on the Grand Canal, Dublin', x; 'The Hospital', x
Keats, John, xii, 5, 83
Kennelly, Brendan, 11
Kerrigan, John, 111, 113; 'Ulster Ovids', 115
King, Truby, 135
Kingsley, Charles, *The Water Babies*, 134

Larkin, Philip, xii, 1, 31; 'Sunny Prestatyn', 83; *The Whitsun Weddings*, 2
Lasdun, James, *After Ovid: New Metamorphoses*, 47, 48
Lawrence, D.H., 1, 52; *Etruscan Places*, 160
Leavis, F.R., 52
Levi, Peter, 18
Lewis, C.S., 53
listing and naming, 6–8, 26, 28, 91, 93–95, 104–06, 147, 162
Longfellow, Henry (later Major) Wadworth, 16
Longley, Captain Richard C. (ML's father), 134, 136–37, 156; war service, xi, xvi, xviii, 25, 85–86, 96, 138, 144–45, 165
Longley, Constance (ML's mother), 125, 133–37
Longley, Edna (ML's wife), 122
Longley, Michael: aesthetics of poetry, 21; at Arts Council of Northern Ireland, xiv, xviii, 75; as successor of MacNeice, xviii; attitude to landscape, 58–59; autobiographical voice, 41–42, 138–39; balancing of opposites, 78; botany in, **101–19**, 147; 'Captain Longley', 134, 137, 145; classical forms in Irish context, 10–12; classicism, x, 33,

35–50, 131–32, 134; conflict and violence in, 24–27, 76–80, 85–87, 89–99; eroticism, 5–6, 36, 101–04, 114–18, 125–26, 1343; exuberant eclecticism, 1; and father's war service, xi, 25, 85–86, 96, 138, 144–45, 165; filming in England, xv; fundamental interconnectedness, xii–xiv, xvi, xix, **73–99**; futility of war, 97–98; gender and violence, 131–33, 137, 138; 'Grandpa George', 132–33, 134, 137; haunting by violence, 79–80; hedonism in, 15; Homeric poems, xxi, 36, 40–49, 89–90, 97–98, 123, 138–41; humour in, 18, 31, 49; illustrations for *Poetry Review*, 133–34, 135–36; influence of MacNeice, 2–10; an informing vision, xiii; intertextuality, 84, 87–88, 112, 113; Irishness, xv; 'a lapsed classicist', 29–30, 35, 39, 40, 46; liberal scepticism, 74; listing and naming, 7–8, 26, 28, 91, 93–95, 104–06, 147, 162; a literary personality, 131; long line in, 29–30, **121–41**; love poet, xii; love-death antinomy, xv, xix, 156; lyric distillation, 41, 44–46, 47, 48, 50; lyric intimacy, 128–29; lyric meditations, 42; a lyric poet, xxi; and MacNeice, 2–10, 58; macrocosm and microcosm, ix, xx, xxi; a master of the sentence, 3; metric, **13–33**; natural history poet, **101–19**; neo-classical imitator and translator, xii; on lyric poetry, xv; Ovidian poems, 47–49; a philosophical poet, xii; place and belonging, xiv–xv; poems about fathers and mothers, 89–90; poems about poetry and poets, 31; poet of the Troubles, xii; a poet's obligations, 25; practical criticism, 3; Protestant, middle-class Belfast upbringing, xi; psychic pain, 109, 110; 'quilting' poems, 161–62; relationship with mother and father, 109, 110, 125, 133–37, 156; relationship with nurse, 109, 125, 133, 135–36; relationship with twin, 133–37; response to conflict and violence, xvi, 27, 74–76, 80–83, 93; resurgence, x–xi; romanticism in, 39, 40, 45, 46, 49, 57–58; sacred concepts of his poetry, 90; satire in, 31–32, 44–45; school-teaching, xviii; 'secret' Protestant wit, 56; sectarian murder in, 25–26, 155; shorter poems, xxi, 48–49, 98–99; and socio-religious demarcations, xi–xii; specialization in Classics, xii; and the Irish poetic tradition, **1–12**; and the West, **51–64**; transcending gender, 123, 134; two 'homes', xiv–xv; 'Universal Civilian', 27; violent imagery, 85

'According to Pythagoras', xii–xiii, 74–75, 118, 122; 'After Horace', 31–32, 49, 96; 'Alibis', 80, 106–07, 127–28; 'The Altar Cloth: in Memory of Marie Ewart', 143–44, 153, 157, 158; 'Altera Cithera', 36, 38, 89; 'An Amish Rug', 62, 115, 161; 'An No More Singing', 67; 'Anticleia', 42, 90, 140, 141; 'Argos', 90; 'Autumn Lady's Tresses', x, xiii, 115, 127, 152; 'The Balloon', 90, 92, 140, 141; 'Baucis and Philemon', 48, 98; 'A Bed of Leaves', 109–10; 'Behind a Cloud', 97; 'Between Hovers', x, xiii–xv, 94, 151, 157; 'Birds and Flowers', 164;

'Birthmarks', 78; 'Blitz', 164; 'Bog Cotton', 88, 111–12, 119; *Broken Dishes*, ix, xx, 143; 'Brothers', 128; 'The Butchers', 42–45, 90, 122–23, 124, 125, 138, 139; 'The Cairn at Dooaghtry', 90; 'Camouflage', 55–56, 83; 'The Camp-Fires', 8, 11–12, 97; 'Casualty', 74, 77, 78, 86; 'Ceasefire', x, 82, 129, 138, 165; long line in, 122–25, 139; 'The Centaurs', 80–82; Chinese Objects', xx, 98, 99; 'Chinese Occasions', xx, 98, 109; 'Chinese Whispers', 99; 'Circe', 10–11; 'The Comber', 151–52; 'Company', 126–27; 'The Corner of the Eye', 59; 'Couchette', 156, 165–66; 'Couplet', 99, 115; 'Cupid', 37–38; 'Damiana', 143, 155; 'Dead Men's Fingers', 131–32, 136; 'Death of a Horse', 145, 146; 'The Design', 161, 162; 'Detour', x, xviii–xix, 69, 151; 'The Dry Cleaners', 7; *The Echo Gate*, xvi–xvii, 29, 88, 107–08, 110–11, 121, 131–32, 136, 137; 'Edward Thomas's War Diary', 87; 'The Eel-trap', 99, 152; 'Epithalamion', 15, 17; 'Etruria', 156, 157–61, 162, 166, 169–70; 'Eurycleia', 41–42, 90, 108–09, 139, 140, 141; 'Eva Braun', 164; 'The Exhibit', 164–65; *An Exploded View*, xxi, 21, 36, 57, 59, 91, 106, 127, 164; 'The Fairground', 79–80; 'Finding a Remedy', 110–11; 'The Fishing Party', 7; 'Fleance', 87; 'Flora', 107; 'Florence Nightingale', 30; 'A Flowering', 49, 115, 123; 'Form', 99, 125, 127, 130; 'The Fox', 167; 'The Garden', 154; 'Gathering Mushrooms', 65; 'Geisha', 164; 'Ghetto', 27–28, 43–44, 91–92, 93, 131; 'The Ghost Orchid', 96, 98, 99, 118–19; *The Ghost Orchid, see Ghost Orchid*; 'A Gift of Boxes, II', 99; 'Goldcrest', 95; 'The Goose', 74, 77–78, 86; *Gorse Fires see Gorse Fires*; 'Gorse Fires', 70; 'Grace Darling', 30; 'Graffiti', 18, 83; 'The Greengrocer', xviii, 147; 'Halley's Comet', 62; 'Heartsease', 154; 'The Hebrides', 15, 17, 57–60, 82–83, 98; 'The Helmet', 97–98, 123–24; 'The Horses', 146; 'Household Poems', 104; 'The Ice-cream Man', xv–xvi, 7, 93, 94, 104–06, 110, 147; 'Il Volto Santo', 156; 'An Image from Propertius', xxi; 'In Aillwee Cave', 109; 'In the Iliad', 154; 'In Mayo', xix–xx, 61–62, 151; 'In Memoriam', xx, 85, 138; 'In Memory of Charles Donnelly', 94; 'In Memory of My Parents', 92; 'Insomnia', 127; 'Invocation', 163–64; 'January 12, 1996', 144 165; 'Journey out of Essex', 17; 'Jug Band', 92; 'Kestrel', 98; 'The Kilt', 96–97; 'Kindertotenlieder', 91; 'Kingfisher', 59–60; 'Laertes', 42, 89–90, 139, 140, 141, 156; 'Landscape', 83; 'The Lapwing', 152–53, 154; 'Letters', xviii, xxi, 21–24, 83; 'Light Behind the Rain', 83, 115; 'The Linen Industry', 160; 'The Linen Workers', xv, xviii, 85, 86–87; eroticism in, 6, 114, 115, 116–18; 'Lore', 110; *Louis MacNeice: Selected Poems*, 6; 'Love Poem', xix; 'The Mad Poet', 32–33; 'Man Lying on a Wall', 26, 83, 121; Man Lying on a Wall, 61, 107, 121, 132; 'Martinmas', 83, 115; 'Massive Lovers', 98; 'Master of Ceremonies', 132–33;

'Mayo Monologues', 30–31; 'Meniscus', 83; 'Metamorphosis', 83; 'A Misrepresented Poet', 3–4, 5, 9; 'Mole', 87; 'Mountain Swim', 115; 'The Moustache', 144–45; 'Mr 10½: after Robert Mapplethorpe', 101, 103–04, 127; 'The Mustard Tin', 149–50, 162; 'Narcissus', 10–11; 'A Nativity', 83; 'Nausicaa', 10–11; 'Nightmare', 80; *No Continuing City*, 10–11, 17–19, 54–55, 57, 74, 155; 'Northern Lights', 7–8, 89, 138, 140, 141; 'The Oar', 49; 'Oasis', 98; 'Obsequies', 118; 'Odyssey', 10–11, 17; 'Oliver Plunkett', 118; 'On Mweelrea', 5, 83, 115; 'On Slieve Gullion', 79; 'Options', 80, 164; 'The Ornithological Section', 15; 'Out There', 60–61, 99, 127, 128; 'Pale Butterwort', 153; 'Paper Boats', 162; 'The Parody', 154; 'The Parting', 124; 'Partisans', 99, 124, 125; 'Pascoli's Portrait', 150, 156; 'Patchwork', 115, 163; 'Peace: after Tibullus', xvi–xvii, 30, 48, 74, 78, 88–89, 111, 132, 137; 'Perdix', 98; 'Peregrine', 95; 'Persephone', 83; 'A Personal Statement', 15, 16–18, 23, 56, 76–77; 'Phemios and Medon', 98, 122; 'Phoenix', 48–49; 'Phosphorescence', xxi, 152; *Poems 1963–1983*, ix 121, 122, 132, 133; 'Poetry', 145; 'At Poll Salach', 165; 'Poppies', 122–24; 'A Poppy', 148–49; 'A Prayer', 165; 'A Questionnaire for Walter Mitty', 18; 'The Quilt', 161–62; 'Readings', 134; 'Remembering Carrigskeewaun', 8, 128; 'Remembering the Poets', 143, 155; 'River and Fountain', 96, 98; 'The Rules of Baseball', 127; 'The Scales', 46; 'Scrap Metal', 166; 'Sea Shanty', 90; 'Self-heal', 114; 'The Sewing Machine', 161, 162; 'The Shaker Barn', 155; 'She-wolf', 166; 'Sheela-na-gig', 115; 'Sitting for Eddie', 129; 'Smoke in the Branches', 79; 'Snow Hole', 112, 126; 'The Snow Leopard', 148; 'Spiderwoman', 48, 127; 'A Sprig of Bay', 144; 'Spring Tide', 107–08; 'Sulpicia', 30, 83, 89, 115; 'The Sunburst', 161; 'Swans Mating', 66; 'Sweetie Papers', 153–154, 164; 'Terezín', xx, 28–29, 164; 'To James Simmons' 83–85; 'To the Poets', xxi; 'Trade Winds', 7, 162; 'Tuppenny Stung', 41, 132, 133, 135–37, 139–41; *Tuppenny Stung: Autobiographical Chapters*, 75–76, 109, 110; 'The Velocipede', 63, 92; 'View', 83; 'The Vision of Theoclymenus', 154; 'The War Graves', 145, 147–48; 'Water-burn', 152; 'Watercolour', 129–30; 'The Waterfall', 158; *The Weather in Japan*, see *Weather in Japan*; 'The White Garden', 99, 109, 130–31; 'Wounds', xx, 25–26, 28, 138, 145, 156; Troubles and other conflicts, xvi, xviii, 74, 78, 85–86; 'Wreaths', 74, 78, 86; 'X-Ray', 110; *see also* poetry

Longley, Peter (ML's twin brother), xi, 133–37

Longley, Sarah (ML's daughter), xvi

Longley, Wendy (ML's sister), 134, 135

Longworth, George (ML's grandfather), 132–33, 134, 137

Louisburgh, xviii

Lowell, Robert, 1; 'Waking Early Sunday Morning', 21

Lucretius, xii

Lucy, Seán, 54
Lyon, John, 47–48

McDonald, Peter, xi, 118, 122
McGuire, Edward, 129
MacNeice, Louis, 1, 10, 31, 58, 59; Irishness, 9, 79; liberal scepticism, 74; list-making, 6–8; Longley as successor, xviii; love poetry, 4–6; a master of the sentence, 3; a philosophical poet, xii; and socio-religious demarcations, xi; subject of 1996 Symposium, ix; *Autumn Journal*, 3–4; 'Autumn Journal', 8; Autumn Sequel, 18–19; 'Budgie', x; *The Burning Perch*, x, 4; 'Charon', x; (ed. E. R.Dodds) *The Collected Poems of Louis MacNeice*, 2–3; 'Country Week-end', 7; 'Flower Show', 7; 'Letter from India', 21; 'Mayfly', 5, 6, 118; 'Meeting Point', 6; 'Memoranda to Horace', 144; *Selected Poems*, xviii; 'Snow', 2, 7; *Solstices*, 4; 'The Strand', 8; 'The Taxis', 151; 'Trains in the Distance', 3; 'Trilogy for X', 5–6
Mahon, Derek, 13, 39, 73, 84; and metric, 29, 33, 39, 131; 'Letters' addressed to, 21; at Trinity College, 1, 2; 'A Disused Shed in Co. Wexford', 91; 'The Hudson Letter', 131; 'A Rage for Order', 122; 'The Yaddo Letter', 131
Mapplethorpe, Robert, 103–04, 114, 115; 'Mark Stevens (Mr 10½)', 101–02
Marvell, Andrew, 21, 54, 58, 109; 'The Garden', 55; 'Upon Appleton House, to my Lord Fairfax', 55, 109
Mayo, County, xiv–xv, xviii, 57, 63, 64, 157
Miller, Liam, 2

Milton, John, 21, 51, 52, 54, 58; 'Lycidas', 94
modernism, 2, 14, 33
Moebius Band, 83–84
Montague, John, 98
Moore, Henry, 115
Morgan, Jeffrey, 107, 129–30
Morrison, Jim, 82
Morrison, Toni, *Playing in the Dark: Whiteness and the Literary Imagination*, 20
Movement poets, 31
Muldoon, Paul, 13; 'Duffy's Circus', 79; 'Meeting the British', 82; 'The Mixed Marriage', 82; 'Mules', 82
Murphy, Tom, 11

Nairac, Robert, 79
Nazi atrocities, 90, 93
ni Houlihan, Kathleen, 89
Northern Ireland Senior Certificate, 2

O'Brien, Sean, 14
O'Donoghue, Bernard, 39
O'Keeffe, Georgia, 104, 115
O'Neill's bar, xii
Opsahl Report on Northern Ireland (1993), 129
Orange Order, xi
Orkneys, 156
Ormsby, Frank, 85
Ovid, 11, 36, 46–50, 89, 109; *Metamorphoses*, xii, 36, 40, 46–47, 49, 75, 115; *Tristia*, 155
Owen, Wilfred, xii

Pageant of English Verse, A, 2
Paulin, Tom, 122, 125
Peace People, xvii, 88, 132
pigs and boars, 80
poetry: aesthetics of, 21; artistry of, 13–14; Basho, 98; Catholicism and, 59, 61; Chinese and Japanese, 98; classical, 10–12, 30, 40–46;

contemporary and modern, 21–22, 29, 31, 32, 41, 48, 50; early Irish, 98; elegies, xx, 128–29, 148; loss and celebration, 143–44, 148, 153, 157, 165; pastoral, 94–95; for victims of violence, 87, 91, 92–94; in English, ix, 33, 52–53, 54; English, 1, 9–10, 15–16, 38, 52–54, 55, 61; epic, xxi, 11, 36, 98; epistolary, 21–24; erotic, 5–6, 36, 101–04, 115–18, 125–26, 136; freer or free verse, xxi, 18, 19–20, 27–30; Gaelic, 58; haiku, xx, 163, 164, 165; hedonistic, 14–15; Japanese, 164, 165; love, xix, 4–6, 36–38, 42, 125–27, 143; love-elegies, xvi–xvii, 36, 38, 81, 143; lyric, 19, 36, 40–50, 62, 83, 117–18, 126; 'metric' defined, 14; moral aesthetics, 52, 53, 54; 'moral project' in, 15, 17, 19, 21, 28, 29, 31, 33; of natural history, 10, **101–19**; peace, xvi–xvii, 74, 78, 88–89, 96, 97; poet's voice/acoustic, 14, 17–18, 27; and Protestantism, 52–54, 61, 62; sequences, xxi, 30–31, 43, 98; of sexual longing, 115–16; sonnet, 45–46, 148; war, 85, 88, 112–13, 145–46
Poetry Review, 133
Poland, 156
Pope, Alexander, 21
postmodernism, 31–33, 47, 49, 96
Pound, Ezra, xxi, 2, 14, 24
Private Eye, 35
Propertius, Gaius Sextus, xii, 36, 37, 38, 89, 132, 143
Protestantism, 52–54, 59, 61, 62
Pythagoras, 75

Queen's University, Belfast, 3

Raine, Craig, 13
Reading, Peter, 13, 52
Review the, 'The State of Poetry', 9

Rilke, Rainer Maria, 2; *Duino Elegies*, 106
Rimbaud, Arthur, 1
Rodgers, W.R., 75
Roethke, Theodore, 108
romanticism, 39, 40, 45, 46, 49, 57–58
Rosenberg, Isaac, 10, 85, 104; 'Break of Day in the Trenches', 88, 112–13; 'Dead Man's Dump', xii
Royal Belfast Academical Institution, xii

Satie, Erik, 62, 63
Scandinavia, 156
Scott, Sir Walter, *Waverley*, 58
Seferis, George, 'The King of Asine', 147
Shakespeare, William, 22, 52, 54
Shan, Han, 51
Shan, Po, 51, 56, 57
Shankill Butchers, 90
Sharp, Nancy, 5
Shelley, Percy Bysshe, 51, 52; 'Adonais', 94
Shriver, Don, 75–76
Sidney, Sir Philip, 53
Simmons, James, 21, 84, 85
Smith, Stan, 73, 76
Somerville and Ross, *The Real Charlotte*, 60
Somme, xvi, 85–86
Sophocles, xii, 137
Sorley, Charles, 148
Spanish Civil War, 94
Spenser, Edmund, 58, 62; *The Faerie Queene*, 52–54
Stallworthy, Jon, 5
Stanford, W.B., 57
Stevens, Wallace, 1, 5
Swift, Jonathan, 52
Synge, John Millington, 58

Tanigawa, Fuyuji, 164
Tennyson, Alfred, Lord, xii, 15, 16
Thomas, Dylan, 1

Index

Thomas, Edward, xii, 10, 104–05; 'Aspens', 159; 'The Cherry Trees', 165; 'In Memoriam (Easter, 1915)', 165; 'The Wasp Trap', 159
Tibullus, Albius, xvi, xvii, 30, 38, 88, 89, 143
Trinity College, Dublin, xii, 1, 57
Trojan war, xvii
Troubles, 88, 94, 146; Longley and, xii, 27, 80, 85, 90, 111; Longley's response to, xv–xvii, 4, 73–74
tsan ('bore into'), 51, 57
tsan Zen, 57, 59

Ulster Division, 25
University of Ulster, 1996 Symposium, ix, xv, xxi
Untermeyer, Louis, 125

Vietnam War, 97
Virgil, 39, 86, 148

Weather in Japan, The, ix, **143–67**; belonging in landscape, 151–52; Cardoso affiliation, 156, 158, 160; elegies, 143–44, 148, 153, 157, 165; innocent victims, 146–47; 'momentous' themes, 164–65; 'quilting' poems, 161–62
Welch, Robert (ed.), *Oxford Companion to Irish Literature*, 39
Wheatley, David, xx
Whitman, Walt, 16
Wilbur, Richard, 1
Williams, C.K., 29
Williams, Hugo, 101
Williams, William Carlos, 99
Wills, Clair, 122, 125, 138
Winters, Yvor, 23, 24; *In Defense of Reason*, 15; *Primitivism and Decadence*, 14
Wordsworth, William, 51, 54
World War I and II: effect on poetry, 3, 10, 27, 88, 112–13, 148–49, 154, 162; innocent victims, 146–47; Longley's father's service in, xi, xvi, xviii, 25, 85–86, 96–97, 138, 144–45, 165
Wright, Frank, *Northern Ireland: a Comparative Analysis*, 138

Yeats, W.B., 1, 11, 58, 84, 118; 'Coole Park and Ballylee, 1931', 117; 'In Memory of Eva Gore-Booth and Con Markiewicz', 21; 'An Irish Airman Foresees His Death', 21; 'The Man Who Dreamed of Faeryland', 8; 'The Second Coming', 82; 'Under Ben Bulben', 13, 21

Zen, 51, 56, 57, 99
Zen garden, 163
Zen Protestantism, 59

OHIO UNIVERSITY LIBRARY

Please return this book as soon as you have finished with it. In order to avoid a fine it must be returned by the latest date stamped below. All books are subject to recall after two weeks or immediately if needed for reserve.

CF